PENGUIN BUSINESS

CORPORATE STRATE

A Management Classic

SERIES EDITOR: GEORGE BULL

H. IGOR ANSOFF is President of Ansoff Associates, in San Diego, California. A graduate of Stevens Institute of Technology and Brown University, Professor Ansoff worked for the RAND Corporation as a project officer and with Lockheed Electronics Company, where he became vice-president and general manager of the Industrial Technology Division. His business career was followed by one in the academic world. He has held appointments at the Graduate School of Industrial Administration, Carnegie-Mellon University; served as the founding dean at the Graduate School of Management at Vanderbilt University; as Professor at the European Institute for Advanced Studies of Management; as Professor at the Stockholm School of Economics, and is at present Distinguished Professor of Strategic Management at the United States International University in San Diego, California. *Corporate Strategy*, first published in 1965, was Professor Ansoff's first book and it is published here in a revised edition. It was followed by *From Strategic Planning to Strategic Management* (1979); a theoretical book, *Strategic Management* (1979); and a summary of advanced practice, *Implanting Strategic Management* (1984). Professor Ansoff has also published over ninety articles in the field of strategic management.

EDWARD J. MCDONNELL is Professor of Business Administration at Los Angeles City College in Los Angeles, California. A graduate of Pepperdine University and the University of Southern California, he is currently a doctoral candidate at the United States International University in San Diego, California. His business career has included positions in sales and construction contracts management. He is also a business consultant.

SIR JOHN HARVEY-JONES, MBE, was Chairman of ICI from 1982 to 1987. He is, among other things, a non-executive Director of Grand Metropolitan plc and Chairman of the *Economist*. He has written two autobiographical books, *Making It Happen* and *Getting It Together*, both of which became bestsellers. *Troubleshooter*, written with Anthea Masey, was also very successful, appealing both to the general reader and to the student of business. Its sequel, *Troubleshooter 2*, is published by Penguin. Sir John lives near Ross-on-Wye in Herefordshire.

Corporate Strategy

Revised Edition

H. Igor Ansoff
Assisted by Edward J. McDonnell
With an Introduction by J. H. Harvey-Jones

Penguin Books

This update edition of *Corporate Strategy*
is gratefully dedicated to
the thousands of readers who have used
the original book since 1965

PENGUIN BOOKS

Published by the Penguin Group
Penguin Books Ltd, 27 Wrights Lane, London W8 5TZ, England
Penguin Books USA Inc., 375 Hudson Street, New York, New York 10014, USA
Penguin Books Australia Ltd, Ringwood, Victoria, Australia
Penguin Books Canada Ltd, 10 Alcorn Avenue, Toronto, Ontario, Canada M4V 3B2
Penguin Books (NZ) Ltd, 182–190 Wairau Road, Auckland 10, New Zealand

Penguin Books Ltd, Registered Offices: Harmondsworth, Middlesex, England

First published in the USA by McGraw-Hill 1965
Published in Great Britain by Penguin Books 1968
Revised edition 1987
10 9 8 7 6

Printed in England by Clays Ltd, St Ives plc
Filmset in 9 on 11½ pt Monophoto Times

CONTENTS

Despite the fact that the world of business prides itself on its self-analytical and ordered approach to things, businessmen are no less prone than the next man to fashion and crazes. As the ground of what constitutes business success is ploughed over again and again 'new discoveries' are made, new methodology is produced and new panaceas for success are recommended, and as eagerly sought.

The attempt to study management seriously in these ways is really relatively new and modern, although studies of human organization and motivation date back to the very beginning of civilization. One of the major fascinations of business is the breadth of issues which have to be taken into account and the fact that the businessman is continually selecting from an enormous range of options those items on which he or she will concentrate. Since the field is so broad and problems of definition are so difficult, it is perhaps not surprising that over the years first one aspect, and then another, of business has been the subject of intense study and therefore of emulation throughout the business world. One can see this starting with the early work of Taylor and work measurement and work study. Such concepts seem a very long way away from our contemporary views as to how to motivate people, but in their day they were seen as having a crucial effect upon business effectiveness. The idea that men and women can be timed and programmed as exactly as a machine seems in today's age of automation and robotism a terrible misuse of the human spirit. But at the time it did constitute an attempt to study in a rational way what actually happened at work and, therefore, started an inexorable path of trying to build up business concepts from the smallest visible factor.

A little later the business world was heavily influenced by Sloan's views on organization and divisionalization, a subject which is covered in *My Years with General Motors*, also published in the Penguin Business Library. In many ways his theories derived from classic military theory, but, when applied to the organization of business, where at that time it appeared that the advantages of scale would never be overcome, they enabled a degree of decentralization which was a considerable step ahead from earlier thinking. Much more recently in the same fields of thought we have seen the whole interest in social sciences and the theories of people such as Herzsburg, and Maslow's theories of the hierarchies of human needs.

Looking back it is easy to discern the periods during which the pursuit of growth and scale, or the urge for internationalism, were viewed by most business people as the key driving force. The planning era, if one may call it that, occurred some time ago and has been discredited as we have moved on to the greater belief in the development of common values in the organization, and are rediscovering again today the necessity to be close to the market.

The planning period, which was followed of course by such theories as the experience curve, business categorization and so on, became discredited because, as the planning became more elaborate, the results that were predicted frequently failed to come through. In quite a number of cases, as the planning became more detailed, so it became increasingly divorced from the actions of the organization, particularly in large companies structured on a decentralized basis. It is of particular interest to me to see that, despite the very sharp changes of approach to business from the early 1960s to today, the wheel seems to have turned full circle and business has again rediscovered the concept of strategy.

Possibly because resources are now recognized as being more limited, partly because, at least for the time being, the high rates of world inflation appear to have abated, there is a growing realization developing in the business world that the task of leadership, as well as providing the framework, values and motivation of people, and allocation of financial and other resources, is to set the overall direction which enables choices to be made so that the efforts of the company can be focused.

Looking back at the planning period it seems likely that some of these failures were due, in fact, to the way in which the planning process was carried out.

In many large organizations planning became the job and responsibility of an increasingly specialized planning department, who were divorced from the everyday business and sought to apply theoretical measures of a quantified type to the complexities of the business decisions.

All too often in those days one was faced with plans produced by the staff that seemed somewhat remote or at variance with one's own experience of the actual behaviour of the market in which one was operating. But another and even more worrying variant of the same problem arose when the plans laid would have been helpful in a business sense, but were not followed through because of the illusive lack of commitment in a decentralized organization.

Those of us that have worked in large organizations are uncomfortably aware that one of the facts of decentralized leadership is that instructions from the centre can almost always be circumvented if there is no belief in them further down the line. No form of instruction can be sufficiently detailed that it cannot be evaded by someone who is determined not to follow it; the problem has increasingly appeared to be how to develop planning processes which involve those who have to carry them out and thus acquire their commitment to success and to following the plan as a part of the actual process of developing it.

The focusing has to be done to a considerable extent by a shared vision of where each individual's responsibility fits into the overall pattern of direction in which the company is going. There is no question that the differentiation between successful and unsuccessful companies is a clear sense of mission on the part of the successful company. It is a comfortable feeling that everybody knows what the objective is and recognizes how he or she can help to achieve it.

I have always believed that my ideal organization would be one where everybody from the shop floor to the managing director would give the same simple and short response to the question of 'what is the most important issue facing your company at present?' The task of leadership, after all, is to obtain extraordinary results from ordinary people. Results greater than they themselves believe they can achieve and greater than the more poorly led or poorly directed competitors are achieving. This is one of the many reasons why the Japanese are such formidable competitors. They spend tremendous amounts of time deciding what they are going to achieve with massive involvement at all levels. When they have achieved this clarity there is little problem of communication since everyone has been involved in the production of the plan and understands the objective and their role in it.

This problem of focus is being given a particularly sharp emphasis at present. Most of us in business are recognizing that, for the last decade, we have been, and are likely to be for some time yet, in a period of low growth by comparison with the very high growth rates achieved by the world economy from 1946 onwards. Business depends on growth to a considerable extent, not only to improve its productivity, but also to give within its own organization those opportunities for growth and advancement which are such key motivators of the individual.

The reaction of many businesses to the problems of low growth has been to seek to continue to grow by the acquisition of other companies and this trend has recently accelerated very sharply. Bearing in mind also that the expectation of stock markets is for continual improved performance, and indeed that the mission of the manufacturer is continuously to make more year on year with less use of resources, it is not surprising that the present phase of growth by acquisition is such a marked one. But acquisition, as so many studies have shown, can all too often 'end in tears'. There are more unsuccessful acquisitions than there are successful ones and one of the main features of the successful ones is that they form part of a carefully thought-out strategy where the acquirers can bring synergy of one kind or another to the company they are acquiring.

In addition to this trend there are a number of other trends in the world today which put a particular premium on strategic clarity. In Europe particularly we are conscious that the old familiar national organization of businesses is no longer appropriate in a competitive sense to the problems of tomorrow. Individual national markets in Europe are far too small to support world competitive companies, thus my own company, for example, makes more than 70 per cent of its sales outside our own home market. The days when every country in Europe had one of every sort of manufacturing business are long since gone, and this process of restructuring again involves uncomfortable choices and the need for clarity as to those areas in which to seek comparative advantage and a stronger competitive position.

Lastly, I suppose there can be none of us who are not all too aware of the fact that there is a new technological revolution occurring. In my own company we are perhaps particularly aware of some of these trends. Increasingly, technological advances are being made across the interstices of established technological areas and increasingly new technologies are opening up hitherto unsuspected opportunities. The effect of this from a strategic point of view is that we now see links and synergies between widely differing types of business. The ability to produce new polymeric materials in either film, fibre, sheet or moulded form is, for example, of increasing importance. The physical properties that may be derived from such products by these different methods of presentation are also of great significance. As another example, the use of modern information technology in itself is a powerful competitive weapon and there are many examples of imaginative use of this technology to secure nearly impregnable competitive advantage.

The common ground between all the changes which are going on is the need to have sat back and thought one's way through very carefully to decide the prime factors affecting the business for the future and then to have derived from this the optimum directions in which the company can go.

Never have we needed more clarity than we do now as to what the specific objectives are that our own company uniquely can pursue; never have we needed more commitment to those objectives, and more readiness and willingness to avoid being drawn down the many fascinating highways and by-ways which divert attention and weaken the concentration on our own chosen path to competitive success.

It is in this context that the reissuing of Igor Ansoff's book is so appropriate. It is a remarkable tribute to Professor Ansoff's foresight and analytical ability that the book, which was first issued in 1965, continues to sell in such quantity and must rank as one of the most successful business books of all time. It is really a must for any chief executive officer or any board member, since one of the business trends which one can so readily discern is the belated realization that the development of the strategic plan for the group cannot be delegated. It is the unique responsibility of the chief executive to ensure that the process of development of the plan is carried out. But the planning really has to be done by the board as a whole. Not only because, in theory at least, they are the most experienced members of the company and have the deepest knowledge of the company's strengths and weaknesses, but also because there is now a growing realization that the development of a plan is not of itself enough. Of course, the paradox of the board setting the strategy is that almost inevitably they are further away from the market-place and, while they may have the advantage of 'helicopter vision', they are almost certainly less sensitive to current trends and changes in the market place.

The consequence of these events is that while the planning has to be done by the board as a whole, it must be done in a way which involves those who will ultimately be responsible for carrying out the plan and who will also have the most intimate and up-to-date knowledge of the practical problems with which they are struggling, be they technological, financial or of a management type, as well as the current 'feel' and possible future needs of the market-place. This form of involvement will produce a large number of choices from which the company as a whole has to select and it is that selection process which forms the basis of the development of the company strategy which is a subject of Professor Ansoff's book.

Bearing in mind the almost limitless confusion which exists in the field of planning and strategic thinking in companies, and the ability on occasions to produce even more confusion of aim and purpose rather than additional clarity, it should be no criticism of the book that Professor Ansoff develops processes and disciplines, and a methodology of such rigour that, superficially at least, the corporate strategy could be drawn up by an unintelligent computer. As many of us know that is unlikely to produce competitive advantages, since what one computer can do another can do with equal ease.

What the book does do is to produce an invaluable check-list of the points that should be looked at when developing a strategy and makes the vital point of the need to continue iteration. Iteration is necessary not only because the development of a corporate strategy must be practical and must be achievable, albeit very frequently with some difficulty, but also because of the vital need to gain the commitment of those who will ultimately have to carry the strategy out. If there is a weakness in the book, it is the emphasis on the methodology and the lack of emphasis on the fact that the way in which the strategy is developed is, in itself, a means of promoting the best opportunity by which the strategy itself will be followed.

It is perhaps as well for all of us who have made our lives in business that there is still room for flair, intuition, perception, foresight and luck. Without these no business will succeed and without these the development of strategies for many businesses could be safely left to Professor Ansoff's excellent book.

J. H. Harvey-Jones
June 1985

PREFACE

to the Revised Edition

This book updates my earlier *Corporate Strategy*, first published in 1965, which dealt with management of the firm's adaptation to a changing environment.

When Andrew Franklin of Penguin Books and Professor Tom Kempner asked me to revise *Corporate Strategy*, my first reaction was that nothing short of complete rewriting would do the job. The reason was that, having closely followed the past thirty years of evolution of strategic management, and not having re-read *Corporate Strategy* in about twenty of those years, I have come to regard it as obsolete.

Upon re-reading the book, I was delighted to discover that a substantial part remains relevant today. However, the book is dated in several important aspects. The first, and easiest to correct, are the dated examples sprinkled through the book.

The second aspect is caused by the enormous progress in the theory and practical technology of strategic management which has occurred since the 1960s. Subsequent to *Corporate Strategy*, I had published two comprehensive books, one theory and the other on technology which reflect this progress. Therefore, I decided to revise *Corporate Strategy* into a practice-oriented overview of the modern concepts, with references to other works in which an interested reader will find greater depth.

The third deficiency which dates *Corporate Strategy* has been insightfully diagnosed by Sir John Harvey-Jones in his brilliant introduction to this book. This deficiency is the almost exclusive focus of *Corporate Strategy* on analytic reasoning.

The past thirty years of experience have shown that strategic planning works poorly, if it works at all, when it is confined to analytic decision-making, without recognition of the enormous influence which the firm's leadership, power structure, and organizational dynamics exert on both decisions and implementations.

To remedy this deficiency, I have added Part 2 to the original book, which introduces the reader to the political, sociological, and psychological variables embedded in the work of management.

The term 'strategic management', used as the title of this book encompasses three principal ingredients. Analytic *formulation of corporate strategy* is the first ingredient, treated in Part 1. Part 2 treats the other two closely related ingredients: *design of management capability* and *management of discontinuous change.*

This book is written in the inductive mode. The basic concepts are defined and discussed first, and are then integrated into a conceptual framework.

A reader who would like a quick overview of the book, may prefer to start with Chapter 19 as it is written as a summary of the material in both parts of the book.

H. Igor Ansoff
San Diego, California
May, 1987

AUTHOR'S PREFACE

to the Original (1965) Edition

This book is concerned with *business strategy formulation* in the social-economic environment of the United States. The concepts and methodology presented are applicable to other environments and other types of institutions. However, the approach, the terminology, the examples, and the concepts are all derived from the American business scene.

This book is concerned with *management*, the active process of determining and guiding the course of a firm toward its objectives. In contrast to more common descriptive theories used in the economic theory, the interest is normative: we seek to develop a practically useful series of concepts and procedures which managers can use to manage.

Management of a business firm is a very large complex of activities which consists of analysis, decisions, communication, leadership, motivation, measurement, and control. Of these, we single out the process of decision-making, since it is the corner-stone of successful management. Peter Drucker has said, 'The end-products of management are decisions and actions.' Decisions, whether explicitly or implicitly arrived at, precede every action. Our interest is in the characteristics of these decisions, regardless of the organizational process by which they are made: through an authoritarian management structure, through participative management, or by default.

Our interest is in a particular part of the total 'space' of decisions which confronts a business manager. These are the *strategic decisions*. Presently such decisions will be defined more carefully. For the time being let us describe them as decisions on what kind of business the firm should seek to be in.

In viewing the problem of strategic decisions the approach is analytic. Management was born and developed as an art. Early in the twentieth century, pioneers like F. W. Taylor, Elton Mayo, and Henri Fayol began to apply science to management. The post-World War II period has seen a blossoming of applications of operations research and management science to problems of the firm. Historical progress has been from the 'inside out'. Taylor, Mayo, and their generation concerned themselves with problems of individual and group productivity within the manufacturing organization.

Post-war efforts have spread to a wide range of internal operating problems of the firm. Analytic approaches to the external or strategic problems of the firm have come last. Over the past ten years a number of writers have provided *partial* analytical insights into strategic business problems. The purpose of this book is to synthesize and unify these into an overall analytic approach to solving the *total* strategic problem of the firm.

Finally, we have attempted to make the analytic framework *practical*. This calls for a compromise between mathematical precision on the one hand and realism in the problem statement on the other. The compromise is consistently made in favour of the latter. What has emerged is a qualitative–quantitative framework stated in business language and directly usable for solving real-world business problems. In fact, the framework is an outgrowth of several concrete problems which the author has helped solve.

Methodologically, the 'scientific' method of operations research and management science is not wholly applicable to the strategic problem. In fact, the method falls short in several important respects. A partial result of this book, therefore, is a *new* methodology which appears more suitable for problems of the type considered here.

In summary, this book provides a practical method for strategic decision-making within a business firm. It is addressed to working managers responsible for such decisions: the chairman of the board, board members, the chairman, the chief financial officer, and the development and planning staffs which report to them. Drafts of this book have proved useful in teaching graduate and executive training courses in the area commonly known as 'business policy'. It is my hope that other teachers and students of management will find it similarly useful.

The chapters in the book have been arranged to enable a busy executive to become acquainted with the concepts and the general approach without becoming involved in the technical details of its development. Such readers may wish to proceed from Chapter 7 directly to Chapter 10.

ACKNOWLEDGEMENTS

This book is dedicated to my many friends and colleagues who contributed to my understanding of strategic management since *Corporate Strategy* was first published.

My particular debt is to: Richard G. Brandenburg (USA), Roger Declerck (USA and Belgium), Gay Haskins (Great Britain), Gunnar Hedlund (Sweden), Jan Joule (Holland), Werner Kirsch (Germany), Gen. Ichi Nakamura (Japan), Gian Franco Piantoni (Italy), Jean François Poncet (France), Maurice Saias (France), John Stewart (USA), Philippe de Woot (Belgium).

As on so many previous occasions during forty years of marriage, my dear wife remains a source of unswerving support and inspiration.

I am very grateful to Edward J. 'Mac' McDonnell, whose name appears on the title page for an outstanding job of blending the old and the new into the manuscript of this book.

PART 1

Strategy Formulation

Part 1 presents an updated version of the book *Corporate Strategy* which first appeared in 1965.

CHAPTER 1

Structure of Business Decisions

... The strategic aim of a business [is] to earn a return on capital, and if in any particular case the return in the long run is not satisfactory, then the deficiency should be corrected or the activity abandoned for a more favorable one.

ALFRED P. SLOAN, JR

The Problem

As every experienced executive knows, a major part of a manager's time is occupied in a daily process of making numerous and diverse decisions. The demands on the decision-maker's time always seem to exceed his capacity; decisions of great potential import come mixed with trivial but time-consuming demands; the nature of decisions is multifaceted and continually variable. This diversity generally tends to increase with the level of responsibility and becomes particularly pronounced for the top executive of the firm. On a single day he may be called upon to decide on a future course of the firm's business, to reconcile an organizational conflict between two executives, and to resolve a host of day-to-day operating problems.

In seeking to understand this very complex decision process we can proceed along two complementary lines. The first, and by far the more ambitious one, is to discover how people in general and executives in particular, make decisions, either individually or in groups. Given the alternatives and their consequences, what kind of group interactions are they involved in, what mental process do they go through, and what rules do they apply in arriving at the preferred choice? This direction, which goes under the general name of *decision theory*, has received much attention for many years from diverse scientific disciplines: philosophy, psychology, mathematics, and economics.

The other direction is to focus attention on *practical prescriptions* which can improve managerial decision-making through systematic and logically sound procedures. This involves study of the structure and dynamics of actions and decisions, identification of the key problems, enumeration of controllable and uncontrollable variables, establishing relationships among them, and developing procedures which enhance the firm's chances of meeting its objectives.

This is a somewhat less ambitious task than theory building, for it does not attempt to explain the underlying causes of the many varieties of organizational behaviour.

The two approaches (they are frequently called *descriptive* and *prescriptive*) are complementary: a clear theoretical understanding of *how a firm does work* provides an invaluable point for deciding *how it should work*.

Ideally, development of theory should precede practical prescriptions. But in management practice it has worked the other way around: beset by problems posed by novel challenges, practising managers invented practical prescriptions long before theoretical insights were available to explain and to validate them.

In the particular area of strategic management, which is the concern of this book, a large body of prescriptions has been accumulated since the 1950s, but it was not until 1979 that a first comprehensive formulation of a theory of strategic behaviour was published.[1] *

Most of the material in the first part of this book is based on practical prescriptions, invented largely within business firms. Happily, a comparison with the now available theory, as well as the accumulated experience from practice, validates the prescriptions. But both practice and theory also show that these prescriptions do not go far enough and, if practised by themselves, they may produce unsatisfactory results and give rise to an organizational phenomenon known as resistance to change.

It is for these reasons that the original version of this book, published in 1965, was enlarged by addition of a new Part 2, titled 'Strategy Implementation'.

The historical lesson is that strategy planning, which is the concern of the first part of this book, is a valid managerial instrument, provided it is combined and blended with the appropriate planning and execution of implementation. But systematic strategy formulation is a potentially frustrating and ineffective instrument if it is uncoupled from implementation. In this book the coupled approach to strategy planning and implementation is called *strategic management*.

Classes of Decisions

The adjective 'business' has traditionally meant that the firm is an

---

* Superior numbers refer to references at the end of the book.

economically or 'money.' motivated *purposive* social organization. This implies that a set of objectives or purposes can be identified in most firms, either in explicit form as a part of the firm's business plan, or implicitly through past history and individual motivations of the key personnel. Traditionally the measure of success in a business firm has been profit – the excess of returns to the firm over the costs incurred – and it is this measure that has distinguished a business firm from other forms of social organization such as the government, the church, the armed forces, nonprofitmaking foundations, etc.

As will be seen in Chapter 3, the role of profitability as the corner-stone of business has recently been subjected to sharp questioning. Further, measurement of profitability presents some difficult theoretical as well as practical problems. However, for the purpose of discussing business decisions we need only what mathematicians would call a 'weak' assumption, namely, that, however measured and however variable, a set of objectives can be ascribed to each firm, and that this set is the major guidepost in the decision process.

The second major characteristic which is essential to an understanding of decision-making is that a firm seeks its objectives through the medium of profit and, more specifically, through conversion of its resources into goods and/or services and then obtaining a return on these by *selling* them to customers. There are three types of basic resources: physical (inventory, plant), monetary (money, credit), and human. All three are used up in the conversion process: plant becomes obsolete, money gets spent, and executives get old. In this respect, survival of the firm depends on profit; unless profits are generated and used for generation of future profit and replacement of resources, the firm will eventually run down.

From a decision viewpoint the overall problem of the business of the firm is *to configure and direct the resource-conversion process in such way as to optimize the attainment of the objectives*. Since this calls for a great many distinct and different decisions, a study of the overall decision process can be facilitated by dividing the total decision 'space' into several distinct categories. Our approach will be to construct three categories called respectively *strategic*, *administrative*, and *operating*, each related to a different aspect of the resource-conversion process.

Operating decisions usually absorb the bulk of the firm's energy and attention. The object is to maximize the efficiency of the firm's resource-conversion process, or, in more conventional language, to maximize profitability of current operations. The major decision areas are resource allocation (budgeting) among functional areas and product lines, scheduling of operations, supervision of performance, and applying control actions. The key decisions involve pricing, establishing marketing strategy, setting production schedules and inventory levels, and deciding on relative expenditures in support of R & D (research and development), marketing, and operations.

Strategic decisions * are primarily concerned with external, rather than internal, problems of the firm and specifically with selection of the product-mix which the firm will produce and the markets to which it will sell. To use an engineering term, the strategic problem is concerned with establishing an 'impedance match' between the firm and its environment or, in more usual terms, it is the problem of deciding what business the firm is in and what kinds of businesses it will seek to enter.

Specific questions addressed in the strategic problem are: what are the firm's objectives and goals; should the firm seek to diversify, in what areas, how vigorously; and how should the firm develop and exploit its present product-market position.

A very important feature of the overall business decision process becomes accentuated in the strategic problem. This is the fact that a large majority of decisions must be made within the framework of a limited total resource. Regardless of how large or small the firm, strategic decisions deal with a choice of resource commitments among alternatives; emphasis on current business will preclude diversification, over-emphasis on diversification will lead to neglect of present products. The object is to produce a resource-allocation pattern which will offer the best potential for meeting the firm's objectives.

Administrative decisions are concerned with structuring the firm's resources in a way which creates a maximum performance potential. One part of the administrative problem is concerned with organization: structuring of authority and responsibility relationships, work flows, information flows, distribution channels, and location of facilities. The other part is concerned with acquisition and development of resources: development of raw-material sources, personnel training and development, financing, and acquisition of facilities and equipment.

* Here, we use the term strategic to mean 'pertaining to the relation between the firm and its environment'. This is more specific and different from a more common usage in which 'strategic' denotes 'important'. Depending on its position, the firm may find operating decisions to be more important than strategic ones.

Interactions Among Decision Classes

The characteristics of the three classes of decisions are summarized in Table 1.1. While distinct, the decisions are interdependent and complementary. The strategic decisions assure that the firm's products and markets are well chosen, that adequate demand exists, and that the firm is capable of capturing a share of the demand. Strategy imposes operating requirements: price–cost decisions, timing of output to meet the demand, responsiveness to changes in customer needs and technological and process characteristics. The administrative structure must provide the climate for meeting these, e.g., a strategic environment which is characterized by frequent and unpredictable demand fluctuations requires that marketing and manufacturing be closely coupled organizationally for rapid response; an environment which is highly technical requires that the research and development department work in close cooperation with sales personnel.

In this sense 'structure follows strategy' – the environment determines the strategic and operating responses of the firm, and these, in turn, determine the structure of authority, responsibility, work flows, and information flows within the firm. A. D. Chandler [2] has illustrated this relationship of strategy and structure through a historical analysis of American business. As the country's economy developed, different strategic opportunities became available to business. As firms took advantage of these opportunities and thus changed their previous strategies, operating inadequacies developed which dictated new forms of organization. Chandler traces the development of the modern concept of centralized policy making with decentralized operations control to its strategic and operating antecedents. Alfred P. Sloan in his memoirs [3] has diagnosed one of the major requirements which strategy has imposed on structure: to organize the firm's management in a way which assures a proper balance of attention between the strategic and operating decisions.

Such balance is difficult to achieve. In most firms everyone in the organization is concerned with a myriad of recurring operating problems. Management from top to bottom continually seeks to improve efficiency, to cut costs, to sell more, to advertise better. Problems are automatically generated at all levels of management, and those which are beyond the scope of lower management authority become the concern of top management. The volume of such decisions is great and constant, particularly because of the need for daily supervision and control. In fact one of the major concerns of top management is to avoid overload by establishing decision priorities and by delegating as much as possible to lower managers.

By contrast, strategic decisions are not self-regenerative; they make no automatic claims on top management attention. Unless actively pursued, they may remain hidden behind the operations problems. Firms are generally very slow in recognizing conditions under which concern with the operating problem must give way to a concern with the strategic. Usually when such conditions occur, operating problems neither cease nor slacken. On the contrary, they appear to intensify.

Conditions in the environment of the 1980s demonstrate these competing claims on operating and strategic responses. On the one hand many firms are buffeted by forces of change: technology obsolescence, saturation of demand, rapid obsolescence of products. On the other hand, the very same firms have to meet competition of an intensity which they have never experienced before: the opening of the global market place and the entry of low-cost producer countries into markets which have traditionally been secure from foreign competition.

The immediate demands on management time and effort raised by such operating problems can readily obscure the fact that the basic ills lie not in the firm but in its environment. Even when a continuous downward trend in profitability or obvious signs of market saturation strongly point to the need to revamp the entire product-market position, a natural tendency is to seek remedies in operational improvements: cost reduction, consolidation, a new advertising manager, and, the most popular remedy of them all, reorganization of the company. And yet the main problem may be that the demand for the firm's products is on a rapid decline.

The situation in 1986 in the personal computer industry is a case in point. Reports from firms experiencing difficulties due to declining sales, reductions of profits, loss of market share, etc., record retrenchment measures such as personnel reductions, closing of facilities, efforts to reduce overhead costs, discounting, etc.

Since strategic problems are harder to pinpoint, they require special attention. Unless specific provisions are made for concern with strategy, the firm may misplace its effort in pursuit of operating efficiency at times when attention to strategic opportunities (or threats) can produce a more radical and immediate improvement in the firm's performance.

A proper balance of managerial attention requires three kinds of provisions. One is to provide management with a method of analysis which can help to formulate the firm's future strategy. This problem is discussed in the first part of this book.

Table 1.1. Principal Decision Classes in the Firm

	Strategic	Administrative	Operating
Problem	To select product-market mix which optimizes firm's ROI* potential	To structure firm's resources for optimum performance	To optimize realization of ROI potential
Nature of problem	Allocation of total resources among product-market opportunities	Organization, acquisition, and development of resources	Budgeting of resources among principal functional areas Scheduling resource application and conversion Supervision and control
Key decisions	Objectives and goals Diversification strategy Expansion strategy Administrative strategy Finance strategy Growth method Timing of growth	Organization: structure of information, authority, and responsibility flows Structure of resource-conversion: work flows, distribution system, facilities location Resource acquisition and development: financing, facilities and equipment, personnel, raw materials	Operating objectives and goals Pricing and output levels Operating levels: production schedules, inventory levels, warehousing, etc. Marketing policies and strategy R & D policies and strategy Control
Key characteristics	Decisions centralized Partial ignorance Decisions non-repetitive Decisions not self-regenerative	Conflict between strategy and operations Conflict between individual and institutional objectives Strong coupling between economic and social variables Decisions triggered by strategic and/or operating problems	Decentralized decisions Risk and uncertainty Repetitive decisions Large volume of decisions Suboptimization forced by complexity Decisions self-regenerative

* ROI stands for 'return on investment' (this concept will be explored fully in Chapter 3).

The second provision is to provide a method by which management can determine the administrative structure which will be needed to manage under the new strategy. This is discussed in Chapters 12 to 15 in Part 2.

The third provision is to provide a method for guiding the transformation from the present to the future strategy and from the present to the future administrative structure. This will be covered in Part 2 in Chapters 16 to 18.

Priority Balance between Strategic and Operating Decisions

The balance of management attention to strategic and operating decisions is ultimately determined by the firm's environment.

If the demand in the firm's markets is growing, technology is stable and customer demands and preferences change slowly, a firm can remain successful by focusing its attention on the operating activities, and letting its products, markets and competitive strategies evolve slowly and incrementally.

In such environments a majority of firms typically focuses its attention on the operating decisions. Strategic decisions seldom find their way into the corporate office, and the strategic evolution of the firm is 'from the bottom up', initiated and implemented through cooperation among the R&D, marketing and production departments.

A minority of firms in growing and stable environments is strategically aggressive. These are the firms led by restless and ambitious entrepreneurs who are bent on expanding the firm beyond the limits made possible by its markets.

If the environment turns turbulent and changeable, and/or demand approaches saturation, firms no longer have the option of a dominant concern with operations. Continued success, and even survival, is possible only if management gives a high priority to the firm's strategic activity. Sooner or later, a majority of firms in the industry have to become vigorous strategic actors. The alternative is to go bankrupt.

The history of the modern business firm shows three important shifts in priorities between strategic and operating activities. These shifts are discussed in the next section.

Evolution of Challenges

Modern business history starts in the United States roughly in the 1820–30s. First, construction of a network of canals, and then of a nationwide railroad system, triggered a process of economic unification of the country. A stream of basic inventions: the steam engine, the cotton gin, the Bessemer steel process, the vulcanization of rubber, etc., provided a technological base for a rapid industrial take-off. Technological invention proceeded alongside the social invention of one of the most successful and influential organizations in history – the business firm.

By 1880–1900 a modern industrial infrastructure was in place. It unified the country into an American common market. The firm emerged as a privileged and central instrument of social progress. The period from 1820 until roughly 1900 which became known as the *Industrial Revolution* was one of extraordinary strategic turbulence. The early industrial entrepreneurs devoted most of their energies to creating modern production technology, surrounding it with organizational technology, and staking out their market shares. Their concern with creative strategic development left little time for attention to effective operations management.

From 1900 on, focus shifted to developing and consolidating the industrial structure created during the Industrial Revolution. This new period, which lasted until the 1930s, has been named the *Mass-production Era*. As the name suggests, the focus of industrial activity was on elaborating and perfecting the mechanism of mass production which progressively decreased the unit cost of products.

The concept of marketing was straightforward and simple: the firm which offered a standard product at the lower price was going to win. This was succinctly summarized in the phrase of Henry Ford I, who in response to a suggestion in favour of product differentiation, responded to his sales people: 'Give it [the Model T] to them in any color so long as it is black.'

There were many problems to be solved, but worrying about strategic challenges was not one of them. The industrial lines were well drawn and most offered promising growth opportunities. The inducement to diversify into new environments appealed only to the most adventurous firms. A majority were satisfied with their own growth prospects. It was obvious that the steel companies were in the 'steel industry', automobile companies in the 'automotive industry', etc. As a result the focus of managerial attention was focused inward on the efficiency of the productive mechanism.

The result was a set of managerial perceptions, attitudes and preferences which later came to be known as 'production mentality'.

On the political front, the business sector was well protected against outside interference. Political and social controls were minimal. Government 'interference' with the free enterprise was infrequent. When needed, the government could be expected to provide a protectionist economic policy. When business flagrantly transgressed social norms, government reacted by limiting freedoms of business action, with measures such as anti-trust or anti-price collusion legislation. But these were occasional events; most of the time the boundary of the business environment remained inviolate. The business of the country was business. It was this sense of the centrality of the business sector that led 'Engine Charlie' Wilson, president of General Motors, to say: 'What is good for General Motors is good for the country.'

For the first thirty years of the century, success went to the firm with the lowest price. Products were largely undifferentiated, and the ability to produce at the lowest unit cost was the secret to success. But toward the 1930s the demand for basic consumer goods was on the way toward saturation. With 'a car in every garage and a chicken in every pot' the increasingly affluent consumer began to look for more than basic performance. Demand for Model T types of products began to flag.

In the 1930s General Motors triggered a shift from production to a market focus. The introduction of the annual model change was symbolic of a shift of emphasis from standard to differentiated products. By contrast to earlier 'production orientation', the new secret to success began to shift to a 'marketing orientation'. Mr Ford, having tried to replace a standard Model T with a standard Model A, was forced to follow the multi-model suit of General Motors. Promotion, advertising, selling and other forms of consumer influence became priority concerns of management.

The shift to the marketing orientation meant a shift from an internally focused, introverted perspective to an open extroverted one. It also meant a transfer of power, and power struggles were a frequent outcome within firms. But, beyond power struggles, managers resisted the shift because it required costly, time-consuming and psychologically threatening acquisition of new skills and facilities, development of new problem-solving approaches, changes in structure, in systems and acceptance of new levels of uncertainty about the future.

In process industries and in producer-durable industries, the marketing concept was slow to penetrate. When confronted with saturation, firms in such industries frequently settled for a stagnating of growth under production orientation, rather than undertake the pains of a shift to the marketing outlook. It was not until after World War II that many of these industries were propelled by new technologies, first into a belated marketing orientation.

Consumer industries and technologically intensive producer industries were early in embracing the marketing orientation. An overswing frequently occurred: marketing began to dominate operations at the expense of the production efficiency. As a compensation for this, a 'total marketing concept' emerged, which balanced the conflicting demands of marketing and production. Such balanced sharing of priorities gradually emerged and is still to be found in most progressive firms.

In low-technology consumer industries the advent of the annual model change generated a demand for incremental product improvements, better packaging, cosmetic appeal, etc. But, with significant exceptions, the change in products and markets was evolutionary, rather than revolutionary. *Focus on exploitation of current markets and products dominated the concern with future profit potential.* In technology-based industries, new product development became an important activity early in the century. An historical milestone was the establishment of intra-firm research and development, laboratories in companies such as Du Pont, Bell Telephone, General Electric; a step which institutionalized innovation within the firm.

During the Industrial Era, most of the major changes in the environment originated from leading, aggressive firms which established the style and the pace of progress. Thus, with considerable justification, business could claim to control its own destiny. To be sure, business initiative sometimes produced an invisible chain of adverse consequences which led to periodic 'loss of control', such as recurring recessions. But these were viewed as the price of competitive freedom well worth paying for by 'blowing off' of 'economic steam' to enable progress to resume. These periodic 'surprises' were seen as an exception in an otherwise surprise-free world.

From the mid-1950s accelerating and cumulating events began to change the boundaries, the structure, and the dynamics of the business environment. Firms were increasingly confronted with novel, unexpected challenges which were so far-reaching that Peter Drucker called the new era an 'Age of Discontinuity'. Daniel Bell labelled it the *Post-Industrial Era* – a term we shall adopt for our discussion. Today, in the 1980s, change continues at a pace which makes it safe to predict that the current escalation of turbulence will persist for at least another ten to fifteen years. It is harder to predict whether, beyond this horizon, the acceleration will persist or (what is more probable) whether the environment will settle down to absorbing and exploiting the accumulated change.

To an outside observer, business problems of the Industrial Era would appear simple by comparison to the new turbulence. The managers' undivided attention was on 'the business of business'. They had a willing pool of labour (so long as the wage was right) and they catered to a receptive consumer. They were only secondarily troubled by such esoteric problems as tariffs, monetary exchange rates, differential inflation rates, cultural differences and political barriers between markets. Research and development was a controllable tool for increased productivity and product improvement. Society and government, though increasingly on guard against monopolistic tendencies and competitive collusion, were essentially friendly partners in promoting economic progress.

But managers inside firms had found the problems of the Industrial Era very complex, challenging, and demanding. Outside the firm, managers had to fight constantly for market share, anticipate customers' needs, provide timely delivery, produce superior products, price them competitively and assure the retention of customer loyalty. Internally, they had to struggle for increased productivity through better planning, more efficient organization of work and automation of production. Continually, they had to contend with union demands and still maintain the level of productivity, retain their competitive position in the market, pay confidence-inspiring dividends to stockholders and generate sufficient retained earnings to meet the company's growth needs.

Thus, it was natural for busy managers to treat the early Post-Industrial signs in much the same way they had treated periodic economic recessions. Inflation, growing governmental constraints, dissatisfaction of consumers, invasion by foreign competitors, technological breakthroughs, changing work attitudes – each of these changes was at first treated as a distraction from 'the business of business', to be weathered and overcome within a basically sound preoccupation with commercial marketing and operations.

Just as in the earlier shift from production to the marketing orientation, the shift to a Post-Industrial orientation is still unrecognized or resisted in many firms, because it introduces new uncertainties, threatens a loss of power by the entrenched managers, requires new perceptions and new skills. The resistance to change frequently leads to a gap between the behaviour of a firm and the imperatives of the environment. The firm continues to focus on marketing and disregards the technological and political changes, continues to rely on past precedents when experience is no longer a reliable guide to the future. Such managerial attitudes are well summed up by a popular French saying: 'plus ça change, plus c'est la même chose'.

But it is not the 'même chose'. The underlying cause of the new change is society's arrival at a new level of economic affluence. The Mass-Production Era was a drive to meet the basic physical comfort and safety needs of the population. The Mass-Marketing Era lifted the aspirations from the comfort and safety levels to a drive for affluence. The Post-Industrial Era is the arrival of affluence.

Satisfaction of survival needs and growth in discretionary buying power change consumer demand patterns. Industries that served the basic needs in the Industrial Era reach saturation. These industries do not necessarily decline, but their growth slows down. New industries emerge that cater to the affluent consumer – luxury goods, recreation, travel, services, etc.

Technology fundamentally affects both supply and demand. Massive wartime investments in research and development spawn new technology-based industries on the one hand, and brings about obsolescence in others. Internal to the firm, fuelled by technological progress, the 'R & D Monster' acquires a dynamic of its own, which spawns unasked-for products, increases the technological intensity of the firm and directs the firm's growth independently, and sometimes in spite, of the aspirations of the management.

The arrival of affluence casts doubt on economic growth as the main instrument of social progress. Social aspirations shift away from 'quantity' to 'quality' of life. Industrial bigness increasingly appears as a threat both to economic efficiency through monopolistic practices, and to democracy through 'government-industrial' complexes. Large enterprises are challenged on their immoral 'profiteering' practices, lack of creativity and their failure to enhance efficiency while increasing size. Acquisitions of other firms is challenged because it is seen to destroy competition. Studies are prepared for dismemberment of giant firms. The growth ethic, which had provided a clear guiding light to social behaviour, begins to decline. 'Zero-growth' alternatives are advanced, but without a clear understanding of how social vitality is to be retained when growth stops.

Realignment of social priorities focuses attention on the negative side-effects of profit-seeking behaviour: environmental pollution, fluctuations in economic activities, inflation, monopolistic practices, 'manipulation' of the consumer through artificial obsolescence, blatant advertising, incomplete disclosure, low-quality after-sale service. All these effects begin to appear to be too high a price to pay for the laissez-faire conditions of 'free enterprise'.

The firm is now assumed to be able not only to maintain affluence under stringent constraints (which only twenty years ago would have been considered subversive and socially destructive) but also to undertake 'social responsibility'. Thus, *one of the consequences of affluence is the loss of social centrality for the institution that created it.*

Having 'filled their bellies', individuals begin to aspire to higher levels of personal satisfaction both in their buying and in their working behaviour. They become increasingly discriminating – increasingly demanding 'full disclosure' about their purchases, demanding 'post-sales' responsibility from the manufacturer, unwilling to put up with ecological pollution as a by-product. They begin to lose faith in the wisdom of management and its knowledge of 'what is good for the country'. They challenge the firm directly through 'consumerism' and put pressure on government for increased controls.

Within the firm, the traditional solidarity of the managerial class begins to disintegrate. Middle managers begin to reject the role of working for the exclusive benefit of the stockholders. The traditional aspiration of every manager to become the president of the firm is not shared by the new generation, which wants the firm to become more socially responsible, and to offer opportunities for individual self-fulfilment on the job. Thus middle managers begin to identify with the interests of technocracy, rather than with those of the top management, or the stockholders.

As another result of affluence, developed nations turn their attention to social problems that remained unsolved while the focus was on economic growth: social justice, poverty, housing, education, public transportation, environmental pollution, ecological imbalance. The private sector is now called upon to perform a twofold role: (a) to restrain and remove its problem-causing activities (such as pollution), and (b) to take responsibility for positive social progress.

New demands for social services create potential new markets, but they are not easy to serve because they have remained previously unattended, precisely because they were inherently unprofitable.

Thus, socio-political relations of the firm with the environment, which lay dormant during the Industrial Era, acquire a life-or-death importance to the firm. They become important as a source of information and opportunities for new commercial activities, as a source of new social expectations from the firm, and as a source of threatening constraints on the commercial activity.

At first glance, the turbulence in the Post-Industrial environment may appear as a return to the days of the Industrial Revolution. But today's turbulence is much more complex. In the earlier era, creation of marketable products and of the markets was the major concern of the entrepreneurs. They dreamed grandly and had the genius and the energy to convert dreams into reality. But their priorities were almost wholly entrepreneurial. Having created the business sector, they often lacked the motivation and the capacity to settle for the job of competitive exploitation of their creations. Other managers, no less talented, but less visionary and more pragmatic, replaced them and began to elaborate and perfect the production mechanism of the firm and to realize growth and profit. Later, marketeers injected new vitality in the environment. Thus, the industrial environment up to the 1950s was a 'sequential' one. In succeeding periods the key to success shifted, and managerial preoccupation with the previous priority also shifted to the next one.

But in the 1970s the new priorities do not replace, but rather, add to the previous ones. Competition is not slackening but intensifying, as a result of internationalization of business, scarcities of resources, and acceleration of technological innovation. Production and distribution problems are growing bigger and more complex, and to these are added concerns with technological breakthroughs, with obsolescence, with structural changes in the economy and in the market, and in the firm's relations with government and society. *Thus, strategic concerns come on top of, not in exchange for, the historical operating preoccupation with competition and or production.*

Problems for Management

To summarize, the relative priorities of strategic and operating decisions have changed and shifted over the past 150 years. During the last half of the nineteenth century strategic concerns dominated the operational. During the first half of the twentieth century operating profit making replaced the strategic as the central concern of management. Starting in the 1950s, concern with assuring future profitability has become increasingly important. But, unlike during the last half of the nineteenth century, this does not mean a recurrence of the strategic decisions as a dominant priority. As concern with future profit rises, so does the concern with competitive success in today's market place. *Thus, in the second half of the twentieth century strategic and operating decisions require equal attention.*

This duality of priorities has major consequences for the firm's administrative decisions. As we shall see in the second part of this book, strategic and operating activities require very different supporting administrative structures. Thus, most firms which have spent fifty years perfecting effective administrative structures in support of operating activities, face the difficult task of adding a structure needed to support the strategic work of the firm.

Furthermore, strategic and operating structures are not only different but also inimical to each other. Thus, having built the strategic capability, firms need to assure cooperative coexistence of the two.

Resolution of these issues will be our major concern in the second part of this book. For the moment, we focus our discussion on the making of strategic decisions.

CHAPTER 2

A Model for Strategic Decisions

There are more things in heaven and earth, Horatio, than are dreamt of in your philosophy.

WILLIAM SHAKESPEARE

The Problem

The end product of strategic actions is deceptively simple: a combination of new products, markets and technologies is developed by the firm. This combination is arrived at by addition of new product-markets, divestment from some old ones, and expansion of the present position. The change from previous posture requires a redistribution of the firm's resources – a pattern of divestments and investments in company acquisitions, product development, marketing outlets, advertising, etc. At first glance, strategic decisions resemble capital-investment decisions, which deal in a similar manner with resource allocation to fixed assets and machinery. Since a well-developed theory is available for capital-investment decisions, it is useful to start the discussion by reviewing the applicability of this theory to the strategic problem.

This analysis will show that the resemblance is more superficial than real and that the differences between the two types of decisions are so great as to require new concepts and methodology of the strategic problem.

A framework containing such concepts and methodology will be described at the end of this chapter as an introduction to the detailed analyses in later chapters.

Capital Investment Theory (CIT)*

Capital investment analysis starts with identification and enumeration of fixed asset and equipment proposals for the next budget period. For each proposal, positive (revenues) and negative (costs) cash flows are computed over the life-time of the project. For proper comparison, these flows must be marginal to the other flows within the firm: only additional revenues and

---

* For the sake of brevity, in the following pages we will occasionally use CIT to denote capital investment theory.

costs generated by the project must be considered. If it turns out that the lifetime of some projects exceeds the budget period, the period is extended for purpose of analysis. It is essential to the traditional capital investment theory that all of the projects which will become available during the forthcoming budget period be anticipated at decision time.

With the projects enumerated and the flows determined, the worth of each project is evaluated with respect to both its net returns to the firm and the entailed risk.* Three common methods for evaluation are the payback period, the internal rate of return, and the net present value.[1]

With individual evaluations in hand, the preferred projects can be chosen by several techniques such as minimum rate of discount for relatively simple problems, and linear programming for more complex ones.

At first glance, this procedure for plant and equipment decisions appears applicable to deciding what markets to enter or what products to develop. In fact, some writers have extended capital investment theory to apply to the entire spectrum of business investment decisions.[2] Our objective in this chapter is to see where product-market investments differ from capital investments and what modifications in the method are needed for a practical approach to strategic decisions.

It will presently be seen that for the purpose of establishing the dimensions of the strategic problem, we shall use C I T as a 'whipping boy'. This should not be interpreted as criticism of the capital investment theory in its use for capital decisions.

Steps in Problem Solving

Simon has shown[3] that solution of any decision problem in business, science, or art can be viewed in four steps.

1. *Perception* of decision need or opportunity. Simon calls this the *intelligence* phase.
2. *Formulation* of alternative courses of action.
3. *Evaluation* of the alternatives for their respective contribution.
4. *Choice* of one or more alternatives for implementation.

A comparison with the preceding section shows that capital investment theory is concerned with the last two steps, evaluation and choice. Perception of the need for decision and formulation of alternatives are

---

* In traditional capital investment theory, the problem of risk is handled rather superficially. Much is left to the intuitive judgement of the decision-maker.

assumed to take place prior to and outside of the framework of analysis.*
As one writer puts it, 'to solve (the first two steps) there is simply no
substitute for reflection . . . There is no magic wand we can wave to produce
alternatives'.[4]

1. *Perception of Need.* As suggested in Chapter 1, perception of need is a
major issue in strategic decision-making. A method which fails to provide
for the choice between continuing concern with the operating problem as
against attention to the strategic, leaves a key part of the problem to
intuition and judgement. A firm, say, in the heavy chemicals industry needs
a mechanism for monitoring the trends in the return on investment (which
has been declining) and the rate of growth in demand (which has been
slowing down); it needs a mechanism for recognizing whether the time has
arrived to diversify. All of this should take place *before* individual
diversification opportunities are sought and analysed.

Thus, CIT is incomplete for our purposes. This is a major deficiency.
Our requirement is for a method which provides for continuing intelligence
activity and for diagnosis of the need for strategic action.

2. *Search for Alternatives.* Traditional capital investment theory requires
that all of the alternatives be known at decision time. In the strategic
problem this is a rare situation. At the beginning of any planning period
only a few of the alternatives will be known in sufficient detail to permit
construction of cash flows. Usually, these will include the firm's traditional
product-markets, current R & D projects, and perhaps some names of firms
which are known to be interested in a merger. Other alternatives will present
themselves throughout the planning period in a continual stream: product
inventions in the firm's laboratories, new market opportunities, firms
available for acquisition, and joint-venture opportunities. In strategic
decisions such conditions of partial ignorance about future opportunities
are the rule rather than the exception; a method which fails to provide for
them is not addressed to a business firm.

Under conditions of partial ignorance a firm is confronted with two
problems. The first is how to conduct an active search for attractive
opportunities.† The second problem is to allocate the firm's limited resources
among the opportunities which have been uncovered and the possibly more

* In fact, this feature is characteristic of a great majority of so-called management
science models.

† To be sure, the firm can take a completely passive attitude and wait for opportunities to come to it. However, it will be shown in Chapter 6, that for most firms
this leads to uncoordinated, inefficient, and potentially costly management practices.

attractive ones which are 'just around the corner'. This is the classic 'bird in the hand versus two in the bush' dilemma which is common to many decision situations in practice.

Capital investment theory is silent here, since it assumes that *all* of the decision alternatives can be enumerated and their outcomes measured. A practical method for strategic decisions must, therefore, broaden this theory by adding provisions for search and for project evaluation under partial ignorance.

3. *Project Evaluation.* CIT uses long-term profitability over the lifetime of the project as the yardstick for evaluation. Efforts to apply such a single yardstick to the strategic problem run into theoretical as well as practical difficulties.

On the conceptual level, viewpoints have been advanced by business writers and economists that profit is not the sole objective of a business firm and that a 'vector' of objectives, only one of whose components is profit, should be used.* Such a vector is usually composed of conflicting objectives; when the firm's performance is optimized on one, it is degraded on others. For example, in the 1980s American firms are under strong pressures from both large and small shareholders to show consistent near-term profits. On the other hand, environmental turbulence makes it necessary to reduce these profits through investment in R&D if long-term profits and survival of the firm are to be assured. CIT, which uses the single yardstick, is not equipped to handle either the multiplicity of objectives or the problem of conflict between them.

On the practical level it turns out that, even for the profitability component of the vector, attempts to compute cash flows for long-lived projects are frustrated by the rapid decrease in reliability of data for long-term forecasts. Since strategic decisions are concerned with projects which have a long profitable life, CIT turns out to be the least reliable of methods in most important situations.

Further, on the practical level, limitations of data usually lead to cash flows which are typical of a product-market area, not ones that are specific for the opportunities in question. However, what the firm needs is not typical but *particular* flows which will reflect the unique competitive advantages of the product-market opportunity, such as superior quality, timing of product introduction, customer appeal, and competitors' reactions. While CIT implicitly requires that such effects be taken into account, it provides no method for doing so.

* This viewpoint will be discussed at length in Chapter 3

A related and equally important difficulty is encountered in efforts to make project projections marginal to other projects in the firm's product-market posture. This requires that cash projections take account of the joint economies and diseconomies between the project and present operations of the firm on the one hand, and between the project and all other projects under consideration on the other. As every practising manager knows, joint effects are just as difficult to reduce to pounds as uniqueness is; the task becomes prohibitive for 'breakthrough' types of products. At the same time, as we shall discuss later, proper use of joint effects and of unique characteristics are primary competitive tools in a firm which aspires to be a better-than-average business competitor. Again CIT assumes that joint effects will be taken care of *outside* the method.

Requirements and Background for a New Method

The preceding discussion shows that, to be applicable as a practical method for product-market decisions, capital investment theory must be broadened, amended, and supplemented. It must be broadened to monitor the business environment and to search for new product-market entries under conditions of partial ignorance. It must be amended to deal with multiple conflicting objectives. It must be supplemented to identify unique product-market opportunities and joint effects. Since all of these requirements are far-reaching and fundamental, they are recorded below and will be used throughout this book as a checklist in the development of a strategic decision method. The method *must*:

1. Include all four, rather than the last two, steps of the generalized problem-solving sequence. Emphasis should be on the first two steps, monitoring the environment for changes and searching for attractive product opportunities.

2. Handle allocation of the firm's resources between opportunities in hand and probable future opportunities under conditions of partial ignorance.

3. Evaluate joint effects (synergy) resulting from addition of new product-markets to the firm.

4. Single out opportunities with outstanding competitive advantages.

5. Handle a vector of potentially antagonistic objectives.

6. Evaluate the long-term potential of projects even though cash-flow projections are unreliable.

This is an imposing list of requirements, which suggests that capital investment theory in its traditional form applies to product-market decisions only under very special conditions, i.e. when these requirements can be neglected for one reason or another. This conclusion was reached by a majority of the business community in the early days of current interest in the strategic problem of the firm. As a result, business managers began to develop practical approaches which bore little resemblance to CIT project evaluation schemes found in textbooks on economics and finance. With time these approaches found their way into business publications and thus have provided insights into the true nature of strategic business decisions.

Practical insights into 'how we did it' have been summarized in many publications. A talented and prophetic Frenchman, Henri Fayol,[5] anticipated imaginatively and soundly most of the more recent analyses of modern business practice. Recently two important books have taken a view of the business firm which is closely related to our present interest. Within a historical perspective Chandler[6] has analysed the relationship among the firm's environment, its business strategy, and its organizational structure. Sloan[7] has presented a highly illuminating history of some forty years of strategy formulation and implementation in the world's largest firm.

Aside from differences of viewpoint and concepts, these two efforts complement one another, since each concerns itself with a different aspect of the total decision problem. Chandler focuses on the administrative consequences of changes in the firm's strategy, while Sloan deals with strategy formulation and the redesign of the administrative structure. In the following pages we deal with the same subjects, but from a *prescriptive* rather than a historical point of view.

When concern with strategy surfaced in the 1950s, there were two needs. Since the previous theoretical literature was, at best, marginally applicable to the strategic problem, there was a need for a comprehensive theoretical statement of *strategic behaviour* of organizations.

Since the 1950s, several important contributions were made to theory, notably by Henry Mintzberg. In 1979 Ansoff published the first comprehensive applied theory of strategic behaviour.[8]

The second need was for a practical methodology of strategy analysis. The original version of this book was one of the first comprehensive statements of methodology of strategic formulation, at a time when doubts were voiced about feasibility of systematic strategic analysis. Since then, doubts have disappeared and practice of systematic strategy formulation has flourished. The strategy problem has expanded beyond strategic to administrative decisions, and the most recent concern has been a focus on managing the process of strategic change.

In preparing this revised edition of the original book, it was decided to leave the original ideas in place because the methodology for strategy analysis found in the book is still comprehensive and valid for today's needs. However, it was necessary to update several concepts, notably that of strategy.

Since this book is intended as an introduction to strategic management, a treatment of the more analytic techniques has been omitted. The reader will find a summary of these techniques in Ansoff, *Implanting Strategic Management*.

Part 2 has been added in order to give the reader a modern perspective on the corner-stones of strategic management which complement strategy analysis. This includes the concepts of management capability and of management of resistance to change.

The Two-level Approach

In the opening parts of this book, we have discussed the limitations of capital investment theory as a tool for strategic analysis. As an alternative frame of reference we could have used *portfolio selection theory*. While C I T deals with selection of physical assets for the firm, portfolio selection concerns selecting securities, either for an individual investor or for an investment firm.

H. Markowitz[9] has written a pioneering work on portfolio selection. His work shows an even greater divergence from the strategic problem than we found to hold for C I T. However, an approach taken by Clarkson[10] has many features in common with the present problem. A comparison of Clarkson's method with this book shows that our approach, when simplified for application to an investment trust, has a close similarity to Clarkson's.

Clarkson's formulation is significant to this discussion, because it sheds light on yet another requirement which is not even suggested by capital investment theory. This is the fact that, unlike C I T, the *decision rules for search and evaluation of products and markets are not the same for all firms*. In application to personal investment policies Clarkson shows that a person's profession, adequacy of current earnings, tax bracket, and legal restrictions on estate all affect the choice of the preferred portfolio of securities. This preference will naturally undergo changes as the above conditions change in the course of the investor's life. Similarly, the decision rules for product-market selection vary from firm to firm and, within a firm, from one time period to another. This is a direct consequence of requirements 1 and 5 listed in the preceding section.

Since objectives are no longer a simple yardstick, they will vary from one type of firm to another depending on the firm's past profitability, its prospects, and its stage in the life cycle. For example, an infant firm trying to gain a toehold will focus attention on current profitability, whereas a large firm entrenched in the market-place will turn attention to long-term growth prospects. Since a firm has to search for opportunities, it will also tend to adapt search rules to the particular opportunities which confront it. Thus a firm with large fixed investments will narrow its search to opportunities to which this investment can be applied, while a firm with highly liquid assets may range wide in search of new product-markets.

The fact that decision rules vary is the foundation for our approach to the problem. Our concern must be not only with *evaluation* of projects for given rules, which is the main concern of CIT, but also with *formulation* of the rules for each individual firm. Further, the focus of interest is on the formulation aspect. While project evaluation is quite similar to CIT, formulation of decision rules requires a novel approach. Formulation of rules plays a determining role in the overall process because, as Simon has shown,[11] it tends to predetermine the final choice of the individual product-markets. It is clear, for example, that if a firm decides to confine search to its traditional industry, this decision will heavily predetermine the future pattern of profitability even before individual products and markets are identified.

We shall deal with the strategic problems on two levels and in two steps. On the first level we shall consider the characteristics of the firm's total position, to derive decision rules for search and evaluation of opportunities. Drucker and Levitt[12] have aptly characterized this step as deciding what kind of business the firm is in and what kind of business it should be in. Two decision rules in their totality describe this concept. One, which sets the yardsticks for the firm's performance, deals with the objectives of the firm. The other, which defines the desirable characteristics of products and markets, deals with the product-market *strategy*. The two sets of rules have a means-ends relationship; objectives set the goals, and strategy sets the path to the goals.

On the second level the rules are applied to individual opportunities whenever they occur and however they come about. Here the approach is somewhat similar to CIT. The differences are in (1) application of strategy to screen the opportunities, (2) use of a vector of objectives, and (3) use of additional qualitative yardsticks to refine measurement of profitability.

Outline of the Adaptive Search Method for Strategy Formulation

As the title indicates, the method uses a search procedure in arriving at a strategy. This is accomplished through a 'cascade' approach: at the outset possible decision rules are formulated in gross terms and are then successively refined through several stages as the solution proceeds. This gives the appearance of solving the problem several times over, but with successively more precise results. The first step is to decide between the two major alternatives: to diversify or not to diversify the firm. The second step is to choose a broad product-market scope for the firm from a list of broad industrial categories. The third is to refine the scope in terms of characteristics or product-markets within it.*

For example, a firm in the basic chemicals industry may analyse its past performance and prospects and arrive at a decision to seek diversification. As the second step it would decide that a closely related industry is the natural direction to follow and pick fertilizers as its preferred area. This would be followed by a detailed analysis of the firm in relation to the competitive characteristics of fertilizer firms. The end product would be specific decision rules such as the competitive and joint effect interactions desired for the new entry. Thus armed with a concept of the business it wishes to become, the firm would begin to seek out, create, and evaluate opportunities.

Another important characteristic of this process is feedback. Since the cascade is a process of search for the best solution, information may develop at later stages which casts doubt on previous decisions.

Thus the chemical firm may discover that it does not have as good a match with the fertilizer business as appeared on preliminary rough examination. It will then re-examine the previous choice of the product-market scope.

The procedure within each step of the cascade is similar: (1) A set of objectives is established, (2) The difference (the 'gap') between the current position of the firm and the objectives is estimated, (3) One or more courses

---

* This approach of successive convergence on the solution should be contrasted with the more usual method in management science in which an effort is made at the first stage to enumerate all of the final alternatives and then to construct an evaluation scheme to compare them.

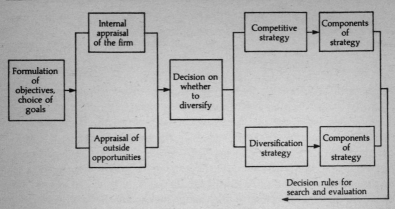

Figure 2.1. Decision Schematic in Strategy Formulation

of action (strategy) are proposed, (4) These are tested for their 'gap-reducing properties'. A course is accepted if it substantially closes the gap; if it does not, new alternatives are tried.*

To continue our simple example, the chemical firm may choose 12 per cent annual rate of return on investment (ROI) as its sole objective (this is highly unlikely in real life, but helps the example; see Chapter 3). It finds that past history and current trends show that 8 per cent ROI is the best that can be attained with maximum effort in the chemical business. The gap is 4 per cent. Trends in the fertilizer industry indicate an average 14 per cent return for the industry. To attain a 12 per cent average, a certain size of acquisition is needed. A test is made to see whether an acquisition of such size within a reasonable period of time is within the firm's resources. If the answer is yes, the fertilizer industry is selected; but the result is provisional, because later stages of analysis may show that the chemical firm's chances of doing *as well* as the average in the fertilizer industry are not very great, or that a much larger investment will be needed than was originally anticipated.†

The example points to another feature of the method which introduces the word 'adaptive' into the title.

* Again a comparison with more usual management science approaches shows a difference. In the adaptive search method the firm is 'satisficing' rather than 'optimizing' its behaviour. Hence no assurance is obtained that the decision rules selected represent in any case 'the best of all possible choices'.

† The pristine beauty of this example should not deceive the reader, it is merely illustrative. Many were the times when the author wished that strategic problems were this clear cut and simple.

Suppose that the firm cannot find any industry through which it can attain a 12 per cent ROI. In that case the goal will have to be revised downward. Or a more happy event, suppose the fertilizer entry looks so promising that even 15 per cent would be reasonable. Up goes the goal.

Thus the method has what Reitman[13] calls 'open constraint' property; both the objectives and the evaluation of the present position are subject to revision as a result of insights obtained in the process of solution.

To summarize briefly, the adaptive search method was described above in its application to formulation of a product-market strategy for a business firm. Its salient characteristics are (1) a 'cascade' procedure of successive narrowing and refining the decision rules, (2) feed-back between stages in the cascade, (3) a gap-reduction process within each stage, and (4) adaptation of both objectives and starting-point evaluation.*

The concepts of strategy and of objectives are the keys to successful application of the method. Therefore, the next few chapters will explore how product-market decisions relate to these concepts in practice. Then, a decision flow diagram will be constructed which applies the adaptive search method to the problem in hand. Although somewhat prematurely, we would like to give the reader a simplified schematic of this diagram as a means for relating various chapters to the final product. This schematic is shown in Figure 2 1, where for simplicity all feed-back relations have been omitted.

* For more detailed discussion of methodology see notes 14 to 20.

CHAPTER 3

Objectives

... with regard to an individual enterprise, the question of profit is of great importance as an economic indicator of its efficiency.

NIKITA KHRUSHCHEV

We, as business people, can fulfil our obligation to society in the everyday process of running our businesses . . . Businessmen should be proud of the contribution they are making . . . not apologetic because they are making money.

MEYER KESTENBAUM

The Problem

In Chapter 1 we described a business firm as a *purposive* organization whose behaviour is directed toward identifiable end purposes or objectives. When made explicit within the firm, objectives become tools of many uses in appraisal of performance, control, coordination, as well as all phases of the decision process. Their potential pervasiveness is such that objectives have been used as a basis for an integrated view on the entire management process which has become known as 'management by objectives'. Our interest in this book is in only one of these uses, namely, the role which objectives play in strategic decisions. This means that we shall be concerned with objectives of the firm as a whole and shall not deal with the very important problem of the organizational hierarchy of objectives which are essential to the operating problem of the firm. Nor shall we be concerned with the process by which objectives are derived, whether they are imposed from above by top management, generated through a synthesis of lower-level objectives, or arrived at through a bargaining process among participants in the firm. We shall, however, be concerned with the business, economic and social variables which determine the objectives, regardless of the process by which they are formulated.

The central question, which must be resolved before specific values are assigned, is what kind of objectives should the firm seek: maximum profit, maximum value of stockholders' equity, or a balanced satisfaction of its 'stakeholders'.

One way to an answer is through philosophy – a study of ethical, aesthetic, and economic values within the firm and the socioeconomic-political environment. The answer, hopefully, would be a statement of what the firm's role and objectives *should* be in modern society. Several philosophically different approaches will be discussed below; while each has apparent merit, none appears to have a clear advantage over the others.

Another way to the answer is through a historical analysis of business objectives that have been used and how they have evolved. Since explicit use of objectives is a relatively recent management technique, this approach is difficult. Little appears to have been done in this direction except a survey of current practice.

A third approach is to construct a list of objectives which is consistent and usable on one hand, and which can be observed in current business practice on the other. This is the approach we shall use in this chapter. Starting with an assumption that long-term profitability must be the central objective in the firm, we shall construct a system of objectives which are commonly used in business practice.

As the first step, this chapter is devoted to laying foundations. Several currently popular philosophies of objectives will be described and compared, a new philosophy will be formulated, and the central business objective will be described. The next chapter will take up the task of converting this theoretical formulation into a usable system of objectives.

Current Philosophies

At first glance, the question of the objectives of a business firm would appear to be non-controversial. Traditionally and historically, a business firm has been regarded as an economic institution; it has developed a measurement of efficiency – profit – which is common and unique to business. It would seem, therefore, that profit-seeking, or maximization of profit, would be the natural single business objective.

In actual fact, objectives are currently one of the most controversial issues of business ethics. Distinguished writers have sought to remove profit from its position as the central motive in business and replace it with doctrines such as equal responsibility to stockholders, long-term survival, or a negotiated consensus among various participants in the firm. Some have branded profit as immoral and socially unacceptable. The situation is confused to the point where Soviet leader Nikita Khrushchev and some of his successors proclaim the importance of profit, while a distinguished American business leader feels compelled to defend the role of profit in

American society.[1] Several reasons can be advanced for this confused state of affairs.

The first is the growing conflict between long- and short-term demands for the firm's resources. During the eighteenth and nineteenth centuries, before technology made necessary long-term product research and long-term anticipation of capital-equipment needs, it seemed appropriate to use short-term profitability as a yardstick of the firm's success. Increasingly in the twentieth century, and more rapidly after World War II, the influx of technology and increasing capital-equipment needs have forced concern with long-term problems. And yet, if short-term profitability were to remain the principal performance yardstick, investments in projects with long-term maturity would naturally be neglected. The result would be a threat to the very survival of the firm in the long run. To assure survival, the concept of the firm's objectives must be expanded to cover the long-term horizon.

The microeconomic theory of the firm – a major body of theory which gave rise to the nineteenth-century concept of profit maximization – could not accommodate this expansion for two reasons. First, because it is basically a steady-state theory concerned with successive equilibrium conditions and thus not capable of dealing with distinctions between short- and long-range horizons; and, secondly, because it does not recognize the exchange between investments for current profit and those for future returns.[2]

A number of economists and business writers have offered alternatives to short-term profit maximization such as maximization of the company's net present worth, maximization of market value of the firm, or profit-constrained maximization of growth. Each of these, taken by itself, is logically persuasive, but none appears superior on philosophical grounds nor conclusively supported by data derived from experience.

A sharp break with the profit maximization tradition was made by Drucker, who proposed survival as the central purpose of the firm. This is to be accomplished through pursuit of a set of 'survival objectives' based on five 'survival functions' which the firm must fulfil to stay alive. Although 'adequate' profitability is among the objectives, according to Drucker, '"profit maximization" is the wrong concept whether it be interpreted to mean short-range or long-range profits'.[3]

The problems resulting from the deficiencies of the historical short-term profit maximization concept are by no means resolved. They are further compounded by the growing importance of the firm as a social institution.

In reaction to the public outrages at the 'smash'n-grab imperialism' of the nineteenth century, business has acquired a sense of social responsibility to society in general and participants in the firm in particular. Thus Frank Abrams speaks of the firm's responsibility to 'maintain an equitable and working balance among the claims of the various directly interested groups – stockholders, employees, customers, and the public at large'.[4]

While, as we shall see later, 'responsibilities' and 'objectives' are not synonymous, they have been made one in a 'stakeholder theory' of objectives. This theory maintains that the objectives of the firm should be derived by balancing the conflicting claims of the various 'stakeholders' in the firm: managers, workers, stockholders, suppliers, vendors. The firm has a responsibility to all of these and must configure its objectives so as to give each a measure of satisfaction. Profit which is a return on the investment to the stockholders is one of such satisfactions, but does not necessarily receive special predominance in the objective structure.[5]

The philosophy of objectives has been further complicated by structural changes within the firm. One such change has been a major shift from ownership by a few individuals to ownership by many small shareholders. It created professional management cadres, working for a salary, virtually in control of the firm's fortunes, and guided by personal ambitions of their own. The objectives of top management can and frequently do come in conflict with objectives of other stakeholders in the firm and in particular with those of the equity owners. Thus, the desire of a chairman to remain in control of a firm until his retirement age would lead him late in his career to become a cautious and conservative decision-maker. At that very time the firm's long-term survival may well depend on radical strategic changes such as abandoning the traditional line of business and diversifying. Faced with the conflict between his own security and the firm's welfare, the president presumably would avoid leading the firm into such change and would, instead, assure other managers, stockholders and the board that there is no need to rock the boat, that the problem is really not that serious.

Some writers who raise this problem of the management-owner conflict cite other important examples but propose no constructive solutions for guiding the firm's behaviour. Others argue that the conflict is more apparent than real and that professional interests and ethics of the manager are, in the last analysis, consonant with the maximum profitability concept.

Another structural change in the firm has been growth in size and complexity. The resulting philosophy of decentralized profit and loss responsibility, which in America culminated in the 1920s in the doctrine of centralized policy-making with decentralized operations control, has led to a wide delegation of decision-making power in the firm.[6] Thus the decision process now consists of many local decisions which are based on local limited information and are in potential conflict with one another. Somehow these add up to consensus decisions on central issues of the firm.

This change has dealt a severe blow not only to the economist's concept of profit maximization but also to the validity of the microeconomic theory in explaining behaviour of the firm. A 'managerialist' point of view came into being which, in a substantial body of writings, subjected the microeconomic theory to thorough criticism. While the managerialists have offered a number of substitute explanations of the behaviour of the firm, until the 1960s none had produced a practical guide to business decisions.

Substantial progress toward this end has been made by Cyert and March in *A Behavioral Theory of the Firm*.[7] In consonance with the managerialist outlook, they argue that 'organizations do not have objectives, only people have objectives'. Therefore, the objectives of a firm are in reality a negotiated consensus of objectives of the influential participants. This has the ring of the stakeholder theory, except that in the former the resolution of conflicting claims is presumably made by a benevolent judicious agency (top management?), whereas Cyert and March suggest that the consensus is negotiated by the participants and is renegotiated as it becomes unstable because of changes in power position or in outside business conditions.

The great value of the Cyert and March theory lies in the fact that it offers for the first time a common framework for the economic and the managerialist points of view by admitting both economic and social variables into the decision-making process. A recent contribution was made by Ansoff who added *power* to the economic and social variables as a major factor in objectives' formation.[8]

Basis for a Practical System of Objectives

The preceding survey leaves the subject in a rather unsatisfactory state. If one were interested in the objectives as a detached observer, the variety of opinions would offer much material for further comparison and speculation. Since our specific interest is in objectives as tools for management, choices and commitments must be made from a particular point of view.

Thus it is clear that the choice of philosophy will have to be made by each firm for itself. The management responsible – the board, the corporate management. the key operating managers, as well as other influential stakeholders – must arrive at a consensus within the present power structure of the firm.

Although the choices and priorities will be different among firms, the objectives lists of most firms will contain the following:

(1) Economic objectives aimed at optimizing the efficiency of the firm's total resource-conversion process.

(2) Assurance of an attractive return on investment over the long-term. Such an objective will be on the lists of most firms, because it is an essential survival objective: if the return is not attractive, the investors will abandon the firm; if the return becomes chronically negative, the firm will go out of business.

In most firms, economic objectives such as (1) and (2) exert the primary influence on the firm's behaviour and form the main body of explicit goals used by management for guidance and control of the firm.

(3) Social or non-economic objectives, which respond to the needs and aspirations of the firm's participants.

(4) Objectives which respond to the aspirations of powerful external constituencies (e.g. the individual shareholders or other powerful stakeholders outside of the firm such as share-holding pension trusts). Objectives such as (3) and (4) exert a secondary modifying and constraining influence on management behaviour.

(5) In addition to proper objectives, two related types of influence are exerted on management behaviour: responsibilities and constraints.[9]

a. Objectives are decision rules which enable management to guide and measure the firm's performance toward its purpose.

b. Responsibilities are obligations which the firm undertakes to discharge. They do not form a part of the firm's internal guidance and control mechanism. For example, the responsibility for the support of the Ford Foundation does not affect in any way the Ford Company's decisions about how to sell automobiles, what types of new models to develop, what new markets to invade, or the choice of non-automotive diversification moves.

c. Constraints are decision rules which exclude certain options from the firm's freedom actions. For example, the minimum wage level is usually a legal or contractual constraint, not an objective, unless the firm consciously chooses to raise it either above the legal minimum or above the level negotiated with the union.

In the perspective of the discussion in the preceding section our basic philosophy can be viewed as an attempt to reconcile several of the points of view. The benefit of the doubt is given clearly to the 'traditional' approach of the economist, but with the addition of a long-term view of profitability. At the same time, the influence of the key managers is admitted as a modifier to the final system of objectives.

Our approach is not necessarily more rigorous or conceptually attractive than several of the approaches discussed earlier. We do have in our favour the fact that our method is related to experience and, as will be shown in the next chapter, we have the benefit of a clear relationship between objectives and common business performance measurements. Thus the approach has merit to the extent to which current practice is *good* practice.

The Basic Economic Objective

We assume that the business firm does have objectives which are different and distinct from individual objectives of the participants. This does not say that the latter are not important and influential in modifying the former, but it does say that objectives for an institution known as a business firm can be inferred from its relationship to the environment, from its internal structure, from the functions it performs, and from its past history. This does not lead to the conclusion that objectives of all firms are identical, but rather, as we shall see, to a conclusion that they are drawn from the same master list.

Our second major assumption is that, to assure survival and success, the firm must optimize the efficiency of its resource-conversion process, i.e. the return to the firm, or profit, is optimized in relation to the resources employed to produce it.

To make this concept meaningful, we need the idea of the *time horizon* of a firm – the period over which the firm seeks to optimize its resource-conversion efficiency. Most large publicly held corporations are legally and practically assumed to exist in perpetuity. i.e. their time horizon is infinite. There are many cases of smaller and closely held firms where the time horizon is finite. For example, owners of a small electronics firm, who seek to build the firm up to a point at which it can be sold under attractive capital gains terms, would view their time horizon as terminating at the time of the sale or merger, since new sources, management and perspective would come into play at that time.

We define an *objective* as a criterion by which the firm's success (or failure) is determined. An objective contains three elements: the particular *attribute* that is chosen as a measure of fulfillment of the criterion; the *yardstick*, or scale, by which the attribute is measured; and the *goal* – the particular value on the scale which the firm seeks to attain.

For the key economic objective, return on the firm's equity has been selected as the attribute* and the average rate of return on equity over the time horizon as the yardstick for the overall objective of the firm. The goal is to optimize this return. To put this in more concise terms, the primary economic objective is to optimize the long-term rate of return on the equity employed in the firm.

The key idea is selecting *profitability* (a measure of return on resources) rather than *profit* (excess of revenues over cost) for the principal attribute.

In economic theory maximum profit is reached at a level of sales at which incremental costs of goods just balance the incremental revenues The implied assumption is that the resources employed in the firm can be adjusted at will and scaled down or up to the exact amount needed to sustain the optimum level of sales.

In practice the resources in a firm are not flexible, and a change in equity base is always associated with tangible costs to the firm. Expansion of equity entails underwriting fees plus other less tangible but frequently important costs due to changes in the pattern of ownership. Contraction of equity base is more costly, since it usually involves liquidation of fixed assets at a considerable discount from their original cost to the firm. Further, the process of equity liquidation is time-consuming and could not be carried out without serious effect on market evaluation of the firm by the investing public.

In summary, the problem of the firm in practice is how to make available resources yield the best possible return, rather than to maximize profit on the assumption that the resources base can be adjusted at will.

The second distinctive point in our formulation of objectives is selection of the *rate of return on the investment* as the yardstick of profitability. We could have chosen others; Solomon, for example, chooses the *difference* between net present value of revenues and present value of investment.[10]

There is no absolutely 'correct' yardstick – each has its advantages and dangers.† Our choice is suggested by the following reasons: (1) Rate of return on investment is a common and widely accepted yardstick for

* Business literature has reflected a lively controversy over whether the owners' equity or total assets, or working capital plus fixed assets is the appropriate denominator for R O I computations. Our view is that equity provides an all-inclusive measure of top management's performance, including skill in use of outside financing. On the other hand, the other denominators may be appropriate for appraisal of performance on management levels charged primarily with *operating* responsibilities.

† For example, unthinking use of a ratio for profitability measurements can lead to the unrealistic conclusion that the best way to maximize performance is to reduce equity to zero, which will make the return theoretically infinite!

measuring business success. (2) Unlike other formulations, it permits us to sidestep the presently unresolved problem of what constitutes the appropriate rate of discount for future uses of capital.* (3) Rate of return is a common and convenient yardstick for comparison of business prospects in different industries.

Thus far, the profitability objective is realistic and can be measured by a commonly used business ratio. We are, unfortunately, very far from a usable objective. We specified the time horizon of the firm as the period over which profitability is to be measured, and recognized at the same time that for most firms the horizon is infinite! We require that profitability be maximized, and yet in Chapter 2 a big point was made of the fact that many of the alternatives the firm will encounter are not known at decision time.[11] The next task, therefore, is to tackle these problems. In the process we shall make progress in meeting requirements (2) and (6) set forth in Chapter 2, p. 41.

* Mathematically inclined readers will easily see that the average of ratios of return by period is equivalent to the average of ratios of present value of return to the present values of investment taken by period.

CHAPTER 4

A Practical System of Objectives

Long-Range Goals:
1. Health – more leisure.
2. Money.
3. Write book (play?) – fame////??
4. Visit India.

Immediate:
Pick up pattern at Hilda's.
Change faucets – call plumber (who?).
Try yoghurt??

FROM THE DIARY OF A LADY
QUOTED IN THE *New Yorker*

The Problem

We shall approach practical objectives through a series of approximations. Keeping the maximization of the rate of return as the central objective, we shall develop a number of subsidiary objectives (which the economists call *proxy* variables) which contribute in different ways to improvement in the return and which are also measurable in business practice. A firm which meets high performance in most of its subsidiary objectives will substantially enhance its long-term rate of return.* As will be seen, this road has its own obstacles: the difficulties of long-term maximization are replaced by the problem of reconciling claims of conflicting objectives.

Proximate Objective and Partial Ignorance

The first step is to deal with the problem of the time horizon. For most firms this will be very distant, theoretically at infinity. In contrast, the period for which reasonably reliable profitability forecasts can be constructed is relatively short and varies between three and ten years. When taken beyond five years, most profit forecasts become unreliable because of

---

* The defect in our approach is that we cannot prove that the result will be a 'maximum' possible overall return.

a great many uncertainties in the future state of technology, the company's share of the market, future management skills, general economic climate, and political climate.

We shall refer to the period for which the firm is able to construct forecasts with an accuracy of, say, plus or minus 20 per cent as the *planning horizon* of the firm. This divides the firm's time horizon into two parts: what we shall call the *proximate period* (three to five years) which extends to the planning horizon, and the *long-term* period from the planning to the time horizon. The latter may be very long indeed.

Within the proximate period, data are adequate for a reasonable estimate of return on investment. There is no need, therefore, for proxy objectives. Values of ROI can be selected as reference goals and thenceforth used for evaluation of different product-market entries. The question of relative risk of different opportunities is of great importance. Since ROI is what is usually called an expected value measure (it uses probable values of contributing variables) it does not discriminate between risky opportunities and less risky ones.

Unfortunately, theory has produced very few useful insights for dealing with risk. In most formulations the final exchange between prospective gain (ROI) and the risk is left to the decision-maker. Therefore, for practical purposes we suggest that, following customary practice, the firm establish three levels of ROI, each adjusted to the relative riskiness of opportunities. The reference level is the value of the ROI which will be determined as *the* proximate objective by methods which will be presently discussed. This level will be applied to a majority of opportunities which are judged to be 'normally' risky. A high level of desired ROI is then set up for opportunities which are judged to be very risky, and a correspondingly low level of acceptable profitability for opportunities which are a near 'sure thing'.*

The next issue is how to select the reference level for ROI. If all opportunities which will lay claim to the firm's resources during the forthcoming budget period could be anticipated in advance, the conventional procedure of capital investment theory could be used. First, tentative values for ROI would be selected for each class and opportunities in each class arranged in order of their ROI prospects. If resources available

---

* For example, some firms require that the expected rate of return on very risky projects be twice that for normal projects. Thus a firm which requires 15 per cent after tax ROI from most projects, may, on occasion, reject opportunities which promise as much as 20 to 25 per cent.

to the firm were used up by opportunities above the minimum required ROI levels a subset with a preferred mix of risks would be chosen. If too few opportunities qualified, minimum required values might be adjusted downward, or only the qualifying opportunities chosen.

As discussed before, in most real-world situations only some of the alternatives are known at the beginning of the budget period. Others are only dimly perceived. How should a firm go about establishing realistic ROI levels so that it does not end up regretting early overcommitment of resources on the one hand, or having been overly 'stingy' on the other? Peter Drucker has diagnosed the problem in more general terms as follows: 'We cannot rest content with developing plans for the events which we either foresee or want to foresee. We must prepare for all possible and a good many impossible contingencies. We must have a workable solution or at least the approach to it – for anything that may come up.'[1]

The resolution of this 'bird in hand versus two in the bush' dilemma is helped by the fact that, as was indicated earlier, the ignorance about future opportunities is not total but partial While many specific products, customers or company acquisitions cannot be identified in advance, the characteristics of the industries in which these will occur, the probability of their occurrence, and their general characteristics can.

For example, a firm interested in entering the computer industry may not be able to specify in advance the individual products and markets it will have two years hence. It can, however, estimate the particular kind of technology which will characterize the product line, the overall growth prospects, the nature of the competition, the typical patterns of return on sales, return on investment, and price/earnings ratios.

Thus, in reality the condition is one of *partial*, rather than total, *ignorance.** If the firm raises its sights from specific product opportunities to the demand and profitability prospects, much information is available for decision-making.*

Thus, the first step in setting objectives is to forecast the future profitability which will be available to successful competitors in the industries in which the firm is doing business. Forecasts should be made for

* Condition of partial ignorance is different from the types of situations treated in the bulk of mathematical theory for decisions under risk and uncertainty. In the latter all of the specific decision alternatives are assumed known. The uncertainty and risk are ascribed in various degrees to the likelihood of their occurrence, or their outcome.

the probable, optimistic, and pessimistic possibilities. (For a technique for making such forecasts, see Refs. 2, 3, 4, 5 and 6.)

Next, the forecasts are used to select R O I values which the firm will seek to achieve in their respective industries.

Next, a *range* of values of R O I is selected for the reference risk class. The value at the high end of the range represents a highly desirable *goal*, the value at the low end the acceptance *threshold* below which opportunities are not accepted. The goal-threshold values are based on the following factors:

1. Past, present, and future R O I characteristics of the industries in which the firm is interested, including the average and the spread, as described above.

2. An estimate of the number of opportunities which the firm may encounter during the next budget period. For company acquisition programmes this would be derived from a count of firms in the industry which are of appropriate size and an assessment of the intensity of diversification activity. For internal product development this would be based on an assessment of the probable output from research and development.

3. The urgency of strategic action by the firm during the forthcoming budget period. If the profitability picture urgently needs a near-term boost, a more modest goal and a lower threshold will be acceptable than would be in a case when the strategic action is taken for its long-term contribution.

4. The amount of resource (or the size of the entry) which the firm wants to commit to product-market changes during the budget period. Again, if the firm's ambitions are modest a high goal and a narrow range are indicated. If much money is to be spent, the firm should be prepared to be less choosy.

The goal-threshold range thus established becomes the proximate yardstick for evaluation of opportunities. Those below the threshold are rejected, those above are evaluated as being more or less desirable depending on how close they are to the goal. The usefulness of the range of values lies in the fact that it permits relative ratings, even when a single opportunity is being looked at. This would not be possible if the problem were approached through setting only one reference value, either the threshold, or the goal.*

---

* In this respect our approach appears to us to be superior to a single level 'aspiration level' approach advocated by H. Simon, W. Morris and others. On the other hand our approach can be shown to be a 'poor man's' practical variant for a mathematical formulation of the same problem which has been offered by Kaufman.[7]

The approach to the partial-ignorance problem described above can thus be seen to take advantage of usually available knowledge of industry characteristics, even when individual opportunities in the industry cannot be anticipated. It presents a very general technique which can be applied to other objectives and to elements of strategy. *Unless otherwise specified, we shall assume that all other decision rules discussed in the book will be expressed in the form of threshold goals.*

Attention should be called to the significant aspect of the adaptive search method which is illustrated above and which will recur repeatedly through the book. This is the circular dependence of the goals on the environment and of the choice of environment on the goals. While the management at the outset will have some ideas about the value of proximate ROI it wishes to achieve, before the final values are selected it will have to modify the original aspirations in the light of the firm's capabilities and of available opportunities. This illustrates what is meant by the 'open-ended constraint' property of the strategic problem.

Long-term Objectives

Exclusive concern with proximate profitability would be almost certain to leave the firm run down at the end of the period. Total emphasis would be on current products and markets: on advertising, promotion, sales force, productivity of the manufacturing organization. But to remain profitable into the long term, the firm must continue to renew itself; new resources must be brought in and new products and markets must be developed. Many key phases of this self-renewal activity have long lead times. Therefore, during the proximate period resource commitments must be made to such long-term needs as research and development, management training, and new plant and equipment.

If the behaviour of the firm were guided solely by the proximate objective, expenditures for such purposes could not be justified and would be given very low priorities. It is essential, therefore, to establish long-term objectives aimed at maintaining and increasing profitability after the proximate period. The obstacle to setting these is that accurate ROI forecasts and measurements cannot be made for the long-term period.

A way around this obstacle is to abandon efforts to measure long-term profitability directly and to measure, instead, characteristics of the firm which contribute to it. One major category of these is concerned with continued improvement of the external competitive position.

1. Continuing growth of sales *at least* at the pace of the industry to enable the firm to maintain its share of the market.
2. Increase in relative market share to increase relative efficiency of the firm.
3. Growth in earnings to provide resources for reinvestment.
4. Growth in earnings per share to attract new capital.
5. Continuing addition of new products and product lines.
6. Continuing expansion of the firm's customer population.
7. Absence of excessive seasonal or cyclical fluctuations in sales and earnings and of consequent loss of competitive position through externally forced inefficiency in the use of the firm's resources.

Each of these factors is a partial indicator of long-term profitability potential; taken together they assure that the firm will have a strong competitive position vis-à-vis the environment.

To make good on this position, internal efficiency must be maintained. An overall, but not necessarily reliable, indicator is the trend in earnings per share. It is unreliable because behind it may lurk a failure to invest in long-term growth such as would occur, for example, if the firm failed to modernize plant or maintain long-lead time inventories. Therefore, more direct indicators of efficiency are needed.

1. If turnover ratios are comparable to or better than those of competition, indications are strong that the firm is making good use of its resources. A key turnover ratio is return on sales; supporting ones are turnover of working capital, net worth, inventory, etc. Another key ratio is debt/equity, which indicates how well the firm uses its borrowing capacity.
2. Depth of critical skills is a key indicator of future profitability. This may be measured by depth of management, of skilled personnel, and of research and development talent.
3. Human and organizational assets must be backed up by modern physical assets. Among the yardsticks are the age of plant, machinery, and inventory.

These *proxy* (lower-level) yardsticks form a hierarchy which relates to the overall long-term objective of the firm in the manner shown in Figure 4.1. The hierarchy shown has no organizational implications, since our interest is primarily in relating internal proxy measurements to overall profitability of the firm.

The structure of Figure 4.1 suggests an answer to a question which is frequently asked: If ROI is the ultimate measure of the firm's performance,

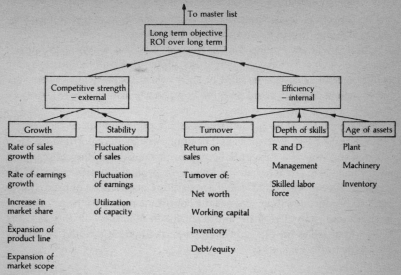

Figure 4.1. Hierarchy of the long term objective

why should management be concerned with the variety of contributing proxy measurements? The answer is that, *theoretically,* long-term ROI does indeed subsume other variables, but since in *practice* ROI can only be reliably computed over the proximate period, the other goals must be brought in as a measure of long-term dynamics of the firm.

Proxy measurements below the level of ROI are also essential for diagnostic analysis of the firm's performance. For example, poor profitability may be traced to incomplete utilization of plant, to the inherent inefficiency of obsolete plant, or to an increase in selling expense out of proportion to the growth in sales. A systematic diagnostic procedure for such analysis has been developed in the so-called 'Du Pont system' of financial control.[8]

The proxy measurements shown in Figure 4.1 have been selected to make use of data which are commonly generated for such diagnostic purposes. This is why Figure 4.1 shows many familiar financial ratios. This overlap is highly desirable, because it avoids the necessity of creating a new system of measurement within the firm.

However, the overlap should not obscure the basically different ultimate uses of information. Traditionally it has been used for diagnosis and trend analysis. We propose that the common yardsticks be put to further uses:

setting objectives, evaluating the firm's position against these objectives, and evaluating prospective product-market entries.

Selection-reference values for this purpose is similar to setting proximate objectives. For a majority of yardsticks shown in Figure 4.1 quantitative goal-threshold values can be set. For a few others qualitative statements are made such as 'acquire basic research competence in very low temperature physics'.

These goals are then applied to respective opportunities as they occur. Not all of the proxy yardsticks will be applicable to all opportunities. Thus when acquisition of a substantial company is considered, the entire gamut of variables which contribute to long-term profitability will probably be relevant. On the other hand, small acquisitions, acquisitions of products, or internal product developments usually contribute mostly to the competitive strength and may offer little improvement in efficiency. In this case the block of variables on the right-hand side of Figure 4.1 would be largely irrelevant to the evaluation.

Flexibility Objective – Another Aspect of Partial Ignorance

Proximate and long-term objectives evaluate product-market opportunities in the light of the probable trends in the industry and the economy. However, the probable trends can be upset by unforeseeable events which may have relatively low probability of occurrence, but whose impact on profitability of the opportunity and on the firm as a whole would be major. The impact may be negative, with catastrophic consequences, or positive (the word 'breakthrough' is often used to describe it), opening wide vistas to the firm. An example of a catastrophic event might be an act of God, such as an early frost in Florida; an economic depression; or a drastic political change, such as a revolution in a South American country in which the firm has major investments. On the more immediate level, catastrophe might be a decision by a single customer, to whom a firm has been selling its entire output for many years, to take his trade elsewhere. Invention of the transistor was a breakthrough for many companies and a catastrophe for others. Acquisition of electrostatic printing patents was certainly a breakthrough for Xerox; so was Land's invention of a new photographic press.

Although some catastrophes can be anticipated, a firm which tries to predict revolutions and inventions is undertaking a highly unproductive job. On the other hand, a firm can effectively buy insurance against catastrophes and put itself in the way of potential discoveries. This can be done by adding another major objective to the firm's master list – a *flexibility objective*. Flexibility can be measured by two proxy objectives: *external* flexibility achieved through a diversified pattern of product-market investments, and *internal* flexibility through liquidity of resources.

External flexibility is best described by the maxim of not putting all of one's eggs in a single basket. This is achieved through a product-market posture which is sufficiently diversified to minimize the effect of a catastrophe and/or to put the firm into areas in which it can benefit from likely breakthroughs. Thus external flexibility can be either defensive, aggressive, or both. A classic example of the search for defensive flexibility has been the desire of many aircraft-missile companies for a fifty-fifty split between government and civilian business. The failure by most such companies to achieve this indicates the difficulty of attaining flexibility.

Defensive flexibility can be measured in several ways:

1. By the number of independent* customers which take a substantial portion of the firm's sales. The single-customer defence industry firm, or a 'captive' supplier to Sears are examples of firms with the least flexibility.

2. By the number of market segments in the firm's posture which belong to different economies. Thus a firm which sells refrigerators in the United States, the Common Market, and Japan has a higher flexibility than a solely domestic supplier.

3. By the number of independent technologies underlying the firm's product-market posture. Thus a firm in electronics, biochemistry, and fibre optics would have a high degree of flexibility.

Aggressive flexibility is more elusive and harder to implement and measure. Instead of minimizing the shock of catastrophes, it maximizes the chance of participating in breakthroughs.

1. One measure is the firm's participation in areas of technology which are in ferment. Although not subject to quantitative measurement, these can be singled out by perceptive management with the aid of competent technical advice. Examples of areas which are currently in ferment and fraught with breakthrough prospects are fibre optics, bionics and composite materials.

* By 'independent' we mean customers whose ability and desire to buy are determined by economic trends which do not usually move together, such as consumer expenditures for durable goods and the defence budget.

2. Another essential measure is the relative strength of the firm's research and development in these areas. Even if the firm does not make the actual breakthrough, with a strong and responsive research and development organization it can exploit expeditiously and intelligently breakthroughs made by others.

Defensive external flexibility is easier to achieve and easier to measure, whereas aggressive external flexibility offers the real rewards. Most firms need to achieve a measure of the former, but only a few will have the type of management, the type of skills, and the resources to achieve the latter. It should be noted that concern with either form of external flexibility is a relatively new phenomenon – a product of the post-World War II period.

By contrast, concern with *internal* flexibility is as old as business itself. Instead of seeking to minimize the size of the catastrophe (the fraction of the firm's sales affected), it seeks to provide a cushion for response to catastrophe. Although it confronts both large and small firms, the latter usually need and do exhibit the greater concern about internal flexibility and must have proportionally better internal ability to respond to catastrophes.

The traditional yardstick of internal flexibility is *liquidity* of the firm's resources, and among the measures are the current ratio, the acid test (an extreme measure of flexibility which measures 'instant response'), the debt to equity ratio, and the fixed to current asset ratio. For high flexibility the debt to equity ratio should be low to provide the firm with reserve borrowing power. On the other hand, a large debt/equity ratio is a measure of the management's use of leverage to increase the efficiency of the firm and hence maximize the return to stockholders. This is another instance of the conflict between objectives, which must be resolved by the management.*

The hierarchy of the flexibility objective is shown on Figure 4.2. In the top box the catastrophies and the breakthroughs are combined under the title of *unforeseeable contingencies*. The specific yardsticks are phrased so as to permit a largely quantitative measure. However, sound qualitative

---

* A study of debt/equity ratios of large 'old line' firms in mature industries suggests at first glance that flexibility is frequently assigned a higher priority than the efficiency objective. However, this may be due more to a lack of entrepreneurial spirit within such firms than to a conscious assignment of priorities. This conclusion is supported by the fact that many such firms are veritable 'banks' with large cash and securities accounts.

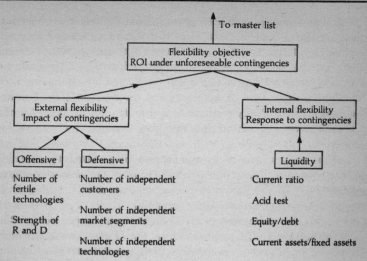

Figure 4.2. Hierarchy of the Flexibility Objective

assessment of external flexibility is probably more important and reliable than efforts to assign numbers.

Non-economic Objectives, Responsibilities, and Constraints

The flexibility objective completes the hierarchy needed for practical elaboration of the central economic objective. While this objective is central and determining in the behaviour of a majority of firms, other influences are present in many firms, which modify the economic objective and sometimes even replace it as the focus. Because of their origin, these will be called *non-economic influences*, even though some of them directly influence the firm's search for profit. It is convenient to separate these into those generated by factors internal to the firm and those due to the external environment. We shall further classify (as defined in Chapter 3) these influences into *operating objectives, responsibilities*, and *constraints*. Since the responsibilities do not interact with the firm's choice of products and markets in the strategy formulation process, they can be treated as voluntarily assumed constraints. The distinction between constraints and objectives resides in the fact that the former represent the *limits* within which the firm must operate, whereas the latter are the *goals* which the firm strives to attain.[9]

Constraints and responsibilities severely limit the freedom of strategic action. Thus, for example, the historical trend in the American government's interpretation of the Sherman and Clayton Antitrust Acts had sharply limited the freedom of diversification for many firms.

The more recent permissive attitude of the Reagan administration was a major stimulus to a wave of takeovers and mergers. Similarly, a sizable philanthropic responsibility assumed by a firm, say, for support of a non-profit foundation can curtail the resources available for growth and expansion.*

One of the major sources of *internal influence* on the firm is the objectives and ambitions of its diverse participants. These are determined by a great many attributes of the participants' backgrounds such as cultural and religious upbringing, racial origin, economic status, age, and career ambitions. Another source may be certain institutional characteristics which have developed historically within the firm. For example, some firms have developed an unwritten but nevertheless carefully followed policy that none of its 'key' management people ever get fired. Once the person gains admission into the 'key' club, he is guaranteed job security till retirement.

As discussed earlier, Cyert and March argue that 'organizations do not have objectives, only people have objectives'.[10] They assert that while the firm may appear to have certain institutional characteristics, these can be traced back in time to the objectives and ambitions of earlier participating individuals who through a 'bargaining' process arrived at certain points of agreement. Later, these characteristics become institutionalized, because new management has either found them desirable for their own purposes or did not feel strong enough to upset them.

Since our interest is not historical, but lies rather in the immediate problem of providing assistance to decision makers, we shall recognize both institutional influences and personal objectives as affecting strategic decisions in the firm.

Institutional influences act largely as constraints on both objectives and strategy. The following institutional attitudes may have an important bearing on the objectives of the firm: job security for key personnel, racial bias in hiring and also in interfirm dealings, maintenance of a favourable image within the community, and promotion of personnel from within the firm.

* This second example is chosen intentionally to stretch the point. Actual records would indicate that most firms engage in philanthropy only when their earnings exceed substantially their expansion needs. This does indicate that economic objectives of the firm are given priority over non-economic influences.

One instance of the evolution of an institutional constraint to a point where it attains the status of the major operating objective has been described by Keynes:

One of the most interesting and unnoticed developments of recent decades has been the tendency of big enterprise to socialize itself. A point arrives in the growth of a big institution – particularly a big railway or public utility enterprise, but also a big bank or big insurance company – at which the owners of the capital, i.e. the stockholders, are almost entirely dissociated from the management, with the result that the direct personal interest of the latter in the making of great profit becomes quite secondary. When this stage is reached, the general stability and reputation of the institution are more considered by the management than the maximum profit for the stockholders.[11]

Objectives of Individuals

Objectives of individuals stem from many diverse origins and are difficult to organize into a hierarchical relationship, such as was presented for the economic objectives. A discussion of the process by which individual drives combine into influences on the firm is beyond the limits of this book (for a model of the objectives formation see Ansoff, *Strategic Management*, 1979). In this book we limit ourselves to a discussion of some of the most important personal influences on the firm.

1. *Maximum Current Earnings*. This personal objective can have a shattering effect on a firm when control is taken over by a person or a group with the explicit aim of siphoning out of the firm most of its liquid or semiliquid assets. While generally regarded as unethical, the practice is prevalent, as exemplified by the recent wave of asset-stripping takeovers. For the duration of such ownership the sole objective is to maximize cash liquidity.

2. *Capital Gains*. During the high-growth phase of the electronics industry many new forms were started by owner-managers with the central objective of quick capital gains and the creation of a public image as a fast-growing, aggressive, competent firm. Since the owner's time horizon was short (up to the point of merger with a larger firm), strategic decision process was focused on short-term profitability to the exclusion of both the long-range and the flexibility objectives. Frequently, unwary purchasers of such companies found themselves in possession of an attractive but hollow shell of an electronics company.

Not all cases of pursuit of capital gains by influential owners lead to such drastic results. However. the near-term capital gains objective can and does place a primary priority on the proximate objective of the firm and on those parts of the long-term objective which contribute to an external image of a growth company.

Among the competing philosophies of objectives, some economists[12] argue that maximization of the market value of equity is the appropriate central objective for the firm. If one assumes that this is sought in the long run and that in the long term 'the truth will out' – the market will assess the firm for its long-term profitability prospects – then optimization of market value is equivalent to optimization of return on investment. The preceding remarks suggest, however, that in the short run very different objectives and strategies follow from the respective philosophies.

3. *Liquidity of Estate.* The desire to enhance the liquidity of the firm's equity frequently arises when controlling owners of closely held companies approach retirement age (or when the owner needs liquidity for other reasons). Two major alternatives to this end are to 'go public', or to merge the firm with another large one which is publicly held and widely traded. The former alternative requires that the firm be made attractive to the investing public which generally has a rather fragmentary and diffuse view of the firm; the latter means attracting an individual buyer who will take a much closer and penetrating view of the property.

The respective alternatives will have generally similar, but specifically different, effects in the firm's objectives. If public issue is the object, emphasis will be placed on current profitability and on a 'growth image' created through the medium of public statements and reports. The aim is to make the firm attractive to individual and institutional investors. If a merger is being sought, more than just an 'image' is needed, because, before acquisition, the firm's operations will be subjected to a careful scrutiny of another management. The image must be backed by evidence of internal efficiency.

4. *Social Responsibility – Enlightened Self-interest.* A sense of personal obligation by management or owner to serve larger purposes of society is sometimes expressed in the form of *enlightened self-interest.* This is exemplified by support for development of computer-based instruction in schools and universities offered by several leading American computer companies. The consequences are not only improvements in social welfare, but also economic benefit for the firm. Since the respective policies stimulate

growth and stability, the firm thus contributes to its own long-term growth objectives.

5. *Social Responsibility – Philanthropy.* Philanthropic objectives of influential participants lead to support of non-profit institutions, such as educational, medical, scientific foundations; public charities; and religious institutions. Since by definition, such activities have no direct relationship to the economic pursuit of the firm, they affect the firm's behaviour primarily through the siphoning effect they have on retained earnings and hence on availability of resources for growth and expansion. Unlike enlightened self-interest, whose size can be readily controlled, certain philanthropic obligations tend to become institutionalized. If such an obligation becomes a major source of income to a permanent institution. the price to the firm for cancelling the obligation may become very high in terms of adverse public reaction.

6. *Attitude toward Risk.* In firms in which management controls the strategic decision process (a situation found, for example, in large widely held companies with strong management representation on the board of directors), personalities, experience, training, and personal objectives of top managers will add up to different overall institutional attitudes toward risk. This may range from highly entrepreneurial risk-taking, such as may be evidenced by a young aggressive management which is 'on the make', to overtly conservative attitudes by older management which seeks to perpetuate itself until retirement age.[13]

Attitude toward risk is a major constraint which must be taken into account in formulating objectives and particularly in establishing their priorities. Many young staff management scientists complain that their superiors are unsympathetic to the recommendations submitted to them and 'do not understand the problem'. In actual fact, this attitude may reflect a particular risk-taking philosophy to which the decision-maker feels entitled in view of the ultimate responsibility which he bears.

The rather complex preceding discussion of non-economic influences has been summarized for quick reference in Figure 4.3. For convenience, the personal objectives have been grouped into two categories: *personal economic objectives*, which includes maximization of current earnings, capital gains, liquidity and equity, fringe benefits, and job security; and *personal non-economic* objectives, which includes philanthropy, personal ethics, social responsibilities, social status, and reputation.

The listings are intended to be suggestive rather than exhaustive, since understanding of both the variables and the mechanism which determines

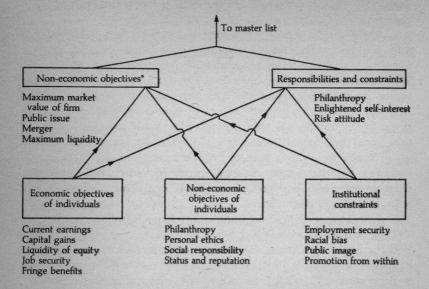

Figure 4.3. Hierarchy of Internally Generated Non-economic Influences

(* Note that the term 'non-economic' means here 'not directly derivable from the firm's basic economic objective'. The impact of such an objective on firm's profit-seeking behaviour can be very far-reaching indeed.)

the firm's non-economic objectives, responsibilities, and constraints is still imperfect and in need of much research. It is our hope that a real-world 'objectives setter' can find guidelines and suggestions in the map of Figure 4.3. The procedure is to single out non-economic influences within the firm which have a strong bearing on the economic objective, and then to assess the extent to which these affect the attributes and the priorities on the firm's master list of objectives.

The Process of Setting Objectives

An effort to establish realistic objectives for a business firm has led us to a complex structure of proxy objectives and sub-objectives. This complexity results from the practical limitations on evaluating long-term profitability of the firm and from the presence of non-economic objectives.

An overall hierarchy of the diverse objectives discussed in the preceding sections is summarized in Figure 4.4. We have tried to identify the principal yardsticks by which the objectives can be measured and also the mechanism by which non-economic objectives and constraints generated within the firm affect the economic objective. In extreme cases this effect was seen to be far-reaching to the point of displacing long-term profitability from its central role in the firm and/or suppressing its relative priority. In a more normal case, the non-economic influences serve to enlarge the master list. As a minimum, they may have some effect on priorities and goal values. Failure to take account of such restrictions may incur unnecessary costs to the firm. As an example, some defence-orientated companies made repeated unsuccessful and costly efforts to enter areas of non-defence business in which they were basically non-competitive because of their very high wage scales. If the wage scales were recognized as a contractual constraint under which defence firms have to operate, the costs of unsuccessful tries would have been avoided.*

The preceding discussion outlined the steps in constructing a master list of constraints and objectives. The next steps are the assigning of relative priorities and goal values to each.

We have already discussed how some of the priorities are imposed by non-economic considerations. Three major economic variables affect priorities: (1) the firm's current and past performance, (2) the total resources available to the firm, and (3) the characteristics and opportunities in the external competitive environment.

If the firm happens to have pursued one of the objectives to the detriment of others, then there is presumptive evidence that reallocation of priorities is in order. For example, a profitable firm which has good growth prospects, but is a captive of a single customer, very likely needs emphasis on flexibility. A currently profitable firm faced with declining markets needs to put a major emphasis on long-term growth. A widely diversified and flexible firm which is not making any money needs to curtail its diversification activities in favour of consolidation and near-term profitability.

One reason why these conclusions need to be regarded as tentative is the fact that availability of resources also affects priorities. A small firm trying to gain a toehold may have neither the financial nor the management resources to do more than concentrate on short-term profitability. When its current position is made secure, it can look ahead to joint emphasis on

---

* It is useful to separate the effect of constraints discussed in this chapter from so-called 'strengths and weaknesses' which will be dealt with later.

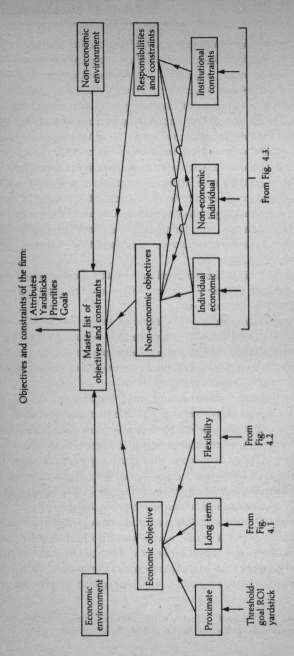

Figure 4.4 Overall Hierarchy of Objectives

proximate and long-term objectives. At the mature stage it can give a high priority to flexibility. As discussed earlier, firms 'safe as houses', occupying near-monopolistic positions, can afford to put major focus on survival, or on 'general stability and reputation'.

However, size is not the only determinant of priorities. Even a very large firm may find its resources too limited to enjoy the luxury of high priority on all of the sub-objectives.

This limitation is highlighted by the recently recognized concept of economic *critical mass*. Critical mass is the minimum investment which a firm must make in an industry before it can become profitable in that industry.

In recent years critical mass has been increasing in most industries as a result of globalization of markets, increasing investments in research and development, and increasing capital intensity.

As a result, the ambitious growth objectives of many large firms (such as American RCA and IT&T) have outrun their resources to a point at which these firms became overdiversified and subcritical in several of their industrial entries. The earnings of such firms fell and they were forced to divest from unprofitable industries, thus modifying their growth objectives.

Finally, and very importantly, the characteristics of the product-market environment have a major effect on priorities. The concept of the industry life-cycle offers a convenient vehicle for discussion. In the early exploratory stages of an industry, the prevalent concern of the participants is external competitive strength and the use of newly available technology to establish new product lines and markets. As the industry becomes structured, internal efficiency becomes the guiding objective, and the emphasis is on developing an effective and efficient business organization. Later, strongly competitive interactions may develop – particularly if the industry is taken over by a small number of competent firms. At this point objectives are again focused on maintenance and enhancement of a strong position vis-à-vis competitors. As the industry approaches maturity, near-term potential becomes dimmed partly through saturation of demand and partly because of the very high costs of further market penetration at the expense of competitors. At this point major emphasis is placed on long-term growth and flexibility.

The preceding remarks clearly show that the choice of objectives is not free. The firm is free to select the basic philosophy, and it has freedom in assigning priorities to non-economic objectives. But when it comes to the economic priorities, the choice is dictated by a number of factors which are

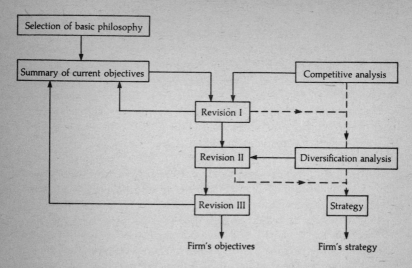

Figure 4.5. Process of Objectives Formulation

(Dotted lines denote part of process which has been oversimplified for this schematic.)

all beyond management control. The same is true of the selection of goals, as was already demonstrated in earlier sections.

Thus realistic objectives cannot be arbitrarily decreed in a smoke-filled boardroom. They must be developed through a continuing interaction of objectives and other elements of the strategic problem. A detailed schematic of this interaction must await later chapters after the other key elements of strategy have been defined and introduced. However, to give substance to the process, a partial schematic is shown in Figure 4.5. It starts with a choice of the basic philosophy. Next, the firm's current objectives are summarized. If these do not exist in explicit form, they should be inferred to the extent possible from the firm's past behaviour and supplemented with 'smoke-filled room' tentative decisions.

In parallel with this effort a *competitive appraisal* of the firm's position is instituted in a manner to be discussed later. Next, the current objectives are evaluated in the light of the appraisal and adjusted accordingly. For example, the current activity may be addressed to an almost exclusive pursuit of current profitability, but the appraisal may show that long-term prospects are poor because of the firm's failure to develop a growth base.

At that point the long-term objective would be given a large increase in emphasis.

If a decision is made as a part of the appraisal that the firm should diversify, or if the management risk attitude is such that it wishes to explore outside opportunities regardless of present prospects, then a *diversification analysis* of available opportunities will be made. Again, the objectives will be reviewed both from priorities and goals. Upon selection of a particular diversification strategy, a final review, this time primarily of the goals, will take place. At that point operating objectives are ready for use.

Objectives are a management tool with many potential uses. In the operating problem they can be used for establishing performance standards and objectives for all organizational levels, for appraisal of performance, and for control decisions. In the administrative problem they can be used to diagnose deficiencies in the organizational structure. In our main area of interest, the strategic problem, objectives are used as yardsticks for decisions on changes, deletions, and additions to the firm's product-market posture.

In this role the mere evaluation of an opportunity on several dimensions of the objectives vector is not sufficient. The final acceptance or rejection requires an *overall* relative figure of merit to be assigned to each opportunity. The use of threshold values for each objective helps somewhat, since it results in a quick elimination of obviously unacceptable opportunities. The presence of priorities helps too, since they emphasize certain characteristics required of an opportunity, such as high growth rate, or a contribution to flexibility. However, at the 'moment of truth' the final yes or no includes a balanced evaluation of all the relevant factors.

This problem of selecting opportunities which are measured by a number of incommensurate components of an objectives vector does not have a satisfactory solution at present.* Among a variety of approaches which have been proposed by management scientists, each has unresolved problems which precludes its unquestioning acceptance by the decision-maker. However, if he is willing to question them and to accept the results for the insights they provide, the manager can obtain substantial assistance from such techniques. In this effort he will require help from a competent management scientist, who not only will perform the evaluation, but also

* We assumed the burden of this problem in Chapter 3 when we decided to face the real-world fact that data are not available to produce a single index number to represent the firm's objective.

will point to the limitations in the underlying assumptions. A specific method for evaluating incommensurate components of objectives will be developed in Chapter 10.

CHAPTER 5

Synergy and Capability Profiles

'Speak English!' said the Eaglet. 'I don't know the meaning of half those long words, and what's more, I don't believe you do either!'

LEWIS CARROLL

The Problem

IN this chapter we begin to explore *synergy*, which is one of the major components of the firm's product-market strategy. It is concerned with the desired characteristics of fit between the firm and its new product-market entries. In business literature it is frequently described as the '2 + 2 = 5' effect to denote the fact that the firm seeks a product-market posture with a combined performance that is greater than the sum of its parts.

In item three on the list of requirements presented in Chapter 2 for a strategic decision method, we described synergy as a measure of joint effects. It will be recalled that this requirement arises from practical rather than theoretical needs. If it were practically possible in each instance to compute the *marginal* cash flows into and out of the firm for each new project, the requirement would not exist, since this aspect of project evaluation would be adequately covered by capital investment theory. Nor would it exist if it were possible to compute quickly and efficiently the new flows for the entire firm each time a new project came along.*

As a substitute for these unfeasible approaches, we shall derive a method for qualitative estimation of joint effects. In the process it will be shown that measurement of synergy is similar in many ways to what is frequently called 'evaluation of strengths and weaknesses'. In synergy, *joint* effects are measured between two product-markets; in strength and weakness evaluation, the firm's competences are rated relative to some desired performance level. The former contributes to the decision to make a new

---

* It would appear, at first glance, that this could be done by 'computerizing' the internal operations of the firm, i.e. by programming its planning process on a high-speed computer. While this step certainly provides for some of the synergistic interactions, it still falls short of the total requirements. To meet the complete requirement we shall require much better models of the firm than are currently available. In particular, models are needed which can measure the potential of the firm as a result of radical changes in its product-market posture.

entry; the latter, to the decision to exploit certain strengths or to remedy certain deficiencies within the firm.

With this in mind we shall develop an estimation technique which is applicable for both purposes. This will be accomplished by means of *capability profiles*. At the end of the chapter we shall have a multipurpose technique which can be used to (1) evaluate any internal strengths and weaknesses within the firm, (2) derive synergy characteristics which the firm can use in its search for opportunities, and (3) measure the synergy potential between the firm and a possible strategic move.

Concept of Synergy

Use of simple mathematical symbols is helpful for a quick summary of the meaning of synergy. Each product-market makes a contribution to the overall profitability of the firm. Each product brings in annual sales of S dollars. Operating costs of O dollars are incurred for labour, materials, overheads, administration and depreciation. To develop the product, to provide facilities and equipment, and to set up a distribution network, a strategic investment of I dollars must be made in product development, market development, tooling, buildings, machinery, inventories, training and organizational development.

The annual rate of return, ROI, on product P_1 can be written in the form

$$ROI = \frac{S_1 - O_1}{I_1}$$

Expressed in words, the formula states that the return on investment from a product can be obtained by dividing the difference between operating revenues and costs during a period by the investment which is needed to put the product on the market. A similar expression can be written for all products in the product line: $P_1, P_2, \ldots, P_n$.

If all the products are unrelated in any way, the total sales of the firm will be

$$S_T = S_1 + S_2 + \ldots + S_n$$

And similarly for operating costs and investment

$$O_T = O_1 + O_2 \ldots + O_n$$
$$I_T = I_1 + I_2 + \ldots + I_n$$

The return on the investment for the firm as a whole will be

$$(ROI)_T = \frac{S_T - O_T}{I_T}$$

This condition obtains whenever the revenues, the operating costs and the investments are unrelated. Therefore, their totals can be obtained through simple additions. In practice this is very nearly true in an investment firm which holds unrelated securities, or in a conglomerate in which there is no interaction among the operating units. A picture of the total profitability is obtained through a simple consolidation of the individual statements.

In a majority of firms, advantages of scale exist under which a large firm with the same total sales as a number of small firms can operate at a cost which is lower than the sum of the operating costs for the separate enterprises. The investment in a large firm can be similarly lower than a simple sum of the respective investments. Using symbols, this is equivalent to saying that for

$$S_s = S_T$$
we have
$$O_s \leqslant O_T$$
$$I_s \leqslant I_T$$

where subscript s denotes the respective quantities for an integrated firm and subscript T, the sum for independent enterprises.* As a result, the potential return on investment for an integrated firm is higher than the composite return which would be obtained if the same dollar volumes for its respective products were produced by a number of independent firms:

$$(ROI)_s > (ROI)_T$$

A similar argument can, of course, be made by keeping the total investment fixed. In this case

$$S_s \geqslant S_T$$
$$O_s \leqslant O_T$$
$$I_s = I_T$$

For a given level of investment, a firm with a complete product line can usually realize the advantages of higher total revenues and/or lower operating costs than competing independent firms.

* The symbol $\leqslant$ means less than or equal to; the symbol $\geqslant$ means greater than or equal to.

The consequences of this joint effect are clearly very far-reaching. A firm which takes care to select its products and markets so as to optimize the effect has great flexibility in choosing its competitive stance. It can gain a larger share of the market by lower prices, it can choose to make a larger investment in research and development than its competitors, or it can maximize its ROI and attract growth capital to the firm. All this can be done while remaining fully competitive with firms whose product-markets are not as carefully chosen.

Types of Synergy

This effect which can produce a combined return on the firm's resources greater than the sum of its parts is frequently referred to as '2 + 2 = 5'. We shall call this effect *synergy*.[1] One way to classify the several types of synergy is in terms of the components of the ROI formula:

1. *Sales Synergy*. This can occur when products use common distribution channels, common sales administration, or common warehousing. Opportunity for tie-in sales offered by a complete line of related products increases the productivity of the sales force. Common advertising, sales promotion, past reputation can all have multiple returns for the same dollar spent.

2. *Operating Synergy*. This is the result of higher utilization of facilities and personnel, spreading of overheads, advantages of common learning curves, and large-lot purchasing.

3. *Investment Synergy*. This can result from joint use of plant, common raw materials inventories, transfer of research and development from one product to another, common technological base, common tooling, common machinery.

4. *Management Synergy*. Although not immediately apparent from the formula, this type is an important contributor to the total effect. As will be shown below, management in different types of industry faces different strategic, organizational, and operating problems. If upon entering a new industry management finds the new problems to be similar to the ones it has encountered in the past, it is in a position to provide forceful and effective guidance to the newly acquired venture. Since competent top-level management is a scarce commodity, very positive enhancement of performance can result in the combined enterprise. Thus synergy will be strong.

If, on the other hand, the problems in the acquired area are new and unfamiliar, not only will positive synergy be low, but there is a distinct danger of a *negative effect* of top-management decisions, especially in areas involving 'high-tech'. For example, management of a firm in such a high-tech industry would be at an actual disadvantage if it attempts, without prior experience, to assume responsibility for pricing and advertising decisions in a highly competitive consumer area, such as the cigarette or the automobile industry.

This example points to the fact that management *synergy*, as well as the other types, *can be negative as well as positive.* An attempt at joint use of a facility which is not suited for manufacturing of a new product (e.g. use of aircraft factories for consumer aluminium products), or of an organization which is not set up to perform a new function (e.g. use of a consumer sales organization to sell to industrial customers) can result in total profitability which is *lower* than the combined profitability of two independent operations.

Table 5.1 demonstrates the possibility of negative synergy through a comparison of competences in the principal functional areas found in typical firms in different industry groups. For purposes of comparison we are assuming that a firm in one of the groups shown in the first column diversifies into an industry group shown in the first line.

Table 5.1 Functional Synergy between Industry Groups

Diversifying industry	Functional capability	New industry		
		Defence-space	Producers	Consumers
Defence-space	GM	High	Low	Negative
	R & D	High	Moderate	Low
	Mfg.	High	Low	Negative
	Mkt.	High	Low	Negative
Producers	GM	High	High	Moderate
	R & D	Moderate	High	Low
	Mfg.	Low	High	Low
	Mkt.	Low	High	Low
Consumers	GM	Negative	Low	High
	R & G	Low	Low	High
	Mfg.	Negative	Low	High
	Mkt.	Negative	Low	High

Legend
    GM – general management
    R & D – research and development
    Mfg. – manufacturing
    Mkt. – marketing

When this book was first written, it was perceived that the best transfer of functional competence would occur in general management, where many practices and skills in accounting, finance, industrial relations, and public relations appeared to be common among industries.

However, the past twenty years of experience have shown that management synergy quickly becomes negative when a firm diversifies into an industry whose environmental turbulence is significantly different from that which, in the past, has characterized their normal areas of operations (for a discussion of turbulence, see Ansoff, *Implanting Strategic Management*).

A recent vivid example of the consequences of negative management synergy is offered by the entry and subsequent exit of the great Exxon Company from the office automation business.

In manufacturing and marketing where organizational forms, cost controls and individual skills become more specialized, differences in synergy appear among the groups. The differences become so great between high-technology industries and consumer groups as to create potentially negative synergy.

It should be noted that the above table describes *potential* (rather than actual) synergy. Whether the indicated joint effects will, in fact, materialize depends on the manner in which the new acquisition is integrated into the parent organization. This problem of management control will be discussed in Chapter 8.

Start-up Synergy and Operating Synergy

As discussed above, the synergistic effect can be measured in either of two ways: by estimating the cost economics to the firm from a joint operation for a given level or revenue, or by estimating the increase in net revenue for a given level of investment. In this section we shall take the first approach and discuss the nature of synergy through analysis of cost economies and diseconomies.

Acquisition of a new product-market area goes through two successive phases, start-up and operating. In addition to identifiable physical costs, such as the costs of facilities and inventories, the costs associated with start-up include the highly intangible costs of learning a new kind of business: setting up a new organization, establishing new rules and procedures, hiring new skills and competences, paying for mistakes in developing organizational relationships and for early bad decisions made in unfamiliar business environment, and costs of gaining customer acceptance.

Although these are one-time costs, most of them are not capitalized, but charged to operating expense during the start-up period. They are difficult to pinpoint, since many of them are not identified (no firm is likely to have a special account labelled 'management blunders made in start-up'), but are evident only indirectly through substandard operating efficiencies.* During the period in which they are incurred they put the firm at a disadvantage with respect to the established competitors in the field, since the latter no longer incur any of these costs.

Whether the firm will, in fact, have to incur these start-up costs depends on how well its skills and resources are matched to the requirements of the new product-market area. If the required new capabilities are very different from those of the firm, then, as discussed earlier, cost dis-economies may result in any of the major functional areas. Thus start-up in new business can have potentially negative as well as positive synergy; a firm with positive synergy will have a competitive advantage over a firm which lacks it.

In addition to the direct and hidden dollar costs, start-up in a new product-market often carries a penalty for time delay. A firm which has the requisite skills and resources, such as suitable production facilities or the appropriate distribution channels for a new market, can quickly transfer them to new activities and thus get a head start on firms which have to build from scratch. The timing advantage in synergy becomes particularly desirable when the new entry is in a dynamic fast-growth stage. Rapid response will have less significance if the firm is considering an entry into a latent demand market (such as RCA's early entry into colour television), or if the new market is stable and slow growing (which would be the case if, for some strange reason, a new firm sought an entry into the textile industry).

Thus, during the start-up phase, synergy can occur in two forms: in the form of dollar savings to the firm thanks to the existence of competences appropriate to the new line of business, and in the form of time savings in becoming fully competitive.

The second category of costs incurred in a new entry is the costs of a going concern: the operating costs and the investment required to support the operation. Here two basic effects operate to produce synergy. One is the advantage of scale – many operations will produce at a lower unit cost when the total volume is increased. For example, purchasing in large quantities offers the advantage of discounts; production in large quantities makes possible more efficient methods and procedures and hence lower direct costs. Many other well-known examples can be given.

A more subtle effect of synergy is a distribution of the burden of overhead

* This is one major reason for the difficulty encountered in determining marginal cash flows for new product-market entries.

expenses over a number of products. This arises from the fact that most overhead functions require a certain minimum level of effort for a wide range of business volume. If volume can be added through a type of diversification which makes use of the existing overhead services, economies will be effected in both the new and the old business. For example, a sales management and administration function must be staffed regardless of whether the firm has one product or a full line; the same research must be conducted regardless of whether it supports one or many products (so long as the products are all based on the same technology).

If top-management talent in a firm is not fully utilized in running the present business, and if its training and experience are relevant, it can provide the most critical ingredient to the new operation. Unfortunately, this potentially strongest component of synergy is also most difficult to measure. Many diversification histories can be cited in which an erroneous estimate was made, either through failure to realize that top management was already fully committed and that new responsibilities resulted in a thin spread of talent or through failure to realize that the new business called for different types of talent and experience and that synergy, in fact, did not exist.

In general, synergy effects during start-up will go hand in hand with operating synergy. However, the strength of the respective effects will differ. For example, a firm with a fully developed position in an area of consumer merchandising, say, in clothing, would have a strong bid for an entry into the toy industry, where similar merchandising experience and talent are required. However, the new entry would require setting up and operating different sales organizations, different manufacturing facilities, different purchases, and different product development. Thus while start-up synergy will be strong in the advantages of timing and basic business know-how, operating synergy will be limited to sales administration and to general management. On the other hand, a firm in women's clothing which adds a line of swimming apparel would have both strong start-up and operating synergy.

Symmetry and Joint Effects

For convenience the preceding discussion has been presented from the viewpoint of the advantages which the diversifying firm can offer to a new product-market entry. It should be made clear that the effects of synergy are symmetric. While the diversifying firm offers benefits to the new product line, it may receive substantial benefits in return. For example, while the parent may strengthen the new subsidiary's research capability, the latter may offer new marketing outlets for the parent's products.

Further, while the viewpoint of cost and investment economics used above is convenient, it fails to account for a full range of potential synergistic benefits. Rather than permit lower costs in support of previous sales volumes, synergy is most frequently sought as a quick way to accelerate growth without additional major investments. This may come from the mutual contributions of *existing* skills and capacities which otherwise might take long to acquire and for which start-up premiums might have to be paid.

A less frequent, but much sought after, effect occurs when by combining resources the joint firm gains access to product-markets to which neither could previously gain access without a major investment. Thus, the recent acquisition by Mercedes of a large electronics company has been explained by Mercedes' management as a move to position the firm for the next generation of automobiles which will be heavy users of electronic controls.

A Framework for Evaluation of Synergy

In principle, all synergistic effects can be mapped on one of three variables: increased volume of dollar revenue to the firm from sales, decreased operating costs and decreased investment requirements. All three must be viewed in the perspective of time. Therefore, a fourth synergistic effect is acceleration of the respective changes in the three variables made possible by synergy.

If this mapping could be carried out in practice, the total effect of synergy could be reflected in the return on investment formula (or some other cash-flow scheme).

In practice, the mapping is frequently not possible, particularly when strategic moves contemplate product-markets in which the firm has little previous experience. Under such conditions, although the primary variables affecting synergy can be identified, as we have done above, it is not possible to quantify and combine their effects.*

As was discussed in Chapter 2, this problem is not unique to measurement of synergy. It occurs in many other parts of the strategic decision process. Our general approach to it in this book is to construct a separate measurement of each important effect and, in a later chapter, to construct a

* Part of the reason is the simple fact that models relating these variables quantitatively are largely unavailable.

Table 5.2. Measurement of Synergy of a New Product-market Entry

Functional area	Symmetry effects	Effects due to pooling of competences						Expansion of present sales	New product and market areas	Overall synergy
		Startup economies			Operating economies					
		Invest-ment	Operating	Timing	Invest-ment	Operating				
General management and finance	Contribution to parent Contribution to new entry Joint opportunities									
Research and development	Contribution to parent Contribution to new entry Joint opportunities									
Marketing	Contribution to parent Contribution to new entry Joint opportunities									
Operations	Contribution to parent Contribution to new entry Joint opportunities									

method for applying these measures jointly to overall evaluation of a project.

A framework for assessing synergy is shown in Table 5.2, which in effect summarizes the developments of this chapter. Synergy effects are first grouped by the primary functional areas of the firm: general management, research and development, marketing and operations (which includes manufacturing, purchasing, inventory control, distribution and warehousing).

Some firms may prefer a finer breakdown of categories. For example, firms which deal heavily in money, securities, and financing will benefit by separating finance from general management. Within each functional area three possible symmetric effects are considered: (1) The contribution which the new product-market entry can make to the firm. (This is a very important effect when the entry is sought through an acquisition of a firm which is comparable in size to the parent. The effect may be negligible when the acquisition is small or the entry is through internal product development.) (2) The contribution from the parent to the entry. (3) Further product-market moves which the two will be able to undertake as a result of the consolidation.

The columns in the table list the variables to be considered in connection with each of the categories. The headings of the columns list the various ways in which synergistic effects may manifest themselves and are self-explanatory in the light of the preceding discussion. It will be noted that a column labelled 'investment' is provided under both start-up and operating synergy. The intent is that a firm will use the former to assess one-time learning costs which do not result in tangible physical facilities, such as marketing start-up costs. The investment entries under operations reflect economics of acquisition of tangible physical assets.

The entries in Table 5.2 should be measurements of the strength of a particular effect. Wherever possible, they should be assigned a numerical value, such as 'reduction of 40,000 square feet in plant requirements' or '20 per cent increase of sales on same investment base'. Failing this, the entries will be relative qualitative ratings. A column is provided for the overall synergy rating, most likely a qualitative one, for each functional area. These in turn can be combined into one overall rating for the prospective entry. Before discussing these entries we need to consider a problem very similar to estimation of synergy, which is frequently called estimation of the firm's strengths and weaknesses.

Strengths and Weaknesses

Management literature dealing with problems of product-market change suggests that one of the early steps following the formulation of objectives should be an analysis of strengths and weaknesses.

The audit has two purposes. First, it can identify deficiencies in the firm's present skills and resources which should be corrected *short* of diversification. Second, it can identify strengths from which the firm can lead in pursuing diversification and/or deficiencies which it may wish to correct *through* diversification.

The strengths from which the firm wishes to lead are readily identified from the preceding discussion as the *synergy* component of the firm's strategy. By searching out opportunities which match its strengths, the firm can optimize the synergistic effects. Thus the problem of strengths and weaknesses and the problem of synergy are seen to be related.

It is also apparent that, when diversification is considered, strengths and weaknesses are relative. Strengths can only be identified relative to the industries into which the firm seeks to diversify. Thus, for example, a superior competence in design of lightweight strong but expensive structures, which is a 'strength' in the aircraft-missile industry, is a weakness when applied to design of industrial machinery.

In order to accommodate synergy and strengths and weaknesses within the same analytic framework, we shall use the method of *profile comparison*. As the first step we shall develop the framework for a *capability profile* which rates a particular pattern of skills and facilities relative to some reference level. We do this by first constructing a grid which matches functional areas in a firm against skills and competences relevant to the functional area, and then by providing a checklist for entries into the grid.

Grid of Competences

The framework we seek must possess two key features. To be widely applicable, it must be constructed in terms of competence areas which are common to most industries; to be applicable to a single firm, these areas must list specific skills and resources which differentiate between success and failure in different types of business. In other words, we are seeking a common framework with differentiated contents within it. Since a fully integrated manufacturing firm has the most comprehensive framework of capabilities, we shall use it as a point of reference. Frameworks for analysis of firms in trade, finance, and services can be obtained through modification of the general model.

The individual skills and resources can be organized along the same major functional areas as in the preceding table:

1. *Research and development* – which we define to encompass the entire process of creating a marketable product. Included are pure and applied research, construction of breadboards and prototypes, industrial design, and preparation of manufacturing drawings. Also included is development of manufacturing processes and techniques. Development of marketing and promotion concepts is included, as well as market research insofar as it is concerned with determining the price-performance characteristics of the product, the size and structure of the market, customer buying habits, etc.

2. *Operations* is concerned with procurement of raw materials, scheduling and controlling production, tooling, manufacturing engineering, quality control, inventory and manufacturing the product.

3. *Marketing* is taken as a broad activity concerned with creating product acceptance, advertising, sales promotion, selling, distributing the product (including transportation and warehousing), contract administration, sales analysis and, very importantly, servicing the product.

4. *General management and finance* is taken to include three areas of activity:

a. Determining the overall pattern of relationships between the firm and its environment. This includes determination of strategy and the total resource allocation, acquisition of new product-market positions for the firm, obtaining necessary financing and maintaining public relations.

b. Providing integrated decision-making, guidance, and control to the functional areas – particularly in areas of pricing, inventory levels, production levels, capital expenditures and individual functional goals.

c. Providing various staff services to the functional areas, such as accounting, industrial relations, personnel training, and performing functions which are most efficiently carried out at centralized levels, such as purchasing.

Within each of these functional areas we recognize four categories of skills and resources:

1. *Facilities and equipment.*

2. *Personnel skills.*

3. *Organizational capabilities* – this includes capabilities such as project management, mass production, large systems management, established standards, policies and procedures for performance of specialized functions.

4. *Management capabilities* – this is described by the types of decisions

and actions for which the management is specially qualified by virtue of training, experience, and present responsibilities. For example, an ability to live with cyclical demand conditions, such as those encountered in the machine tool industry or the textile industry, is a management skill acquired with experience; another is knowledge and understanding of doing complex prime contractor work for the government.

Contents of the Grid

The dual classification presented above offers a grid for assessing a firm's competences. We must next concern ourselves with the contents. The purpose is to develop a master list of entries which will contain the different kinds of capabilities encountered in industries. In view of the great variety of industries such a list cannot be made exhaustive. The purpose is, rather, to provide a master check-list which can be refined by each firm. The following discussion is organized around typical characteristics of principal groups in the United States economy: producers of durables, consumer durables, non-durables, and products and systems for military combat and space missions. Each appears to have a different 'success function' – a different combination of capabilities required of successful competitors.

Many of the capabilities required of firms in manufacturing industries would also apply to firms in service industries. However, both the terminology and the list of items would need to be modified for analysis of capabilities of firms within the two different industrial segments.

A major difficulty in determining the success function of consumer products is that customer acceptance is seldom based on measurable performance characteristics of the product. More frequently it is determined by a complex of factors (the interaction of which is imperfectly understood): apparent performance advantage conveyed to the customer through advertising and sales promotion, price advantage, ready availability of product, fashion, social pressure, artificial obsolescence of preceding products. Since customer acceptance is relatively insensitive to actual performance characteristics, and since quality differences among brands tend to be small, capabilities which are of greatest importance in the consumer business lie in the area of merchandising skills – in advertising, product styling, promotion, distribution and selling. Since demand is sensitive to price, cost-conscious engineering design philosophy is also an important factor.

In industrial products the interaction tends to be somewhat less complex.

The critical factor in product acceptance is its economic justification: demonstrable ability of the product to make money for the buyer (in the form of savings or increased income). Price differential is important, but is related to quality. It is not uncommon in industry to pay a high price for a proven and reliable product. Of great importance is a demonstrated ability of the product to perform reliably. Among key competitive skills in industry are knowledge of the customers' economic justification levels and an ability to design to them, ability to translate new technology into reliable products, special process and manufacturing competences, patent protection, sensitivity to customer needs and requirements and an ability to provide quick and efficient product service.

End products sold to military and space missions succeed primarily if their performance capabilities are in excess of anything which had been previously available. In addition, they must be virtually failure-free during intermittent periods of all-out performance under extreme environmental conditions. A major competitive skill is an ability to apply the most advanced state of the art to products and systems. Organizational competence to manage development and manufacturing of technologically advanced, highly complex systems is another central skill. A very substantial share of military and space business differs from the industrial in that the customer usually buys a design (and a very preliminary one at that) instead of an existing product. This puts emphasis on a very special kind of marketing competence. Technical quality of the design, past performance on similar contracts, technical and scientific reputation, and geopolitical advantages enjoyed by the firm all play an important role in marketing. The salesman is frequently a middleman between engineering and the customer, rather than an active merchandiser.

Since the beginning of the Second Industrial Revolution in the 1950s, a new category of 'high-tech' industries have become an increasingly important segment of economic activity.

The initial success factors in the new high-tech industries were very similar to those for firms which produced for the defence industry: the market share and profits went to firms which pioneered in commercialization of the most advanced technologies. Thus, the advent of 'miracle drugs' after World War II transformed pharmaceuticals into a high-tech industry in which the customers were prepared to pay premium prices for products which treated previously incurable ailments.

The same 'miracle effect' has been observable in the early days of the personal computer industry.

In recent years it has become increasingly clear that the future success in many high-tech industries will be determined by a complex combination of success factors of which advanced technology products will be an important, but not necessarily the determining factor. There is evidence that high-tech industries are learning the importance of customer-tailored design, cost-effective products and marketing concepts. (For further discussion see Note 2.)

In filling out the grid, it is desirable to forego reference to the respective groups and instead to compile a check-list of characteristics of the facilities, skills, organization, and management which may be encountered. The result of such an approach is shown in Table 5.3. An effort was made to make this list comprehensive enough to enable each firm to find items which describe the pattern of its major competences. It is to be expected, however, that many firms will identify additional entries which apply to their particular cases.

As an example, use of the check-list by a firm in road-building machinery may single out the following distinctive entries. In the *facilities and equipment* column: high-bay assembly plant, medium-precision large general-purpose machine tools, up-to-date materials test laboratory, large heavy-duty test track for completed machines, nation-wide direct sales and service offices. Under *personnel skills*: engineering skills in design and manufacture of rugged, medium-tolerance, large machinery, requiring marginal maintenance. *Organizational skills*: job shop for handling large medium-tolerance assembly, strong sales, and field service. *Management skills*: knowledge of dealing with central government and municipalities, experience in running a cyclical business subject to the variations of capital goods cycle and vagaries of government budgets.

Competence and Competitive Profiles

The example describes a part of what we shall call the firm's *competence profile*. It is a list of the major skills and competences in the firm (identified with the aid of Table 5.3) rated with respect to other firms which have the same capabilities. Although most firms would prefer to make the comparison with their own competitors, it is desirable to rate the respective capabilities also with respect to other industries in which they exist. Thus the high-bay large product assembly facilities in the example above would also be found in firms which build railway equipment rolling stock and in materials-handling firms. In assigning the relative ratings some firms may prefer to use a simple two-valued strength or weakness classification. Others would rank the capabilities as outstanding, average, or weak; still others may construct bar-chart profiles.*

The competence profile is the basic reference profile for the firm. It is relatively permanent and will need updating only when major changes occur in the capabilities. The competence profile is a strength and weakness profile only relative to specific areas of competences and skills. It does not necessarily denote strengths and weaknesses with respect to a particular product-market position, since different industries require different balances of capabilities. The major use of the competence profile is in assessment of this balance in four different parts of the strategic problem.

1. *Competitive Analysis*. As will be discussed in detail in Chapter 8, one of the early stages in strategy formulation is to assess the firm's abilities to meet its objectives without changing the present product-market scope of the firm. For this purpose a *competitive profile* is constructed. The relevant profile depends on the characteristics of the future competitive environment of the firm.

If the future environment is expected to be a logical extrapolation of the past, the profile should be based on the profiles of the historically successful competitors. But, if the future environment is expected to be significantly discontinuous from the past, the success factors in the market-place are likely to change, and the historical strength profiles may turn into failure profiles.

This phenomenon is dramatically visible in the 1980s in the personal-computer industry. The historical success lay in advancing the technology of the firm's products. As a result, advanced research and development capability was the key strength of the firm and the other capabilities were rudimentary and dominated by research and development.

In the next phase of the industry's development the dominance in technological advances will no longer be the key strength. Success will be determined by a combination of technological characteristics of the product, their responsiveness to different segments of the market and their cost effectiveness.

Thus, to persist in regarding capability for design of advanced technology products as the key strength and component of future synergy may lead to failure.

When the future is expected to be discontinuous from the past, the

* Similar types of profiles have been used by some firms in evaluation of research and development proposals.

Table 5.3. Check-list for Competitive and Competence Profiles

	Facilities and equipment	Personnel skills	Organizational capabilities	Management capabilities
General management & finance	Data processing equipment	Depth of general management Finance Industrial Relations Legal Personnel recruitment and training Accounting Planning	Multi-divisional structure Consumer financing Industrial financing Planning and control Automated business data processing	Investment management Centralized control Large systems management Decentralized control R & D intensive business Capital-equipment intensive business Merchandising intensive business Cyclical business Many customers Few customers
Research and development	Special lab equipment General lab equipment Test facilities	Areas of specialization Advanced research Applied research Product design: industrial, consumer, military specifications Systems design Industrial design: consumer, industrial	Systems development Product development industrial, consumer, process Military specifications compliance	Utilization of advanced state of the art Application of current state of the art Cost-performance optimization

Operations	General machine shop Precision machinery Process equipment Automated production Large high-bay facilities Controlled environment	Machine operation Tool making Assembly Precision machinery Close tolerance work Process operation Product planning	Mass production Continuous flow process Batch process Job shop Large complex product assembly Subsystems integration Complex product control Quality control Purchasing	Operation under cyclic demand Military specifications quality Tight cost control Tight scheduling
Marketing	Warehousing Retail outlets Sales offices Service offices Transportation equipment	Door-to-door selling Retail selling Wholesale selling Direct industry selling Department of Defense selling Cross-industry selling Applications engineering Advertising Sales promotion Servicing Contract administration Sales analysis	Direct sales Distributor chain Retail chain Consumer service organization Industrial service organization Department of Defense product support Inventory distribution and control	Industrial marketing Consumer merchandising Department of Defense marketing State and municipality marketing

construction of the future competence profiles becomes a much more difficult task than an analysis of historically successful competitors. A description of the process is beyond the scope of this introductory text. (For a detailed description see Ansoff *Implanting Strategic Management*.)

However the competitive profiles are constructed, they are next superimposed on the firm's competence profile to determine the areas in which the firm will be either outstanding or deficient. *These are the future strengths and weaknesses relative to the future success of the present product-market posture.*

2. *Diversification Analysis.* In a later step in strategy formulation, a broad field of outside industries is surveyed to determine attractive areas for the firm. A part of the evaluation will measure the growth and profitability characteristics of the various industries; another part measures the synergy potential between the firm and each new industry, since synergy determines the firm's ability to make a successful and profitable entry. This requires a competitive profile for each industry, describing the pattern of skills required for success. Such profiles can be constructed through a combined use of general industry data and competence profiles of the most successful firms in the industry. Superimposition of our firm's competence profile with the respective competitive profiles measures the 'fit' with each new industry and hence the chances of a successful entry.

3. *Synergy Component of Strategy.* In Chapter 9 the product-market strategy of the firm will be determined through several key components, each of which specifies rules for search and for evaluation of opportunities. Synergy is one of these components. To derive it, a procedure like the above is used, but the competence profile is now compared with competitive profiles for a few selected industries. The major relative strengths and weaknesses of the firm are identified and specified as rules for search. The management has a choice of an *aggressive strategy*, in which the future strengths are used as search criteria, or a *defensive strategy*, in which the search is directed toward remedying the future weaknesses, or both.

4. *Evaluation of Individual Opportunities.* Once search has uncovered a promising acquisition or a new product, a final evaluation must be made. A part of this evaluation is a measurement of synergy as a contributing factor to potential joint profitability. This requires completion of Table 5.2 presented earlier in this chapter. Profiles of the firm and of the acquisition are constructed and superimposed. Then:

a. The resulting pattern is compared with the future competitive profile developed in the competitive analysis above to determine whether the pattern of reinforcements will make any significant contribution to the parent firm's future competitive position. The results can be used to determine the entries in the line 'contribution to parent' in Table 5.2.

b. The superimposed profiles are similarly compared with the future competitive profile in the new entry's industry, thus giving material for the line in the table labelled 'contribution to new entry'.

c. Finally superimposed profiles are compared with typical profiles developed under diversification analysis above to see whether the combination of the two firms' skills will provide an entry into an industry which neither could enter alone. This provides data for the line in Table 5.2 labelled 'joint opportunities'.

This procedure of using paired profiles to fill in Table 5.2 is laborious and should be used primarily at the 'short strokes' of an evaluation of new product-market opportunities or of major acquisition candidates. For a preliminary analysis, profiles can usually be dispensed with and Table 5.2 filled in on a judgement basis.

CHAPTER 6

Concept of Strategy

Strategy is when you are out of ammunition, but keep right on firing so that the enemy won't know.

AUTHOR UNKNOWN

The Problem

During the past twenty years the concept of strategy has become one of the everyday words of managers, and the practice of strategic planning is now widespread among large and medium-sized firms.

This interest in strategy was caused by growing realization that the firm's environment has become progressively changeable and discontinuous from the past and that, as a result, objectives alone are insufficient as decision rules for guiding the firm's strategic reorientation as it adapts to changing challenges, threats and opportunities.

The new decision rules and guidelines, which guide the process of development of an organization, have been defined as *strategy*. It will be recalled from discussion in Chapter 2 that capital investment theory makes no use of the concept of strategy. The need for it arises from characteristics which are peculiar to the strategic problem: the fact that a firm needs direction and focus in its search for and creation of new opportunities and the fact that it is to the firm's advantage to seek entries with strong synergistic potential.

The first two sections of this chapter develop the basic concept of strategy. The next three sections explore the usefulness of strategy and conditions under which explicit strategy formulation becomes necessary. The two following sections define two basic strategies used in modern practice: the portfolio and competitive strategies. The penultimate section then comments on the use of strategies in different types of firms, while the final section differentiates the concept of strategy from the concept of policy.

Concept of the Firm's Business and the Common Thread

Objectives set the performance levels which a firm seeks to achieve, but they do not describe the business of the firm, unless statements such as 'the firm is in 20 per cent ROI business' or in 'flexible position business' are constructed to provide the description.

In a pioneering article published in 1960, Theodore Levitt[1] suggested that a more definitive description of the firm's role in the environment is requisite for growth and success. Such a description should encompass a broad scope of natural extensions of the firm's product-market position, derived from some core characteristic of the present business. Thus railways would view themselves in the 'transportation business' and petroleum companies in the 'energy business'.

While plausible, such broad statements of 'the business we are in' are not sufficiently precise to guide the firm's strategic development. Does it follow from this concept that railways should be in the long-haul trucking industry? The answer would seem to be yes. But how about taxi-cab or rental-car business? These are also transportation industries, but at first glance would seem to have little in common with railways. It is hard to see where the skills, facilities, and experience of railway companies have anything to contribute to the latter areas. Consider the energy business for petroleum companies. Does it follow that they should diversify into fabrication of uranium fuel for atomic power plants, build the power plants, or retail electricity? The respective management, technical, production, and marketing skills are all different. Where is the common core capability?

The weakness with concepts such as 'transportation business' or 'energy business' is that they are too broad and do not provide a 'common thread' -- a relationship between present and future product-markets which would enable outsiders to perceive where the firm is heading, and the inside management to give it guidance.

A separate question is how strong the common thread must be. Royal Little has built the first classic conglomerate company, the Textron Corp., composed of consumer electronics, textiles, helicopters, work shoes and satellite motors, etc. – all without a strongly apparent common thread. Many other firms have followed Little's example in creating numerous conglomerate firms. On the other hand many other firms followed the pioneering example of the Du Pont Company by closely following a very clearly defined common thread.

It is useful to review how firms usually identify the nature of their business. Some firms are identified by the characteristics of their product line. Thus there are 'transistor companies', 'machine-tool companies' and 'automobile companies'. Others are described by the technology which underlies the product line, such as 'steel companies', 'aluminium companies' and 'glass companies'. Each may sell a wide range of different products to different users, but a common thread is provided by a manufacturing and/or engineering technology.

Firms are also described in terms of their markets. Here it is useful to make a distinction between customers and missions. A *mission* is an existing product *need*; a *customer* is the actual *buyer* of the product: the economic unit (such as an individual, a family, a business firm) which possesses both the need and the money with which to satisfy it.

The usefulness of this distinction lies in the fact that sometimes the customer is erroneously identified as the common thread of a firm's business. In reality a given type of customer will frequently have a range of unrelated product missions or needs. He would not necessarily satisfy them through the same purchasing channels, nor use the same approach to buying.

Thus, the individual consumer fills his food needs at the supermarket and his entertainment needs at a television dealer's. Since the product technology, the distribution channels, and the customer motivation are different, no strong common thread is available to a firm which would attempt to sell both food and television sets. Similarly, a company which supplies weapon systems for the Army's combat missions would have a better common thread in supplying control systems to industry than in selling replacement parts for Army trucks.

In selecting a useful range of missions of a particular customer, a firm needs to find a common thread either in product characteristics, technology, or similarity of needs. Thus agricultural machinery firms supply a range of needs of the farmer. All of these are related parts of his overall mission of tilling and harvesting the soil. Similarly, a home-appliance manufacturer offers effort-saving products for the home which may range from washing machines to electronic irons.

In this perspective it is easy to see why the term 'transportation business' fails to supply the common thread. First, the range of possible missions is very broad: intra-urban, inter-urban, intra-continental, and inter-continental transportation; through the media of land, air, water, underwater; for moving passengers and/or cargo. Second, the range of customers is wide: the individual, family, business firm, or government office. Third, the 'product' varies: car, bus, train, ship, aeroplane, helicopter, taxi, truck. The number of practical combinations of the variables is large, and so is the number of common threads.

While such a concept of business is too broad to be useful, the traditional identification of a firm with a particular industry has become too narrow. Today a great many firms find themselves in a number of different industries. Furthermore, the boundaries of industries are continually changing, and new ones are being born. For example, radio. television, transistor, home appliance and atomic energy are all industries which did not exist fifty years ago. The need is for a concept of business which on the one hand will give specific guidance for the firm and on the other hand will provide room for growth. We shall describe such a concept in the next section.

Concept of Strategy

Strategy is one of several sets of decision-making rules for guidance of organizational behaviour. For example:

1. Yardsticks by which the present and future performance of the firm is measured. The quality of these yardsticks is usually called *objectives* and the desired quantity *goals*.

2. Rules for developing the firm's relationship with its *external* environment: *what* products-technology the firm will develop. *where* and *to whom* the products are to be sold, and *how* will the firm gain advantage over competitors. This set of rules is called the product-market or *business strategy*.

3. Rules for establishing the internal relations and processes *within* the organization; this is frequently called the *administrative strategy*.

4. The rules by which the firm conducts its day-to-day business, called major *operating policies*.

A business strategy has several distinguishing characteristics:

1. The process of business-strategy formulation results in *no immediate action*. Rather, it sets the general directions in which the firm's position will grow and develop.

2. Therefore strategy must next be used to generate strategic projects through a *search process*. The role of strategy in search is first to *focus* it on areas defined by the strategy, and, second to *filter out* the uncovered possibilities which are inconsistent with the strategy.

3. Thus, *strategy becomes unnecessary whenever the historical dynamics of an organization will take it where it wants to go*. This is to say, when the search process is already focused on the preferred areas.

4. At the time of strategy formulation it is not possible to enumerate all

the project possibilities which will be uncovered. Therefore, strategy formulation must be based on *highly aggregated, incomplete* and *uncertain information* about classes of alternatives.

5. When the search uncovers specific alternatives, the more precise, less aggregated information which becomes available may cast doubts on the wisdom of the original strategy choice. Thus, successful use of strategy requires *strategic feedback*.

6. Since both strategy and objectives are used to filter projects, they appear similar. And yet they are distinct. *Objectives represent the ends* which the firm is seeking to attain, *while the strategy is the means to these ends*. The objectives are higher-level decision rules. A strategy which is valid under one set of objectives may lose its validity when the objectives of the organization are changed.

7. Finally, strategy and objectives are interchangeable; both at different points in time and at different levels of organization. Thus, some attributes of performance (such as, for example, market share) can be an objective of the firm at one time and its strategy at another. Further, as objectives and strategy are elaborated throughout an organization, a typical hierarchical relationship results: *elements of strategy at a higher managerial level become objectives at a lower one*.

In summary, strategy is an elusive and somewhat abstract concept. Its formulation typically produces no immediate concrete productive action in the firm. Above all, it is an expensive process both in terms of actual dollars and managerial time. Since management is pragmatic result-oriented activity, a question needs to be asked: whether an abstract concept, such as strategy, can usefully contribute to the firm's performance.

In the business firm, concern with explicit formulation of strategy is relatively recent. However, the history of business abounds with clear examples of deliberate and successful use of strategy. Du Pont's deliberate and successful move from explosives into chemicals in the 1920s is one example. Henry Ford's concentration on the Model T for the emerging mass market was another great success, but his strategy of vertical integration was a failure. As an alternative to Henry Ford's strategy, consider Durant's vision of a firm founded on a fully automotive product line, and Sloan's subsequent rationalization of this vision into a clear set of organizational guidelines.

A trained business observer can discern a unique strategy in a majority of successful firms. However, while discernible in most cases, frequently strategies are not made explicit. They are either a private concept shared only by the key management, or a diffuse, generally understood, but seldom verbalized sense of common purpose throughout the firm.

It has been argued by some managers, and with good reason, that this is a desirable state of things, that, because it represents a unique competitive advantage of the firm, strategy should not be made explicit and must be kept private.

Since the mid-1950s, American business literature has increasingly reflected an opposing view in favour of carefully and explicitly formulated strategy. This view favours not only making the strategy a matter of concern to many managers throughout the firm, but also to many of the relevant 'workers', particularly in marketing and R&D, since they are not only making important contributions to strategy formulation, but are also the principal agents of its implementation.

If the value of a concept is to be measured by its contribution to success, we would have to admit that somehow both of the above views are correct: a great many firms have succeeded and are succeeding without the benefit of an explicitly enumerated strategy, while a smaller and growing number have benefited from deliberate strategy formulation.

An explanation can be sought through resolution of another apparent paradox: strategy is a system concept which gives coherence and direction to growth of a complex organization. How is it possible, then, for a large and complex organization, such as a business firm, to attain coordination and coherence without making strategy explicit?

An answer is to be found in the nature of the firm's growth. If a firm is operating in growing markets, if the characteristics of demand change slowly, if the technology of products and processes is stable, if all these conditions exist, strategy needs to change slowly and incrementally. Coherence of behaviour and organizational coordination are attained through informal organizational learning and adaptation. New managers and workers are typically given long indoctrination periods into the nature of the business; their careers are shaped by gradual progression through the firm. In the process they acquire an experiential, almost intuitive, awareness of the firm's strategic guidelines. When environment, technology, or competition change in an orderly manner, these managers are able to adapt their responses incrementally, using their accumulated knowledge and experience. A manager in R&D can be expected to act coherently with managers in marketing and production. The result is reasonably coherent organizational growth. The strategy remains stable and implicit and the firm's products and market evolve in a logically incremental way.

It can be questioned whether such loosely coordinated behaviour produces the best possible growth, but it works demonstrably. Since the first half-century was a period of relatively stable continued growth, the absence of concern with strategy is not surprising.

The second half-century is a new 'ball game'. In many cases the historical organizational dynamics are a path to stagnation and/or decline. Therefore, strategy has emerged as a tool for reorienting the organizational thrust. Given this fact, several questions need to be asked concerning the utility of having a strategy.

The first is whether a systematic explicit strategy is a viable concept. Some writers (significantly, observers, not of the firm but of decision processes in the government) have argued that organizational complexity, uncertainties of information and limited human cognition make it impossible to approach strategy formulation in a systematic manner. Their argument is that strategy formulation must of necessity proceed in the adaptive, unsystematic, informal way observed in most organizations. The answer to this contention is that the proof of the pudding is in the eating. Numerous business firms, which in recent years formulated and announced their strategies, have put this argument to rest.

Given that systematic strategy formulation is feasible, the second question to be asked is whether it produces improvement in organizational performance, if used as an alternative to adaptive growth. Until quite recently we had no satisfactory answer to this question. However, within recent years, several pieces of evidence have been provided.

One of these comes from an extensive study of American mergers and acquisitions by this author and several colleagues. Among other significant results, we found that deliberate and systematic preplanning of acquisition strategy produces significantly better financial performance than an unplanned, opportunistic, adaptive approach. These results are valid under stringent tests of their statistic validity.[2]

Since this study, a number of subsequent research studies confirmed our findings, namely that explicit strategy formulation can improve performance.

When to Formulate Strategy

The third question we need to ask is when does recourse to strategy become essential. One condition is when rapid and discontinuous changes occur in the environment of the firm. This may be caused by saturation of traditional markets, technological discoveries inside or outside the firm, or sudden influx of new competitors.

Under these conditions, established organizational traditions and experience no longer suffice for coping with the new opportunities and new threats. Without the benefit of unifying strategy, the chances are high that different parts of the organization will develop different, contradictory and ineffective responses. Marketing will continue struggling to revive historical demand, production will make investments in automation of obsolete production lines, while R & D will develop new products based on an obsolete technology. Conflicts will result, and reorientation may come too late to guarantee survival of the firm.

When confronted with discontinuities, the firm is confronted with two very difficult problems:

1. How to choose the right directions for further growth from among many and imperfectly perceived alternatives; and

2. How to harness energies of a large number of people in the new chosen direction.

Answers to these questions are the essence of strategy formulation and implementation. At this point, strategy becomes an essential and badly needed managerial tool.

Such conditions were in fact the cause of interest in explicit strategy formulation in the United States during the mid-1950s, when pent-up wartime demand began to reach saturation; when technology began to make obsolete some industries and to proliferate new ones; and when restructuring of international markets presented both new threats and new opportunities for business firms.

An explicit new strategy also becomes necessary when the objectives of an organization change drastically as a result of new demands imposed on the organization by society. This is precisely what is happening today in many non-business purposive organizations: the church, the university, the government. And this was the reason for the efforts to introduce strategic planning into many of these institutions.

Difficulties Encountered in Implanting Strategy Formulation

One major source of difficulty comes from the fact that, in most organizations, the pre-strategy decision-making processes are heavily political in nature. Strategy introduces elements of rationality which are disruptive to the historical culture of the firm, and threatening to the political process.

A natural organizational reaction is to fight against the disruption of the historical culture and power structure, rather than confront the challenges posed by the environment. This reaction has been widely observed during introduction of strategic planning into business firms.

A no-less important difficulty is that introduction of strategic planning triggers conflicts between the historical profit making activities and the new innovative activities. Organizations typically do not have the capability, the capacity or the motivational systems to act and think strategically.

Finally, organizations generally lack the information about themselves and their environment which is needed for effective strategic planning; nor do they have the managerial talents capable of formulating and implementing strategy.

In Part 2 of this book we will be discussing approaches to anticipating and overcoming barriers to implanting strategy formulation in the firm.

Portfolio Strategy

In modern practice two related types of strategy are used to characterize the thrust of the firm's strategic development. We shall call the first the *strategic portfolio strategy* and the second the *competitive strategy*.

The portfolio strategy is the modern version of the 'business we are in' concept discussed in a previous section.

The firm can be conceived of as an assembly of distinctive *strategic business areas* (SBA's), each of which offers different future growth/profitability opportunities and/or will require different competitive approaches. (For a further discussion of the important concept of strategic business areas see Ansoff, *Implanting Strategic Management*.)

One way to state the portfolio strategy is by specifying the kinds of strategic business areas in which the firm intends to do business in the future, as well as the manner in which the SBA's will relate to one another.

There are four components of the portfolio strategy:

1. The first component is the *geographical growth vector* which specifies the scope and direction of the firm's future business.

The original edition of *Corporate Strategy* introduced the concept of the *growth vector* which specified the direction in which the firm intends to develop its strategic portfolio. This was illustrated by means of a matrix, shown in Figure 6.1. *Market penetration* denotes a growth direction through

Product Mission	Present	New
Present	Market penetration	Product development
New	Market development	Diversification

Figure 6.1. Growth Vector Components

the increase of market share for the present product-markets. In *market development* new missions are sought for the firm's products. *Product development* creates new products to replace current ones. Finally, *diversification* is distinctive in the fact that both products and missions are new to the firm. The common thread is clearly indicated, in the first three alternatives, to be either the marketing skills or product technology or both. In diversification, the common thread is less apparent and is certainly weaker.

Specification of the common thread through the growth vector is complementary to the product-market scope, since it gives the directions *within* an industry as well as *across* industry boundaries which the firm proposes to pursue.

With the perspective of twenty years' experience, a somewhat more complex description of the growth vector alternatives becomes apparent. Instead of the two dimensions of the original matrix (product and mission), it is more realistic to describe the geographical growth vector along the dimensions shown in Figure 6.2. The cube shows the three dimensions which the firm can use to define the thrust and the ultimate future scope of the business.

a. The dimension of *market need* (such as need for personal transportation or need for amplification of weak electrical signals).

b. The dimension of *product/service technology* (such as transistor technology, integrated circuit technology, or electro-optical technology).

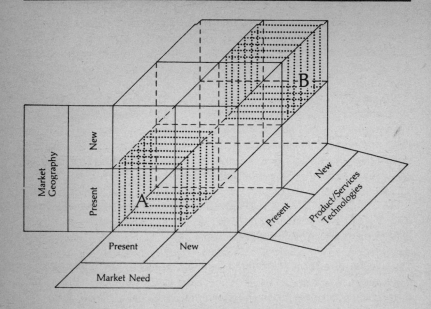

Figure 6.2. Dimensions of the Geographic Growth Vector

c. The *market geography* which defines the regions or nation states in which the firm intends to do business.

As the cube shows, the firm has a variety of combinations and directions in which it can modify its strategic portfolio. The extreme choices are: to continue serving its traditional need and geographical market with its traditional technology on the one hand (see the shaded cube labelled A in Figure 6.2), or to move vigorously to a new position on all three dimensions (see the shaded cube labelled B).

2. The second component of portfolio strategy is the *competitive advantage* which the firm will seek in its respective business areas. Thus the Du Pont Company has traditionally sought to succeed in all of its businesses through products based on patented advanced technology.

3. The third component of portfolio strategy is the *synergies* which the firm will seek among its businesses. In Du Pont's case the synergy was its advanced research and development capability in chemical technology.

4. The fourth component of portfolio strategy is the *strategic flexibility* of the strategic business portfolio.

Strategic flexibility is attained in two ways. The first is externally to the firm through diversifying the firm's geographic scope, needs served, and technologies so that a surprising change in any one of the strategic business areas does not produce a seriously damaging impact on the firm's performance.

The second way to attain strategic flexibility is to base the firm's portfolio on resources and capabilities which are easily transferable among the strategic business areas. Thus, a portfolio of business areas which can be served by a common production system is less vulnerable to strategic surprises than a portfolio which requires distinctive and non-transferable production capabilities for each of the firm's businesses.

As can be seen from examining the four components of the portfolio strategy (growth vector, competitive advantage, synergy, strategic flexibility), optimizing one of the components is likely to depress the firm's performance on the others. In particular, maximizing synergy is very likely to reduce the strategic flexibility. Thus the process of selecting and balancing the portfolio is a complex one.

Competitive Strategy

The portfolio strategy specifies the combinations of different strategic business areas in which the firm will seek to attain its objectives. The competitive strategy, on the other hand, specifies the distinctive approach which the firm intends to use in order to succeed in each of the strategic business areas.

According to micro-economic theory, success in a market-place is totally dependent on the price of the product or service. The logic is that the lowest price will enable the firm to capture a dominant market share. The resulting volume of sales will permit reduction of unit costs through economies of scale, thus making the firm the lowest cost producer in the industry. The firm will thus be able to maximize both its sales volume and its profits.

Two of the underlying assumptions of micro-economic theory are: (1) the products/services offered to the customers are undifferentiated, and (2) the customer seeks to minimize the cost of his purchases as the sole criterion in his decision.

These assumptions were valid in the developed nations during the first half of the twentieth century. Therefore, micro-economic theory offered a valid explanation of practice. As a result the optimal success strategy was simple: minimize the costs of the firm's products and sell at a price equal to or less than the competition. Since this behaviour resulted in optimization of the firm's market share, this strategy was frequently referred to as the *market share* or *market-position strategy*.

For reasons discussed earlier, significant changes occurred in the market-success factors during the second half of the century. Customers were no longer seeking a standard product at the lowest price. They demanded that products have a variety of features and performance characteristics that responded to their particular tastes, social status, buying power, etc. As a result, the ability to offer products responsive to the particular needs of a particular group of customers became a critical success factor and *product differentiation* became an important competitive strategy.

Micro-economic theory makes the implicit assumption that buyers have perfect information and are able to recognize not only price differences, but also differences in features and performance characteristics of the products/services offered to them. But experience has shown that their purchases were affected by the *image* of what products/services could do for them. Further, business firms discovered that customer tastes and preferences can be shaped, and new tastes and preferences can be created, through skilful advertising and promotion. As a result, *market* (*or image*) *differentiation* became another important competitive strategy.

Finally, success in the market-place against competitors no longer guaranteed satisfactory growth and profits, because an increasing number of industries were reaching the stage of demand saturation. If a firm had an aggressive growth objective it could no longer expect automatic growth from the market-place. To meet the growth objective the firm had to formulate and implement a growth thrust strategy, such as a geographic market expansion, market segmentation, stimulation of demand through artificial obsolescence, etc.

Thus, in a brief span of some twenty years new strategies critical to success in the market place were added to the traditional strategy of cost/price minimization.

To summarize, strategies which became important to success during the last quarter of the twentieth century are:

1. (The historical) *market-share maximization* strategy.
2. *Growth* strategy by which a firm assures its future growth.
3. *Market differentiation* (or market niche) strategy of creating a distinc-

tive image in the minds of potential customers for the firm's products/
services.

4. *Product/service differentiation* (or product niche) strategy which differentiates the performance of the product/service from the competitors'
products/services.

Need for Strategy in Different Types of Firms

In an earlier section we discussed the environmental conditions under which
explicit strategy formulation becomes necessary. It remains to discuss the
applicability of the components of the portfolio strategy to different types
of firms:

1. A type of firm which needs the most comprehensive strategy is a fully
integrated synergistic firm. Since its product-market decisions have long
lead times, it needs guidance for R & D, and it must be able to anticipate
change. Much of its investment is irreversible, since it goes into R & D,
which cannot be recovered, and physical assets, which are difficult to sell. It
must, therefore, minimize the chances of making bad decisions.

2. A conglomerate firm has less stringent strategy requirements. It does
not seek synergy among its subsidiaries, nor does it use internal R & D as a
primary source for diversification. Each subsidiary operates independently,
and the common thread among them is primarily financial. The conglomerate does need objectives with threshold-goals type of provisions for
partial ignorance. Its strategy would have no synergy component or growth
vector component. A well-managed conglomerate would include the component of flexibility to protect the firm from strategic surprises. Such a firm
may or may not have a well-defined growth vector to help focus search and
develop local expert knowledge of some industries.

3. At the other extreme from a fully integrated, synergistic firm is a
company which primarily buys and sells. This may be an investment trust, a
pension fund or a real-estate syndicate. Its position differs from conglomerate in that the 'portfolio' of holdings is widely diversified and is
highly negotiable, and the transfer costs are relatively low (sales tax,
commission fees, etc.). Because portfolios are widely diversified, such firms
seldom have the depth of knowledge of individual industries to enable them
to seek a specific competitive advantage. Their planning is usually confined
to objectives which are established on the basis of generally available
industry data. Thus, for example, investment funds choose between the role
of a 'growth fund' and that of a 'current earnings fund'.

Table 6.1. Strategy Requirements for Different Firms

Strategy requirement / Type of firm	P-M scope	Growth vector	Synergy	Competitive advantage	Objectives
Operating firm	√	√	√	√	√
Conglomerate firm	√(?)			√	√
Investment company					√

The three types of company above were described in what might be called their 'pure form'. In actuality there are various shadings of characteristics which make it difficult to place firms into one of the slots. There are different degrees of integration in synergistic companies, some companies act as conglomerates in some parts and are synergistic in others, and some investment firms *do* have industry experts and *do* specialize in certain industries. Therefore, each individual firm will have to determine its strategy requirement using the classification as a guide. Table 6.2 may be useful for this purpose.

It can easily be seen from the table that the synergistic firm requires the most complex strategy.* The remainder of our discussion will continue to deal with the more complex case.

Strategy, Policy, Programmes, and Operating Procedures

The origin of the term 'strategy' lies in the military art, where it is a broad, rather vaguely defined, 'grand' concept of a military campaign for *application* of large-scale forces against an enemy. Strategy is contrasted to *tactics*, which is a specific scheme for *employment* of allocated resources. In applications to business practice, the term *policy* has been often used interchangeably with strategy, thus creating unfortunate confusion between the two different concepts.

In the business vocabulary, long before the advent of strategy, the term policy was widely used in manuals of organization and procedures to denote a specific response to specific repetitive situations, e.g. 'overtime reimbursement policy', 'foul weather policy', 'educational refund policy', 'policy for the evaluation of inventories'. A contingent event is recognized, such as a periodic need to work overtime, or a snowstorm. What needs to be done

---

* Investment funds which trade in listed securities have the additional advantage of knowing the full field of choice. There is no partial ignorance. This and low transfer costs permit an approach to the strategic problem which is much simpler than the present method.[3]

and the outcomes of such contingencies are *well known*; the contingencies are repetitive, but the time of specific occurrences cannot be specified in advance. In view of this, it is not worthwhile to require a new decision on what should be done each time overtime is needed or each time it snows. A better and more economical procedure is to prescribe, in advance, the response to be made whenever a specified contingency occurs. This is done through a written statement of the appropriate policy and of accompanying procedures for its implementation. Since the management decision is thus made in advance of the event, a rule for behaviour can be imposed on lower levels of supervision. Thus economies of management are realized, and consistency of action is assured.

When compared with our definition of strategy this meaning of policy is seen to be distinct and different. Policy is a *contingent decision*, whereas strategy is a *rule for making decisions*. Thus while implementation of policy can be delegated downward, implementation of strategy cannot, since last-minute executive judgement will be required. In technical terms, used by mathematical decision theorists, specification of strategy is forced under conditions of *partial ignorance*, when alternatives cannot be arranged and examined in advance, whereas under conditions of *risk* (alternatives are all known and so are their probabilities) or *uncertainty* (alternatives are known but not the probabilities), the consequences of different alternatives *can* be analysed in advance and decision made contingent on their occurrence. The lower-level executive merely needs to recognize the event and then act in accordance with his instructions.

As mentioned previously, condition of risk may mean assignment of probability either to the *occurrence* of an event or to its possible *outcomes*. When the occurrence is certain, but the outcome is either certain or uncertain, a different kind of decision, called a *programme*, is possible; this is a time-phased action sequence used to guide and coordinate operations. When the occurrence of an alternative is not only certain but also repetitive, the decision takes the form of a *standing operating procedure*.

Thus, the several types of decisions commonly made within a firm can be ranked in the order of increasing level of ignorance: standing operating procedures and programmes under conditions of certainty or partial risk, policies under conditions of risk and uncertainty, and strategies under conditions of partial ignorance.

There is an unfortunate coincidence in our definitions. We speak of 'strategic' decisions,* where 'strategic' means 'relating to firm's match to its environment', and of 'strategy', where the words means 'rules for decision

* Perhaps a better term would have been *entrepreneurial*.

under partial ignorance'. This coincidence should not obscure the fact that all four basic types of decision described above – strategy, policy, programme, and standing operating procedure – occur in all three classes of problems: strategic, administrative, and operating.

It should further be made clear that all of the basic types of decisions may apply on organizational levels below the firm as a whole. Thus, for example, functional organizations, such as research, development, finance, and marketing, have a strong interface with the outside environment and will frequently be faced with conditions of partial ignorance. Under these conditions they will require appropriate strategies, such as R & D strategy, finance strategy, marketing strategy.

CHAPTER 7

Diversification and Internationalization

I don't know of any more difficult management problem than that of diversifying . . .
while diversification is fine as a matter of abstract principle, it can result in so
many different eggs in one basket that nothing really significant is hatched out of
any of them.

JOSEPH T. WRIGHT

The Problem

It was pointed out in Chapter 1 that a firm's concern with the strategic
problem is not automatic and that, in the absence of a trigger signal, most
managements will focus their attention on administrative and operating
decisions. In the first section of this chapter we explore alternative conditions for the trigger signal and suggest an approach to initiating a strategic
analysis.

A milestone in this analysis is reached when the firm faces the decision
whether or not to diversify. The second section explores conditions under
which diversification is indicated and relates the decision to management
attitudes toward risk.

The third section explores alternative directions for diversification and
relates these to the objectives of the firm. The pros and cons of a popular
form, the conglomerate diversification, are explored.

Incremental vs. Discontinuous Change

To review our earlier definition, a strategic portfolio change occurs
whenever a firm changes the markets it serves, and/or the technologies it
uses, and/or geographic locations in which it does business.

We will refer to a portfolio change as *incremental*, whenever the change is
a logical and relatively small departure from the past portfolio. For example,
the expansion of a firm's market to a region within a new country, or an
improvement in a historical technology, would be regarded as incremental
Brian Quinn called such a change process 'logical incrementalism'.[1] Other
writers called it an 'evolutionary' change process.

A change is *discontinuous* whenever it does not directly follow the historical logic of the firm's development, and represents a new departure on one or more of the three dimensions shown in Figure 6.1. In the terminology of this book, a discontinuous change is a significant departure from the historical growth vector.

One test of the degree of discontinuity is the extent to which the firm makes a departure from the market needs which it knows how to serve, from the technology on which the firm's products are based, or from the geographical, economic, cultural, social, or political settings in which it knows how to do business.

Another, and related, test of discontinuity, which will be discussed in detail in Part 2, is the extent to which the change will require revisions in the culture, power structure, systems, organizational structure and reward/incentives within the firm. Another term used in literature for discontinuous change is 'novel change.'

The Trigger Signal

As mentioned in an earlier chapter of this book, from the outset of the twentieth century, firms progressively established R & D departments to provide a capability for incremental strategic change in products/services/technology. Towards the middle of the century, market-development departments came into existence to manage incremental changes in markets and needs served.

While they institutionalized logical incrementalism, these organizational arrangements did not provide the capability, capacity, nor the stimulus for discontinuous changes.

Until the 1950s there appears to have been little understanding of strategic discontinuities, nor of the need to anticipate them. As a result, preoccupation with discontinuities had followed an 'on-off' cycle. A major environmental discontinuity triggered, usually with a substantial lag, urgent attention to strategic reorientation. Once the strategic reorientation was completed, attention was refocused on operating exploitation of the potential of the new strategic posture until the next environmental discontinuity occurred.

A classic historical example of a discontinuous change is offered by the Du Pont Company, which in 1909 became aware of the invention of dynamite which made obsolete the firm's traditional reliance on black-powder technology. Between 1910 and 1918 Du Pont underwent a major strategic reorientation which drastically reduced its dependence on black powder, and transformed Du Pont into a research-based leader in the chemical industry. Having consolidated its position of leadership, Du Pont did not need to confront another strategic discontinuity until the 1950s when a changed competitive environment and expiration of some basic patents again created a new strategic discontinuity.

A. P. Chandler, whose book provided the above example,[2] studied many other cases in which temporary attention to strategy was followed by long periods of preoccupation with operating and administrative problems.

Chandler also showed that awareness of a strategic discontinuity usually comes through a traumatic experience, such as a drastic drop in sales or earnings, a product breakthrough by competition, or a continued failure to meet profit objectives. The unfortunate fact about this route is that when the challenge is finally recognized, the firm is ill-prepared to cope with it. Nor is it an easy challenge to meet, because the symptoms are usually ambiguous. Considerable analysis is required to arrive at a conclusion that the problem is, in fact, strategic; at the same time the tendency is to seek solutions in operating (cost reduction!) and administrative (reorganization!) changes.

For reasons discussed earlier, in the 1900s many firms could no longer treat strategic change as a one-time response, put their strategic posture in order and then revert to operating and administrative concerns. The post-World War II deluge of technology, the dynamism of the world-wide changes in market structure, and the saturation of demand in many first generation industries all have contributed to a drastic shortening of the strategy-operations-strategy cycle which management used to follow.

It appears, in fact, that in many industries, such as electronics, chemicals, pharmaceuticals, plastics, and aerospace, there is no longer any cycle. Strategic change is so rapid that firms must continually survey the environment in search of strategic discontinuities.*

The preceding suggests that:

1. In the present business environment, no firm can consider itself immune to threats of technology obsolescence, saturation of demand and socio-political discontinuities.

2. In some industries, surveillance of the environment for strategic threats and opportunities needs to be a continuous process.

* This increased pace is illustrated by the current rate of merger and acquisition activity, which is one of the major instruments of strategic change. The post-World War II decade has been described as the third great major wave in American business history.[3]

3. As a minimum, firms in all industries need to make regular periodic reviews of their strategic portfolios. It is in response to these challenges that, starting in the 1950s, systematic periodic strategic planning has been gradually developed and adopted by business firms. Today a dominant majority of leading business firms practises some version of strategic planning.

The key question, therefore, is not whether to direct management attention to strategy, but rather how and to what extent. For a firm which faces it for the first time, this question has a chicken and egg quality; a definitive answer cannot be given until a complete strategic diagnosis has been carried out along the lines which will be discussed in the succeeding pages. However, certain preliminary guidelines for decision can be set down.

1. Clearly, the intensiveness of the analysis will be limited by the resources of the firm. A one-man top management will of necessity be forced into a highly condensed review of strategy; a large multi-divisional firm can afford a thorough study.

2. The characteristics of the firm's environments will have a dominant influence.

a. If the environment is highly dynamic, evolution of technology rapid, technology substitution frequent, and/or market structure unstable, the firm will need to put strategic change on a permanent basis. It might as well face this need at the outset, even before the first diagnosis is undertaken.

b. If, on the other hand, the industry is one of the few remaining ones which can be expected to enjoy relative stability in the future, it is best to perform a strategic diagnosis before deciding to institute a permanent strategic-planning process. In such cases the firm may be well advised to secure competent outside help for the initial analysis.

3. The magnitude of the needed strategy realignment will influence the decision. If the problem appears as a minor 'soft spot' in an otherwise healthy product-market position, temporary *ad hoc* arrangements for correcting it may suffice. If a wholesale revision of the position appears necessary, a major allocation of resources on a long-term permanent basis is indicated.

If the final conclusion is that a major strategic-reorientation effort is required, far-reaching organizational changes will probably have to follow. It is important to recognize that traditional organizational forms have evolved for the primary pursuit of the operating problem. Nor does adoption of a strategic-planning system guarantee that strategies will be implemented, nor that the system will not be ejected from the organization.* The costs and the risks attendant on strategic change require that top executive talent takes full-time responsibility for the effort and that it be supported with adequate staff resources and budgets.

Part 2 of this book is devoted to making sure that strategic planning produces results in the market-place and that strategic thinking is implanted in the firm.

Typology of Portfolio Changes

Portfolio strategy is concerned with the assortment of the business areas in which the firm intends to do business, while competitive strategy is concerned with the way it will attack the respective areas.

Portfolio strategy answers the question: in which businesses shall we be; while competitive strategy answers the question: how shall we succeed in each. In this section we identify the alternatives for changing the portfolio.

It is a curious historical fact that in the 1950s, when environmental discontinuities started to buffet business firms, the common reaction was to turn to changes in the strategic portfolio, rather than to re-examination of the continuing validity of the firm's historical strategies within the present portfolio.

In many cases, the reason lay in the fact that attempts to change the portfolio came after years of trying to revive the sagging profits and sales of the present portfolio through heroic measures, such as personnel cuts, inventory reductions, overhead slashing and price wars. Having failed to remedy the difficulties through operating changes within the portfolio, managements turned attention to opportunities offered by fast-growing industries such as electronics, pharmaceuticals and the service industries.

This phenomenon was widely observable in many 'first-generation' industries which were born at the turn of the century and were increasingly suffering from saturation of demand in the 1950s and 1960s.

In many other cases, the push toward new businesses came from invasion of the firm's traditional markets by alien technologies, which made obsolete the traditional technologies of the firm. This occurred, for example, when transistor technology replaced vacuum-tube technology in the markets for amplification of weak electrical signals.

Many firms found that it was more difficult to introduce the new technology into the firm's traditional business areas than to abandon the

* Both Chandler's book and common experience show that in many firms newly created top-level policy makers continue to run rather than plan the company.

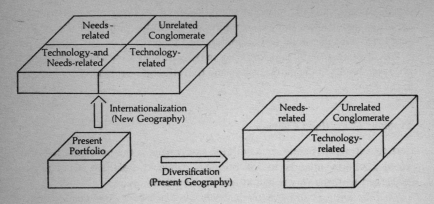

Figure 7.1. Diversification and Internationalization Alternatives

traditional market in favour of entries into new ones. This is what happened to the leading vacuum-tube manufacturers who, at best, became secondary competitors in markets for amplification of weak electrical signals and sought future opportunities in other businesses.

Yet another stimulus to move beyond the present portfolio was an entrepreneurial drive, found in some firms, to expand the firm beyond the limits of its historical businesses.

The path to new horizons took two distinctive forms: one was *internationalization* and the other was *diversification*. This is illustrated in the somewhat complicated diagram in Figure 7.1 which divides the cube of Figure 6.2 into two major types of growth vector illustrated by the upper and lower slices of the cube.

As Figure 7.1 shows, diversification involves departure from familiar business areas, while remaining in the geographical environment(s) in which the firm has previously been successful.

One type of departure, called 'needs-related' in the figure, represents acquisition of a technology new to the firm in order to enable it to continue serving its historical markets. A current example is the acquisition of biogenetic technology by numerous pharmaceutical firms whose products have been traditionally based on chemical-molecular technology.

This particular example calls attention to another important choice made in diversification: to diversify through *acquisition* of an existing firm or through *internal development* by building up the necessary knowledge and capability inside the firm.

Numerous historical and current examples show that internal acquisition of a discontinuously different technology is a very difficult process, as shown by the many instances in which firms abandoned or lost leadership in their traditional business areas when a novel technology displaced the firm's traditional technology from the market-place.

For example, when vacuum-tube technology was displaced by solid-state technology, the historical leaders in vacuum tubes (such as Philips or R C A) yielded leadership to solid-state newcomers such as Texas Instruments, Fairchild Conductors and many others.

A second diversification alternative shown in Figure 7.1 (technology-related) is to apply the historical technology of the firm to new needs (such as the current flood of solid state electronics into the automotive industry). Success in this mode is observable both through acquisition (such as the Ford Motor Co.'s acquisition of Philco) and through internal development which leads the firm to enter markets which it has not served before.

The remaining diversification alternative is to move into businesses which are not related to the firm's present businesses, either through technology or market needs. This is popularly called *conglomerate diversification*. It is usually undertaken through acquisitions.

Conglomerate vs. Synergistic Diversification

As the preceding discussion indicates, the diversification alternatives in Figure 7.1 are arranged according to the degree of synergy between the present businesses of the firm and diversification moves.

At first glance, since synergy offers a firm the advantage of higher consolidated return on investment than can maximally be obtained from a conglomerate firm it would appear that diversification moves should follow the maximum-synergy principle of favouring moves which involve the smallest departure from the firm's normal experience and internal capabilities.

However, since the first edition of this book was published in 1965, a lively argument has continued between proponents of synergistic and conglomerate diversification.

One claim by proponents of conglomerate diversification was simply that synergistic diversification does not work. The claim was supported by studies of post-acquisition results in firms which initially justified their acquisitions on the grounds of synergy.

A closer examination shows that there are two aspects of synergy: the *potential synergy* perceived at the time of acquisition and the *realized synergy* during the post-acquisition integration of the new company. There is both evidence and reason for suggesting that potential synergy will not be realized, unless top management in the acquiring firm forces synergistic sharing on the newly acquired firm. The reason is simply that synergistic sharing is a disturbing and unwelcome phenomenon to general managers responsible for optimizing the performance of the several parts of the firm.

Another claim by proponents of conglomerate diversification is that synergistic diversification frequently confines the firm to a common technology and a common economic-social-political environment, thus making the firm strategically vulnerable to surprises and discontinuities.

This argument is valid, but it does not necessarily lead to the conclusion that synergy must be totally disregarded in diversification. Rather, it leads to the conclusion that a firm's diversification programme must balance synergy and strategic flexibility against each other.

One way to effect such a balance is to make synergy criteria broad enough to permit the firm to enjoy both the advantages of synergy and of flexibility. A recent example is the strategy enunciated by John F. Welch, Jr., the Chief Executive Officer of the American General Electric Company. Somewhat paraphrased, his strategy is to build GE's portfolio on technology-based growth businesses. While providing very significant management synergies (see Chapter 2.3 of Ansoff, *Implanting Strategic Management*) such strategy offers a latitude for minimizing strategic risks through positioning the firm in a diversity of technologies and geographical settings.

A counter-claim by proponents of synergistic diversification, which is supported by both recent events and empirical research[4] is that, indeed, when carefully managed, conglomerates can perform comparably to synergistic companies in non-turbulent growth environments. However, conglomerates typically get into trouble when the environment turns turbulent and highly competitive.

Another counter-argument is that conglomerates make little sense from the point of view of society. They offer no synergistic advantages which can be translated into lower prices to the consumer and they insulate the component companies from the pressures of competition.

As can be seen from the preceding discussion, the synergy vs. conglomerate argument is far from resolved, particularly in the light of the current wave of conglomerate takeovers which are producing megafirms. Some of the new megafirms appear to make synergistic sense, for example, the Burroughs/Sperry merger. Some others appear to serve no useful social or business purposes other than the personal ambitions of the management groups and individuals who engineer them.

In the final analysis, unless government legislation comes into existence which significantly changes the historical competition-preserving legislation (such as the Sherman–Cellar–Kefauver anti-trust laws in the United States) it is safe to predict that, in the foreseeable future, patterns of diversification activity will be determined by two forces. One of these is the business logic of choosing the synergistic rather than the conglomerate route. The other is the personal ambitions, preferences and capabilities of controlling management groups in business firms.

Managers who are 'wheeler dealers', who are motivated by the excitement of the 'merger game', are likely to manage their firms as conglomerates. Managers who are challenged by optimizing the return on the resources invested in the firm, such as John F. Welch, Jr., are likely to opt for synergistic development.

The Internationalization Alternatives

The internationalization alternatives are shown in the upper left-hand corner of Figure 7.1.

The highest synergy move is to offer abroad the firm's traditional products or services. In the early days of the large-scale internationalization activity which started after World War II, such technology/needs-related internationalization was not perceived as discontinuous. The view was that the firm was going to sell its products to the same kinds of customers it had learned to serve in the home country.

But experience progressively showed that the customers are not the same, that their tastes, preferences, buying habits and spending budgets are likely to be very different from those of the domestic customers.

When the economic-political-cultural differences are also taken into account, it turns out that selling one's products in a foreign country can be a very discontinuous strategic move. A very recent example is offered by the divestments from American operations by European firms, which had acquired retail stores and other service establishments in the United States.

The other internationalization alternatives in Figure 7.1 are similar to the diversification alternatives. But it must be kept in mind that each is at least a *two-step discontinuity* from the firm's present business.

Thus, needs-related internationalization leads to the dual difficulties of penetrating a new country *and* offering a novel technology to its markets.

The preceding discussion can be summarized as follows:

1. Internationalization and domestic diversification are alternative routes for expanding a firm's portfolio.

2. With the exception of internationalization in which the domestic and the foreign needs, as well as domestic and foreign technology are related, internationalization is much more difficult and costly than diversification. This is because internationalization involves much more drastic departures from the firm's past experience and competence than similar intranational diversification alternatives. As a result, internationalization is much more risky than diversification.

3. Therefore, the firm should give preference to diversification except in cases in which the firm's objectives cannot be met through diversification. (For further discussion of internationalization, see Chapter 2.6 of Ansoff, *Implanting Strategic Management*.)

Why firms Diversify

1. *Firms diversify when their objectives can no longer be met within the scope of the present portfolio.*

In the area of proximate and long-term profitability objectives the cause may be market saturation, general decline in demand, competitive pressures or product-line obsolescence. A typical symptom is a drop in the rate of return on reinvestments into the present business; another is a 'drying up' of the stream of new opportunities.

In the area of the flexibility objective, the cause may be a disproportionately large fraction of sales to a single customer, a generally narrow market or technological base, or influx of new technologies into the firm's product-market scope.

2. Even if attractive expansion opportunities are still available and past objectives are being met, *a firm may diversify, because the retained cash exceeds the total expansion needs of the present portfolio.*

3. Even if current objectives are being met, *a firm may diversify when diversification opportunities promise greater profitability than expansion opportunities.* This may occur under several conditions.

a. When diversification opportunities are sufficiently attractive to offset their inherently lower synergy.

b. When the firm's research and development organization produces outstanding diversification by-products.

c. When synergy is not considered important by management and hence the synergy advantages of expansion over diversification are not important. This is typically the case in conglomerate firms.

4. *Firms may suffer from the 'grass looks greener in the neighbour's yard' syndrome.* Lacking reliable information about diversification alternatives, such firms tend to plunge rather than probe the diversification alternatives. A much less costly long-run approach is to buy reliable information before plunging.

The above list points to some significant conclusions. As was suggested in Chapter 3, the goals of the firm are not absolute, but are closely related to opportunities. Under reasons (2) and (3) above. firms would pursue diversification when an opportunity to revise the goals upward presents itself. Under reason (1), if analysis of opportunities shows that diversification cannot improve the firm's position, the goals will have to be revised downward.

This absence of an absolute 'proper' set of goals for a firm gives the management great latitude in exercising its risk preferences. Conservative managers would be content to limit interest in diversification to reason (1). Thus if the firm does meet its current objective, diversification will not be pursued. This attitude is not uncommon among top managers whose training and experience has been confined to a single industry, and managers who are approaching retirement.

On the other hand, entrepreneurially oriented managers would view the firm as a pattern of investments to be amended, changed and improved whenever better opportunities arise. They would consider all four reasons as appropriate to diversification activity.

These differences of attitude will obviously have a major influence on the decision to diversify or not. Therefore, in the analysis of this decision in the following chapters we shall provide for both attitudes.

CHAPTER 8

Competitive Analysis

Strategic management is trying to understand where you will sit in
tomorrow's world, not where you hope to sit; assessing where
you can be and deciding where you want to be.

> *Paraphrased from:*
> JOHN F. WELCH, JR, *Chief Executive*
> *Officer, The General Electric Co.*

Two Approaches to Strategic Analysis

Prior to the 1970s a firm's strategic posture in its respective businesses
typically developed without the benefit of systematic planning. Ideas for
new products and markets were generated 'from the bottom up', or
primarily in the marketing and R&D departments. The ideas were a
spontaneous result of creative insights by talented marketers and
technologists. But while spontaneous and sporadically generated, the new
ideas which were accepted for implementation were typically incremental
improvements on products which had succeeded in the past. Maverick ideas
had little chance of being accepted by general management, in the spirit of
the Japanese proverb which says, 'When a nail is crooked, we hammer it in.'

The firm's general management had no direct influence on idea generation
and confined itself to idea evaluation and selection. As the president of a
major pharmaceutical company once said to this author, 'R&D invents
new drugs and I make sure that they are produced and marketed properly.'

Subsequent to the 1970s a large percentage of firms continued to follow
the path of logical incrementalism which was made famous in the 1980s by
the best-seller by Peters and Waterman, called *In Search of Excellence*[1], in
which they advised their readers to 'stick to their (strategic) knitting'.

In logical incrementalism, strategic analysis is focused on the contribution
which new proposals can make to the growth and profitability of the firm,
and there is no concern with the future validity of the firm's traditional
'strategic knitting'. The underlying expectation is that the traditional
markets will continue to grow, and the firm's traditional technology will
evolve incrementally.

If the future environment can be safely assumed to develop in an incremental, orderly manner, guided by extrapolation of past experience, there is much to be said for using the incremental approach to strategic development.

However, if the environment is expected to be turbulent with probable discontinuities in the economic, competitive, technological or socio-political conditions, sticking to the historical 'strategic knitting' becomes dangerous. Firms which persist in incremental evolution and fail to anticipate and prepare themselves for discontinuities are very likely to be left behind in the competitive race.

This is illustrated by the fact that shortly after *In Search of Excellence* was published, several of its star companies, which had built their successes in logical incrementalism, experienced great difficulties when their environments turned turbulent.

In turbulent environments the alternative to logical incrementalism is comprehensive and systematic strategic planning which challenges, re-examines and reformulates the strategic logic of the firm's future development. Nor does strategic planning need to come into conflict with entrepreneurship and creativity, provided management controls the self-bureaucratizing tendency which is inherent in all management systems. (For further discussion of this issue, see Ansoff's article in the *European Journal of Operational Research*.[2])

This book is focused on strategic management in difficult and turbulent environments. Therefore, we will now proceed to outline the method of comprehensive strategic planning. For an excellent exposition of the incremental approach to strategic change, the reader is referred to Chapter 7, note 1.

The Problem

Thus far we have been concerned with development of basic concepts for strategic analysis. The remainder of the book is devoted to using these in constructing a step-by-step logic for the solution of the strategic problem.

As discussed in the last chapter, the initial concern of strategists in the 1950s was with making changes in the firm's strategic portfolio through diversification and internationalization. Both of these activities remained vigorous and increased in intensity during the succeeding thirty years.

But, since the 1960s, an accompanying concern with the firm's *competitive behaviour* in its traditional business areas has become progressively intense.

One trigger for this concern occurred in maturing, first-generation industries, such as steel, machine tools and agricultural equipment. In such industries, operating measures of overhead reductions, personnel cutbacks, productivity improvements and consolidation of operations failed to produce improvements in stagnating sales and falling profits.

Another and very different trigger occurred in a very much larger segment of the economy, which included not only stagnating, but also growth and emerging industries. This trigger was the increasing frequency of discontinuous changes in the firm's traditional markets. As already discussed, these changes came from new technologies, accelerated product substitution, internationalization of competition, government regulation and political upheavals.

In industries in which expectations were for frequent and discontinuous changes, the second trigger created an anomalous situation in which traditional success strategies, honed to perfection through years of experience, became inadequate for the future. It became necessary, not only to re-evaluate the traditional success strategies, but also continually to challenge and re-evaluate the new ones in the future. Thus, for firms in turbulent, changing environments, concern with competitive strategies *within* the current portfolio became a major preoccupation.

The discontinuous changes in the traditional market-place may be so drastic as to make advisable a withdrawal from that market-place. For example, a sudden imposition of import or export barriers by a country in which the firm is doing business, or nationalization of the firm's assets in another country, may leave the firm no other choice than to quit the country.

But many other discontinuities challenge not the basic attractiveness or feasibility of the market, but the ways by which firms will have to attack that market if they are to remain successful in it. Such discontinuities change the types of products or services which will be wanted by the market, the product technologies which will be successful, the promotion and advertising strategies, the channels of distribution, etc.

It is possible that revision of the firm's competitive posture in its traditional markets may raise its future performance prospects to a level which will satisfy its objectives. In such cases diversification may become unnecessary. As a minimum, the prospects offered by the new competitive posture will reduce the need for diversification.

Therefore, it makes sense to start strategic analysis by re-evaluating and re-formulating the strategies within the present portfolio, before proceeding to change the portfolio.

This reasoning is reinforced by the fact that, while changes in the traditional competitive environment may be discontinuous, they are *familiar discontinuities* arising in environments which the firm understands from past experience. On the other hand, internationalization and diversification involve *unfamiliar discontinuities* which move the firm into environments in which it has little prior knowledge or experience.

To summarize in the vernacular, the preceding discussion suggests that before paying attention to the neighbour's lawn it is more efficient and effective to put one's own lawn in order.

Put somewhat differently, this means that if a firm can meet all of its objectives by measures short of diversification or internationalization, it should do so. This conclusion provides the logical structure to our approach to strategy formulation. Since diversification/internationalization is costly and risky, this chapter (*competitive analysis*) is concerned with whether the firm can solve its problems without changing the portfolio.

If the problem cannot be solved within the limit of the present product-market position, presumption is strong that the firm has to diversify; if the conclusion is that the problem *can* be solved internally, the firm may or may not terminate the analysis, depending on the risk preferences of the management.

A decision to look beyond the present portfolio calls for a survey of opportunities outside the firm's present product-market scope (*portfolio analysis*). Comparison of the result with that of the competitive analysis leads to a final decision to change or not to change the firm's portfolio of businesses, and an allocation of the firm's resources among portfilio changes on the one hand and competitive strategy changes on the other.

A decision to change the portfolio (either through acquisitions or internal development) raises the question of whether the new organizational units are to be forced into synergistic interactions with the existing units of the firm, or whether they are to operate independently from the others.

The answer to this question affects not only the administrative strategy by which the firm is managed, but also the portfolio strategy of the firm. This will be discussed in the last part of this chapter.

Because this is an introductory text, the following paragraphs will describe the logic of each of the steps of the analysis; but they will omit the quantitative and qualitative procedures needed to produce the specified outputs. The procedures can be found in Ansoff, *Implanting Strategic Management*.

As will soon become apparent, the flow of decisions leading to strategy formulation is complex, involves many contributing studies and can be very time consuming. One such complete study of a firm consumed between five and seven man-years and cost between $100,000 and $200,000.

Many firms, particularly smaller ones, may not be in a position to make such commitments. It will be helpful, therefore, if the following decision-flow diagrams are interpreted according to the circumstances of the reader. An executive of a small firm can treat them as guidelines for thinking through the strategic problem. He may not be able to afford many of the detailed studies, but he can, by working with a few associates, using the diagrams as a road map and by making qualitative decisions, gain insight into the problems of his firm. On the other hand, line managers in larger firms can use the scheme first to request analytic studies from various staff members, and then to guide the decision process which usually involves numerous participants.

The Logic of Competitive Analysis

The decision-flow diagram for a competitive analysis is shown graphically in Figure 8.1. In order to relate the diagram to the following discussion, the numbers in brackets in the text correspond to appropriate boxes in the flow diagram.

As discussed earlier, strategic analysis may be typically triggered off by a signal of serious trouble or by a change in top management. Forward-looking management may anticipate changes in the environment of the firm and act before difficulties arise. Entrepreneurial management will make strategic change a way of life and periodically review its strategy regardless of performance.

The first step in competitive analysis is to set *tentative objectives* (1). A firm new to strategic analysis may be faced with the problem of making its objectives explicit for the first time. Other firms will conduct a review of current objectives in the light of past performance and make a tentative revision in the priorities and the goals. The procedure for setting these objectives was described in Chapters 3 and 4.

Concurrently, an *extrapolated forecast* (2) of future performance will be made.

The extrapolated forecast is based on four assumptions:

(a) The firm's strategic portfolio will remain unchanged.

(b) Competitive success strategies in the firm's market-places will continue to evolve as in the past.

(c) The demand/profitability opportunities in the firm's market-places will follow the historical trends.

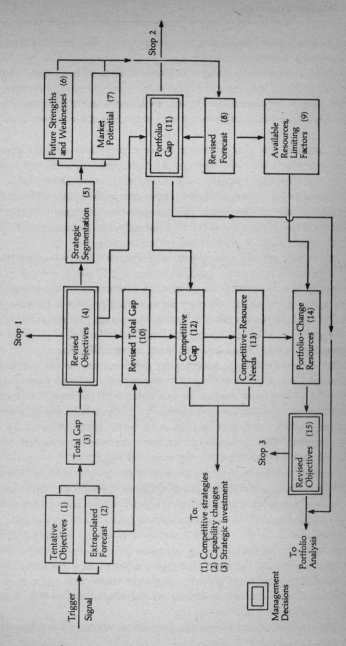

Figure 8.1. Decision Flow in Competitive Analysis

(d) The firm's own strategies in the respective market-places will follow their historical incremental evolution.

To permit comparisons, the performance indices such as sales, profits, etc., used in constructing the extrapolative forecast(s) should be the same as the attributes of the objectives. The extrapolation is made by fitting curves to the firm's historical performance and extending these curves into the future.

A comparison can now be made between objectives and the current forecast to measure the *total gap* (3) – the discrepancy between aspirations and anticipations. For example, a firm whose tentative objectives in the order of priority are 10 per cent ROI, 15 per cent growth rate, with one half of the growth rate to come from new product-markets, may find that the forecast promises to meet the ROI goal but only a 12 per cent growth, and very little expectation of product-market innovation.

As the next step, *revised objectives* (4) are prepared. Clearly, if expectations exceed aspirations (a *negative* gap), objectives are adjusted upward. If the gap is positive, a different order of priority assignment to objectives may become apparent. In the above example increased priority is indicated for the flexibility objective. On other occasions the gap may be generally judged to be too great in the light of the trends and the limitations of the firm, and goal-threshold values are adjusted to lower acceptable values.

If, after these adjustments, a significant gap remains, the analysis moves to the next phase. If there is no gap, conservatively inclined management may choose to terminate analysis at this point until the next review date. Entrepreneurial management will choose to proceed with the purpose of discovering whether the firm can do even better than indicated by the current forecast. This optional management decision is indicated by an arrow and by the word 'STOP', appearing on Figure 8.1.

Throughout the study of the decision-flow process we shall continue to indicate such management decision options at appropriate points in the analysis. It is necessary, therefore, to digress in order to make it clear that the term 'conservative' is in no sense meant to indicate a 'worse' choice, nor 'entrepreneurial' a 'better' one. We use these words to indicate different attitudes towards risk found among managers. By choosing a 'conservative' path, in our sense of the word, management chooses a combination of lower probable gain with a correspondingly lower risk than does an 'entrepreneur' who decides in favour of higher-gain-higher-risk course. Neither is inherently 'right' or 'wrong'.

To return to the decision diagram, revision of objectives is followed by *strategic segmentation* of the environment (5). The problem is two-fold. The first is: should the focus be on the historical performance of the profit centres of the firm, or on the future success conditions in the firm's markets? So long as the environment develops incrementally, the above distinction is not important, because the markets can be expected to want and accept logical extensions of the traditionally successful products and services. Hence, analysis can be focused on the strategies of the historically successful competitors, and the firm's strategies can be revised (if necessary) to imitate the historical successes. This is the approach taken in *competitor analysis* which is widely practised in marketing departments and in the well-known computer-based PIMS approach to competitive analysis.

However, as already discussed, whenever the future environment is expected to be discontinuous, emulation of historical successes becomes dangerous and competitive analysis must be focused not on the firm's history but on the future market needs and on competitive strategies which will be successful in serving these needs.

Since analysis of past successes is much less costly and less speculative than analysis of the future market environment, the decision between the historical and future focus must not be taken lightly. The appropriate choice will obviously vary from firm to firm.

During the past ten years a technique for assessment of the future environment, called *turbulence diagnosis*, has been developed which helps each form to make its choice. (For a technique for turbulence diagnosis, see Chapters 1.2 and 3.4 of Ansoff, *Implanting Strategic Management*.) If the future turbulence is diagnosed as high, the environment, and not the profit centres, should provide the units of analysis. This leads to the second problem in strategic segmentation analysis, namely, what should these units be.

The original edition of this book reflected the practice in the 1950s of using industries (e.g. steel, glass, computers, etc.) as the units of analysis.

Subsequent experience has shown this to be a dangerous approach, because industries typically serve a variety of distinctive market needs, some of which may have excellent and some dismal prospects in the future.

Furthermore, in technologically turbulent environments the traditional industry boundaries become 'porous': vulnerable to invasion from new technologies.

For example, for many years one of the major proprietary markets of the steel industry was the market for beverage-holding containers. But in the 1960s the aluminium can invaded this market and began to displace steel containers. The result was an apparently anomalous situation: while the demand for beverage-holding containers continued to grow, the demand for the steel industry's product began to decline. In the 1980s the picture is even more complicated: steel, aluminium, plastics and paper industries are all in active competition for the beverage-container market.

As a result of the unreliability of industry classification, a new way of slicing the environment came into practice. Several names have been proposed for it. Probably the most frequently used names are 'strategic segment' or *Strategic Business Area, (SBA)*.

An SBA is identified by four factors:

1. A future market *need*.
2. A *technology* which will be serving the need.
3. The *customers* who will have the need.
4. The *geographical setting* in which the customers will have the need.

The reader will note that if the same need can be served by two different technologies, it will create two areas of business opportunities. (For a further discussion of the SBA concept, see Chapter 2.2 of Ansoff, *Implanting Strategic Management*.)

To summarize, the first step in competitive analysis is to determine the units for which competitive analysis is to be carried out. If the future environment of the firm is expected to evolve incrementally, strategic analysis has to be carried out for each profit centre of the firm. If the future will be discontinuous and turbulent, external strategic business areas, rather than internal organizational units, should be the focus of analysis.

Following strategic segmentation, two parallel analyses are made. The first is *future strengths and weaknesses analysis* (6):

1. If the results of the segmentation analysis predict an incrementally evolving future, the firm's competitive profile is constructed and compared to the profiles of successful competitors for each profit centre.

2. If the segmentation analysis results in identification of the Strategic Business Areas, the competence profiles are compared to the future competitive profiles constructed for each SBA. In addition to comparing the firm's capabilities as is done in Chapter 5, modern analysis also compares the firm's *competitive strategy* in each SBA to the *future success strategies*, and the firm's *strategic investment* in the respective SBA's to the *optimal strategic investment* for each SBA.

The other concurrent analysis is of the *portfolio potential* (7). Its purpose is to determine the growth and profitability potential available within the markets of the firm which will be available to the successful competitors.

Table 8.1. Outline for Future Market Potential Analysis

1. Product-Market Structure
   a. Products and their characteristics
   b. Product missions
   c. Customers
2. Growth and Profitability
   a. History
   b. Forecasts
   c. Relation to life cycle
   d. Basic determinants of demand
   e. Averages and norms typical of the industry
3. Technology
   a. Basic technologies
   b. History of innovation
   c. Technological trends – threats and opportunities
   d. Role of technology in success
4. Investment
   a. Cost of entry and exit-critical mass
   b. Typical asset patterns in firms
   c. Rate and type of obsolescence of assets
   d. Role of capital investment in success
5. Marketing
   a. Means and methods of selling
   b. Role of service and field support
   c. Role and means of advertising and sales promotion
   d. What makes a product competitive
   e. Role of marketing in success
6. Competition
   a. Market shares, concentration, dominance
   b. Characteristics of outstanding firms, of poor firms
   c. Trends in competitive patterns
7. Strategic Perspective
   a. Trends in demand
   b. Trends in product-market structure
   c. Trends in technology
   d. Key ingredients in success

Rather than deal with extrapolations of the firm's performance, as was done in the extrapolated forecast, the SBA forecast explores the discontinuities in the economic, competitive, technological and socio-political prospects in the market-place. Trends in growth, profitability, and market dynamics are obtained by applying deviations caused by these discontinuities to the extrapolated trends.

The various trends are put together into projections of performance which a fully competitive firm will be able to attain along the principal attributes of our firm's objectives vector. In summarizing this analysis it is useful to interpret the data within the concept of the *industry life cycle*.* This concept is particularly helpful for avoiding the danger of linear projections of past trends. An outline which has been used for future market potential studies is shown in Table 8.1.

By combining the analyses of strengths and weaknesses with the SBA potential and by referring to the current forecast, it is now possible to construct a new *revised forecast* (8) for the firm. *This is done by assuming that, rather than continue in its present groove, the firm will make an all-out effort to take advantage of its opportunities, short of embarking on diversification.*

The analysis may show, for example, that the current forecast of return on investment is below the maximum expected potential. The strengths and weaknesses profile may show this to be due primarily to the firm's traditional reluctance to shift from distributors to direct sales. This shift is feasible, and an assumption can be made that the firm can raise its ROI to or near the maximum possible.

On the other hand, it may appear that the lag in profitability is to be ascribed to an unfortunate distribution of the firm's manufacturing plants and high attendant distribution costs. Although some improvements can be made, the basic pattern cannot be changed short of costly relocations. In this case a conclusion may be reached that the industry maximum is not attainable; the revised forecast will reflect this decision.

In addition to deficiencies in the firm's capabilities for meeting future competitive conditions, it may turn out that the firm's present strategies in its respective business areas are out of tune with future success factors in the market-place.

For example, the traditionally successful strategy of the Apple Computer Company, based on advanced state-of-the-art computers, which were distinctive and incompatible with IBM computers, was a great success until the mid-1980s. But the changed character of the demand and of industry structure made it necessary to shift to a strategy of market segmentation (Apple has announced that its future focus will be on business and not the consumer market) and of compatibility with IBM.

As can be inferred from the preceding remarks, the preparation of the

* For a discussion of the life-cycle concept see Ansoff, *Implanting Strategic Management* Chapter 2.2.

revised forecast is a complex and laborious process, particularly due to the fact that each business area must be separately analysed one by one. However, the results are useful not only as a forecast of the firm's future performance, but also in a series of decisions on the strategies the firm will pursue in its respective business areas, the capabilities it will build to support the strategies, and the strategic resource allocation among the respective business areas.

At the time the original edition of this book was published, little was known about this aspect of competitive analysis. Since then, business firms, consultants and, to a lesser extent, academics, have contributed to an elaborate body of analytic technology for competitive analysis. (For a detailed description of modern competitive analysis, see Chapter 2.2 of Ansoff, *Implanting Strategic Management*. For a computer-based approach see note 3.)

At this point, the analysis becomes somewhat less than straightforward. It will be recalled that the total gap (3) was determined on the basis of tentative objectives (1) and that a new set of objectives was established (4). Therefore, the total gap needs to be revised. This is shown in box (10) – *revised total gap* – in which the current forecast is compared with the revised objectives. Next, the revised forecast (8) is compared with the revised objectives to determine the *portfolio gap* (11) which will remain after all internal steps have been implemented. The difference between this and the total gap is the *competitive gap* (12) which will be closed. To illustrate this further, Figure 8.2 shows how the respective gaps may look for the firm's sales potential. Similar graphs can be constructed for other attributes of objectives. The two gaps thus show the respective contributions to be made from revising strategies and capabilities in the firm's present markets on the one hand, and changing the portfolio on the other.

Analysis of the gaps leads to another major management decision point. If the competitive improvements promise to close the total gap, many firms will decide against diversification at this point in time. Again management risk preferences play an important role, but in a somewhat different way from the preceding decision point. As discussed earlier, a move to diversification entails, for some firms, not only increased risks but also very high-transfer costs. Such firms are usually highly integrated, with large fixed investments in physical assets and specialized business and technological know-how. They welcome an opportunity to redress imbalances in the present position without diversifying.

On the other hand, firms with highly fluid and negotiable resources and

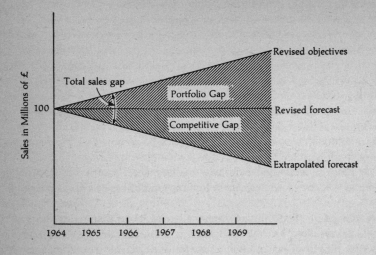

Figure 8.2. Breakdown of Sales Gap

without specialized know-how, such as an investment trust, would have no particular incentive to stop the analysis at this point. The incentive is rather to survey the broadest possible field of opportunities before selecting the product-market posture.

If, for any of the above reasons, the decision is to continue analysis, the next step is to determine the resources available to the firm for implementation of the respective changes. The revised forecast provides a basis for estimating the resources which will be generated (*available resources* (9)) for strategic development. The primary contributors are the net *cash flow*, which will be available above the operating needs, the firm's borrowing power and an estimate of *equity base* which will be available for acquisition activity. The latter is based on the present ownership patterns, the acceptable dilution of present ownership, and the acceptable dilution (if any) of earnings to present stockholders. The result is an estimate of the sterling value of equity available for trading. The usability of the equity for trading will depend on the firm's price/earnings position in relation to potential acquisitions.

Resource analysis should single out the particular resources which may become *limiting factors* (9) in strategic activity. Quite frequently this will be competent general management, but it may also be a limited availability of raw materials, of skilled labour, or of middle management.

Since the intent is to implement fully competitive improvements within the present portfolio before diverting resources to diversification or internationalization, the next step is to make an estimate of *competitive-resource needs* (13). These are costs in terms of sterling, manpower and other resources, over and above the operating costs, which are required to bring about improvement in the firm's competitive behaviour. They include expenditures on product/service developments, development of new markets, new and modernized facilities, administrative changes and increases in research activities.

The *portfolio-change resources* (14) estimate is now obtained by comparing the total available resources (9) with the competitive resources needs (13).

The last step in competitive analysis is another major decision point. The portfolio gap is examined in relation to the diversification resources to determine whether the objectives need another revision (15) and whether the firm should decide against portfolio changes. It is possible that the resources will be insufficient to substantially narrow the portfolio gap. In this case, the objectives may be revised downward to the level made possible by competitive improvements only, and a decision made not to diversify.

It is also sometimes possible to change priorities of objectives to suit the resources. Thus if the aggressive flexibility objective cannot be met through acquisitions because firms with fertile technologies usually sell at a high times-earnings multiple, the objective of defensive flexibility may be given a higher priority because certain unglamorous but steady industries can be acquired at six to ten times earnings.

In addition to the size of the gap, the decision to proceed further will also be influenced by the risk-taking propensity of management as discussed in Chapter 7.

CHAPTER 9

Portfolio Analysis

The Red Queen said, 'Now, *here*, it takes all the running *you* can do to keep in the same place. If you want to get somewhere else, you must run at least twice as fast as that!'

LEWIS CARROLL

Problems in Portfolio Analysis

The purpose of portfolio analysis is to analyse the product-market opportunities which are available to the firm outside its present scope and thus produce the final decision on whether the firm should change the scope of the portfolio through diversification, or internationalization, or both.

In Figure 7.1 we classified portfolio changes into two categories: diversification and internationalization. As the figure suggests, the two activities are quite similar. The primary differences between the two lies in the geographic scope within which the firm seeks new opportunities. A firm seeking a given type of internationalization will encounter all of the problems of diversification, but it must, in addition, learn to do business in a foreign socio-political-economic-cultural climate.

In the following pages we shall discuss characteristics which are common to diversification and internationalization. (Readers interested in the distinctive aspects of internationalization are referred to Chapter 2.6 of Ansoff, *Implanting Strategic Management*.)

Theoretically, the process of diversification is quite simple (see Chapter 2). All opportunities are arrayed, each is tested for its contribution to the firm, and a group of top-ranking ones is selected for addition to the portfolio. As was discussed in Chapter 2, in practice this is a difficult task. A recapitulation of the major problems will help establish the logic for the portfolio analysis.

A major problem is posed by the fact that, instead of a single measurement, the purpose of the firm is described by a multi-dimensional vector of objectives. These objectives are measured in different units (they are not *commensurate*), and optimization on one objective consumes resources which could have been used to optimize the others (they are not *co-linear*). Thus, the proximate objective competes with the long-range objectives, and the flexibility objectives compete with both.

Our approach to this problem will be straightforward. We shall use the respective objectives of the firm as criteria by which opportunities are evaluated and ranked. This process will eliminate certain inefficient opportunities which are inferior to some other opportunities on all objectives. The remaining *efficient list* will provide a basis for selecting opportunities which offer the best balance of contributions to the respective objectives.

A second major problem described in Chaper 2 is partial ignorance, which means that, at the time strategic decisions must be made, it is not possible to enumerate or describe all of the future opportunities for acquisition and/or attractive product and technology developments.

As a result, in competitive analysis, and particularly in portfolio analysis, we are forced to deal with aggregate data which describe characteristics of industries or strategic business areas, and not specific opportunities for strategic action.

This is the reason for the use of the concept of strategy, which specifies the direction in which the firm will develop its future products, markets and technology. It thus provides guidance for the search for and invention of specific opportunities.

Once an opportunity surfaces, strategy is used once again to determine whether the opportunity fits the strategic intent of the firm. If it does not fit, the opportunity is rejected; if it does fit, it is further evaluated for its contribution to the firm's objectives.

If the contribution to the objectives is satisfactory, yet another barrier must be passed. This is the *cost of entry* (*and exit*) into the market for which the opportunity is intended. The cost of entry and exit is important for several reasons:

1. The investment required for a profitable entry must be within the firm's resources which are available for strategic activities.

2. If an acquisition is being considered, the 'going price', as measured by the price-earnings multiple, must be considered. It is frequently the case, for example, that certain industries (electronics in the early 1950s, material handling in the mid-1950s, drugs in the late 1950s) are generally recognized by the investing public as 'growth' areas. As a result, the earnings of firms in such areas become discounted over a long period and the price/earnings ratios tend to rise out of proportion to their real values. A firm contemplating diversifying into such an industry through an acquisition may have to pay a very high entry price, which is not justifiable by the prospective future earnings.

3. The cost of entry and exit is also significant for a different reason. If the market shares in the industry are widely distributed and the minimum investment required to enter is small, great mobility of firms in and out is to be expected. A member of the industry lacks security of his position, because an entrepreneur with a small capital and a 'garage-loft' operation has easy access to the market. This condition is undesirable from the viewpoint of large established companies which lack the flexibility and quick response possessed by small firms. On the other hand, small firms will find such an environment attractive.

Because of the cost of entry considerations, which may eliminate otherwise attractive opportunities, in the portfolio analysis described in the following section, we shall use cost-of-entry criteria to eliminate areas of opportunity which are likely to be unattractive for reasons of cost.

Another problem in portfolio analysis arises from the fact that a majority of diversifying firms expects to integrate the management of new strategic departures into the parent operations, and thus realize synergies from the diversification activities. To provide for this we shall include *synergy criteria* in evaluation of diversification possibilities.

All of the above considerations suggest that a strategic business area, which has very attractive prospects for firms who are already in it, may not be an attractive prospect for the firm which is considering entering the area. The reasons may be several:

1. The cost of entry may not be justified by the future earnings the firm will derive from the SBA.

2. The minimal size of entry (critical mass – see Chapter 5) may be beyond the financial resources of the firm, or, if an acquisition through exchange of equity is considered, exchange of shares will lead to a dilution of earnings of the acquiring firm; or it may lead to loss of control by the acquiring management. Thus, instead of acquiring, the firm will end by being acquired.

3. The competitive environment in the SBA may be unstable.

4. The firm may lack the flexibility and the responsiveness to manage an entry into the SBA.

5. Functional synergies between the capabilities of the firm and the capabilities required in the new SBA may be lacking.

For the above reasons a firm which approaches diversification in a systematic manner must start by analysing the field of potential opportunities and identifying a list of strategic business areas which meet the following criteria:

1. Meet the objectives of the firm in a more cost-effective manner than would be produced by additional investment in the present portfolio.

2. Require minimal feasible investment which is within the limits of the firm's resources available for diversification.

3. Demand an entry cost which is reasonable in the light of the future earnings which the firm will be able to derive from the SBA.

4. Offer attractive synergies both on the managerial and functional levels.

Figure 9.1 presents a decision-flow diagram for generating and analysing a list of potentially attractive business areas. The analysis is triggered either by a need (existence of a portfolio gap), or a management decision to seek out outside opportunities which are more attractive than internal ones.

Logic of Portfolio Analysis

The analysis, shown in flow-chart form in Figure 9.1, commences with the preparation of three lists of objectives and criteria which are to be used for evaluating candidate SBA's (see Box No. 1). These lists are:

1. Objectives which specify the kinds of performance the firm seeks to attain in the near and long term future.

A list of the firm's objectives will have already been chosen during the competitive analysis (see Figure 8.1). Portfolio analysis uses the same list to assess the contributions which different diversification possibilities can make to these respective objectives.

As discussed earlier, typical diversification objectives pursued by firms are growth, profitability, and/or reduction of strategic vulnerability to technical or political surprises.

2. *Cost of entry/exit criteria* specify the terms which the firm is prepared to accept for an entry into new business areas. These frequently include the pay-back period (or some other measure of investment pay-off, such as internal rate of return) during which the firm expects to recover its entry cost. In the case of diversification by acquisition, the criteria list would include a limit on the dilution of earnings per share the firm is prepared to accept; or the criteria may specify the post-acquisition distribution of shares which will assure management control by the acquiring firm.

Since diversification activity involves high-risk decisions, another criteria should be the exit costs which the firm is prepared to suffer, if it is forced to withdraw from a particular entry. This is of particular importance in internationalization moves, as was shown by the high costs which have

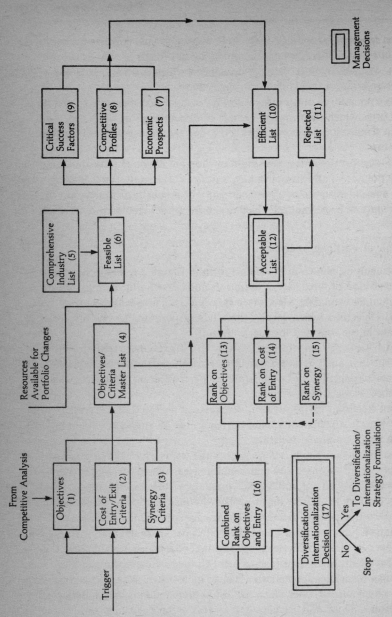

Figure 9.1. Decision Flow in Portfolio Analysis

been incurred by many American firms at the time of a forced exit from countries which require high redundancy payments.

3. *Synergy criteria* specify the mutual support characteristics which the diversification candidates must have in common with other parts of the firm's present portfolio. These are frequently called *common threads* which the firm intends to maintain among its various units as it diversifies.

In the early days of diversification the synergy criteria were focused on the functional areas: marketing, R&D, etc. But later experience has shown that corporate-management synergy is frequently the most important criterion. The reason being that, when corporate-management synergy with the new diversification activity is negative, there is a strong danger that the activity will be 'loved to death' by misguided attention from the corporate office.

As already discussed, recent years' business press has regularly carried anouncements of divestments from diversification moves which were overmanaged by the corporate office to the point of remaining chronically unprofitable.

As Figure 9.1 shows, the three lists of objectives are consolidated into a master list of *objectives/criteria* (4) which is to be used in evaluating diversification alternatives.

The next step in portfolio analysis is to compile a *comprehensive list* (5) of industries or SBA's which the firm is prepared to consider for diversification. It is common to use industries to describe potential diversification moves, because standard industrial-classification statistics, found in most developed countries, offer ready access to data for each industry.

In the 1950s and 1960s, the comprehensive lists were typically focused either on diversification *or* on internationalization alternatives. With the benefit of modern understanding, the comprehensive list can combine domestic diversification moves and internationalization moves.

In the final analysis, the comprehensive list needs to be limited by two considerations: the scope of interests of the firm's management and the resources it is prepared to expend on analysis of the industries on the list.

The costs can be very substantial. In one study which the author conducted in the 1960s, the total cost was $250,000 and the study took two years to complete. On the other hand, the cost can be justified by the fact that changing the basic shape of the firm is a major and a highly risky decision.

Care must be taken to use a level of aggregation of sub-industries, or even sub-sub-industries, which represent areas of opportunity that are distinct from other sub-industries. For example, the consumer electronics industry is an aggregate of sub-industries some of which are mature and not particularly attractive, and some which have very attractive growth prospects.

The next step is to obtain a statement of *diversification resources* (which will be available from the gap analysis described in the preceding section) and to use this statement to reduce the comprehensive list to a *feasible list* (6) composed of sub-industries which the firm can afford to enter.

The selection of these sub-industries should be made by comparing the resources available to the firm with the minimal size of investment into the respective sub-industries which is required to assure a strategic break-even point (critical mass).

In steps (7), (8), and (9), each of the selected sub-industries is analysed along three dimensions:

(a) The future *economic* (growth, profitability and uncertainty) *prospects* which will be available to successful competitors in each sub-industry. Economic prospects should also include estimates of the critical mass and the *optimal mass* of investment which successful competitors will have to invest to become one of the top performers in the sub-industry.

(b) The *competitive capability profiles* (see Chapter 5), which successful competitors will need in the future in each sub-industry.

(c) The *critical success factors* which will have to be incorporated in the strategies of successful competitors.

In step (10) the objectives and criteria master list from step (4) are applied to the results generated for each sub-industry in steps (7), (8), and (9) to eliminate from the feasible industry list sub-industries which are inferior to at least one other sub-industry on all of the objectives and criteria.

The inferior sub-industries are eliminated and form the *rejected list* (11). The promising sub-industries form the *acceptable list* (12) of sub-industries which is ready for final analysis.

The next step is to assess the contributions which each of the sub-industries on the acceptable list can make to the respective objectives and criteria.

Synergy and Management Style

The three ranking lists (13), (14), and (15) provide inputs to the decision on the course of action the firm will pursue in diversification/internationalization. But before this decision can be made, management must decide whether synergy is to be an important factor in the decision.

This decision depends in the first place, on the basic managerial styles which the firm will use, as it makes major changes in the strategic portfolio. As discussed previously, two basic managerial styles are widely observable in practice: the *synergistic style*, under which corporate management vigilantly promotes synergies among the organizational units of the firm, and the *conglomerate style* under which each division or subsidiary is granted full independence to pursue its own growth and profitability.

If the firm has traditionally been a conglomerate, and if management intends to treat new departures in the same manner, the synergy list becomes irrelevant to the decisions about diversification/internationalization.

But if management decides to change its traditionally conglomerate style, or if synergy-minded management decides to continue to act synergistically, the *synergy-rank list* (15) must be used together with the objectives and cost-of-entry lists to develop an overall ranking of diversification alternatives.

The synergy rankings can be viewed as modifiers of the objectives ratings. To the economic and competitive assessment of industries they add an assessment of joint performance advantages which the firm may enjoy in each industry.

However, it is essential to recognize that these are only *potential synergy* advantages, estimated from a superimposition of profiles and that they will not be realized unless the top management of the diversifying firm is prepared to convert the potential into reality.

To illustrate this point, suppose that a manufacturer of medium-sized electric motors in the south of England acquires a Scottish firm which makes fractional-horsepower motors. Strong potential synergy is evident in engineering, manufacturing and perhaps even marketing. However, distance and ambitions of the managers of the two firms interfere, and the two divisions are left to operate completely independently of each other. Actual synergy will be negligible.

Thus commitment to post-diversification synergy must not be made lightly, even by firms which have been synergistically managed in the past. If the corporate management desires to continue presiding over a synergistic firm, it must be prepared to exert the energy and influence necessary to bring about synergistic cooperation between the historical portfolio of the firm's business and the new ventures.

If management decides to follow the conglomerate route, the rank list on objectives (13) and the list on cost of entry (14) are combined to produce an *overall ranking* (16) of potential diversification/internationalization possibilities.

If the synergistic route is chosen, the overall rank list is constructed by combining the objectives, the cost of entry, and omitting the synergy-rank list.

One scheme which was used in an actual diversification study is illustrated in Table 9.1. Shown on the left of the table are the objectives and criteria, each subdivided into a number of elements. The relative priorities assigned by management to the respective objectives/criteria are indicated by the number of elements used. Thus, the economic performance is given a maximum possible of 50 points, while a 20-point maximum is assigned to sales stability. As the columns on the right show, each industry is rated on each element on a scale of 10 to 0.

The subtotals for the objectives and groups of criteria can be used to rank the sub-industries on the acceptable list on the potential contribution to objectives (13), cost of entry (14), and synergy (15).

It can be seen from Table 9.1 that in the referenced diversification study the cost of entry criteria were not recognized. This led to subsequent problems when the firm attempted to diversify into industries which it could not afford.

We are finally in a position where a definitive *diversification decision* (17) can be made. The expansion opportunities analysed in the competitive analysis can now be compared with the lists produced in the portfolio analysis. A choice must be made to pursue competitive improvements, diversification/internationalization, or both. The factors which force the choice one way or another have been discussed in Chapter 7. The following variants of the decision to diversify are possible:

1. In rare cases, when forecasts predict decline and loss of profitability in all of the firm's strategic business areas, the decision should be to initiate wholesale liquidation of the firm's present business and repositioning the firm's resources in diversification/internationalization. A dramatic historical example was the transformation of the Dutch State (Coal) Mines into DSM, a large and successful chemicals firm.

2. Some of the firm's present SBAs may be unattractive, but a majority of the portfolio is sound. The recommended, and less drastic, course of action is to divest from these SBAs and make a major commitment to diversification/internationalization.

3. A variant of the above situation occurs when all of the SBAs promise

Table 9.1. Sample Evaluations of Selected Industries*

Objectives Criteria	Air conditioning	Electronic controls	Metallurgy	Plastics fabrication
1. Expected economic environment				
a. Sales growth	9	10	9	7
b. Profit growth	5	7	· 6	5
c. Price stability	5	7	7	6
d. Excess productive capacity	5	8	6	4
e. Ease of entry by new firms into industry	6	8	7	4
Subtotal	30	40	35	26
2. Stability of sales				
a. Stability of sales over business cycle	4	5	4	7
b. Dependence on single customer	9	7	7	7
Subtotal	13	12	11	14
3. Breadth of product-market base				
a. Entry into fertile technology areas	2	8	7	6
b. Achievement of substantially broadened marketing competence	5	8	6	6
Subtotal	7	16	13	12
Total for Objectives	50	68	59	52

Synergy Criteria	Air conditioning	Electronic controls	Metallurgy	Plastics fabrication
1. Operational compatibility				
a. Use of related technology	3	8	4	4
b. Use of related marketing skills	3	6	6	4
Subtotal	6	14	10	8
2. Potential contribution of diversifying firms to acquired firm				
a. Technological contribution by diversifying firm to acquired firm	4	7	5	5
b. Potential usefulness of diversifying firm's marketing competence to the acquired firm	2	4	2	2
Subtotal	6	11	7	7
3. Potential for joint product development	7	9	6	6
4. Availability of good prospects	5	5	5	6
Total for Synergy	24	39	28	27
Grand Total: Objectives + Synergy	74	107	87	79

* From Theodore A. Anderson, H. Igor Ansoff, Frank Norton, and J. Fred Weston, 'Planning for Diversification Through Merger', *California Management Review*, vol. 1, no. 4, Summer, 1959.

to be profitable, but some are mature. The action is to keep these business areas and to siphon off their cash flow into a vigorous diversification programme. Courses (2) and (3) above, are commonly followed today, as evidenced by frequent announcements in the business press. Thus the great British B A T Company is maintaining its traditional position in the tobacco business and has made major moves into the retailing, fine-paper and financial industries.

4. The fourth case is when, while profitable, most of the present S B As have mediocre future prospects which are inferior to available diversification opportunities. The solution is to cut back strategic resource allocation to the present S B As and invest in diversification/internationalization.

5. It may be that the prospects of the present portfolio are comparable and not significantly inferior to diversification. A wise course of action is to exploit fully the opportunities of the current portfolio and invest only the excess resources (if any) into diversification. (For a possible exception, see case 7 below).

6. The same course of action is advisable when the present portfolio is significantly superior to diversification/internationalization opportunities.

7. All of the above recommendations arise from a comparison of attractiveness of the future prospects of the present portfolio to those offered by diversification/internationalization. Another determinant of the decision is the ability of the present portfolio to meet all of the objectives of the firm.

For example, the growth/profitability prospects may be satisfactory, but the strategic vulnerability of the present portfolio is too high. If, in any of the six cases above, the present portfolio does not meet all of the corporate objectives, a high priority of the diversification activity should be on making sure that these objectives will be met in the future.

The seven alternatives discussed above are summarized in Table 9.2. A shortcoming of the table is that it assumes availability of equally adequate and reliable information about the benefits which can be derived from improvements in the present portfolio, as compared with the benefits of diversification/internationalization.

But typically, even if the firm has undertaken a portfolio analysis along the lines of Figure 9.1, information about diversification/internationalization is typically much less complete and reliable than the information about the future of the firm's historical businesses. (For reasons for this, see Ansoff. Chapter 2.6.1.)

This discrepancy in information may not deter risk-seeking entrepreneurial managers. But prudent risk takers may be reluctant to

Table 9.2. Variants of the Diversification/Internationalization Decision

Condition	Present Portfolio	Diversification/ Internationalization
1. All SBAs are unattractive.	Liquidate.	All resources committed.
2. Some unattractive SBAs.	Partial divestment.	Major resources committed.
3. Some mature SBAs.	Milk mature SBAs.	Strategic resources committed.
4. Diversification SBA's are more attractive than present SBAs.	Cut back commitment to less attractive SBAs.	Significant resources committed.
5. Diversification/-internationalization comparably attractive to present SBA's.	Exploit present portfolio to the fullest extent.	Excess resources to diversification.
6. Present portfolio more attractive than diversification.	Exploit present portfolio to the fullest extent.	Excess resources to diversification.
7. Present portfolio cannot meet all of the firm's objectives.	Follow course according to condition 1–6 above.	Focus diversification on meeting objectives not met by current portfolio.

choose an uncertain 'bird in the bush' against the certain 'bird in the hand'. In fact, experience shows that, when confronted with a need for a substantial repositioning of the firm's resources into diversification or internationalization, many firms not only fail to anticipate the need, but delay their response until the end becomes imperative through chronic decline in sales and loss of profitability.

Aside from the behavioural problems in responding to changes which are discontinuous from the past (which we shall be discussing in Part 2), there is wisdom in proceeding cautiously, whenever the novel fields of opportunity are poorly understood. Such wisdom is observable in the behaviour of successful multi-nationals which frequently follow the path of *gradual commitment* when entering markets in countries in which they have never done business before. (For further discussion, see Chapters 2.6.4, 2.6.8 and 5.4.12 in Ansoff, *Implanting Strategic Management*.)

These considerations do not decrease the validity of the decision alternatives shown in Table 9.2. They do, however, show that availability of information affects the manner in which they are implemented.

CHAPTER 10

Choice of Portfolio and Competitive Strategies

The end products of managers' work are decisions and actions.
                                        PETER DRUCKER

The Problem

The diversification decision moves strategy formulation into its final phase. The first step in this phase is to construct alternative portfolios of product-market entries which are individually large enough to be competitive in their respective markets, which are related to each other, and which can be undertaken within the resources of the firm. The first section of this chapter is concerned with a procedure for constructing such alternative portfolios.

In the process of selecting the diversification/internationalization product-market scope, two problems, which have remained in the background until now, come into focus. The first is how to trade off competing demands of proximate, long-term, and flexibility objectives. Put somewhat more generally, the problem is how to select the preferred product-market scope from alternatives, each of which is measured by several incommensurate yardsticks. Although extensive literature exists on this subject, management science can offer only partial assistance to the decision-maker. Some specific procedures are described in the following section.

The second problem, which so far has been only partially explored in this book, is how to allow for the risk associated with strategic decisions. Several sources of risk and uncertainty are discussed in the third section. This is followed by a brief review of decision rules which are commonly discussed in management science. A somewhat complex procedure is suggested by which several of these rules can be brought to bear on selection of the product-market scope and the growth vector.

The remaining two components of strategy – competitive advantage and synergy – follow selection of scope and help sharpen the firm's search and evaluation of opportunities. Procedures for selecting each component are discussed in the fourth and the fifth sections respectively.

The final section of the chapter discusses the manner in which the requirements for a theory of strategic decisions set forth in Chapter 2 have been met.

Strategic Business (SBA) Portfolios

The diversification decision results in a consolidated list of industries, or strategic business areas, ranked on each of the major objectives. This list is the basis for selection of the diversification scope.

Except in unusual circumstances, no single industry will be preferable to all others for all of the firm's objectives. If the unusual does occur, the choice is clear and the analysis can proceed to selection of other components of strategy. More usually, industries which are preferable for proximate profitability will be inferior to others on long-term objectives. Industries which would contribute most to flexibility will generally be deficient on short-term profitability because of lower synergy with the firm.

To provide the firm with an attractive overall strategic posture it is necessary therefore to consider alternative *portfolios* of industries. One approach to alternatives is to construct all possible combinations of industries from the consolidated rank list and to measure them against objectives and other relevant constraints. This procedure is feasible if the choice strategy can be programmed on a computer. If analysis by hand is to be used, the number of such alternatives may become unmanageable (in one study the consolidated list contained some forty different industries). Under these conditions a judgement trial-and-error method can be used to better advantage to select a handful of the most promising portfolios.

The flexibility objective is attained through a diversity of different entries; it requires, therefore, a large number of entries in the portfolio. The other two major objectives exert an influence towards a small number of entries. The reasons are:

1. A large number of different entries entails an accumulation of entry costs which will depress profitability. The cost of an entry is relatively independent of its size, since the same minimum learning costs have to be incurred for a £500,000 as for a £10-million entry. This applies to all types of firms, but the restriction is less stringent for non-integrated ones. However, even an investment trust faces a fixed commission cost per transaction. A very widely diversified investment portfolio can generate a substantial entry cost.

2. Once acquired, many distinct and different entries will cost more to operate because of a lack of synergy and dilution of management attention.

For a given entry a minimum management commitment is required, regardless of its size. Thus even in an investment trust the investment officer must 'manage' each entry through keeping track of its performance and prospects. Clearly the load on an operating manager is much greater.

3. For each entry there is a minimum *critical mass* below which it is not possible to be competitive and profitable in the chosen SBA. This applies primarily to firms which acquire or create whole operating units, such as divisions or companies. It does not apply to firms which acquire a part of the equity in an operating unit. Although this practice is confined largely to investment firms, some operating firms acquire a part interest in another firm and many go into joint ventures.

Failure to make realistic estimates of the critical mass has been dramatically illustrated in the early days of the mainframe computer industry. A number of firms sought to enter the industry apparently without having anticipated the very high start-up cost and the very large development, marketing development, marketing and service costs. Three medium-sized firms found themselves stretched beyond their means and quit; three very large firms hung on, but showed every evidence of surprise and disappointment at the amount of red ink they were forced to incur. One of these firms (The American General Electric Co.) persisted in the business until it became evident that reaching the critical mass would require an additional investment which exceeded the potential of this giant firm. Having reached this conclusion, General Electric quit the mainframe computer business.

While critical mass is the minimum size of entry needed in order to be competitive, entries which are larger than critical mass are to the firm's advantage, because of large volume and consequent stronger competitive position.

Since the overall size of the portfolio is limited by the total resources available for diversification (see competitive analysis, Chapter 8), the most attractive portfolios will be the result of a compromise between sizes of individual entries and their total number, subject to the critical mass constraint.

A procedure for developing portfolios of diversification/internationalization alternatives is illustrated in Figure 10.1. Several provisional *diversification/internationalization scope alternatives* or portfolios (1) are selected by judgement (or the entire list of possibilities enumerated by a computer). At this point an alternative scope may be as narrow as an industry or part of an industry (if the firm has been fortunate enough to

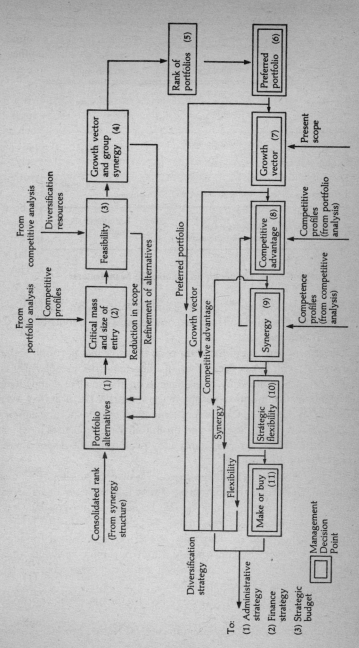

Figure 10.1. Decision Flow in Choice of Diversification/Internationalization Strategy (for competitive strategy start with step 5)

Product　　　Customer	Related technology	Unrelated technology
Same type	Motorcycles lawnmowers, intra-urban personal vehicles	Electric home appliances
Firm its own customer	Gas turbine engines wheels transmissions	Paint, glass, tyres, etc.
Similar type	Farm tractors and machinery	Computers for small business
New type	Diesel locomotives Missile ground support equipment	Petrochemicals drugs

Figure 10.2. Sample Growth Vectors for an Automobile Manufacturer

find one which has good potential for all objectives); or, it may be a combination of several industries selected and matched on their respective contribution to the diversification objectives.

Next, the *critical mass* is estimated for each industry in a portfolio and a tentative *size of entry* (2) is decided upon. The tentative size of entry is based on the decision made by management on the relative competitive position which the firm wants to occupy in the industry. The firm may wish to become one of the top competitors in some industry which, for example, offers the prospects of high growth and profitability. In industries in which the future is problematic but potentially very promising, the decision may be to take a 'foothold' position.

The total resource requirement generated by a diversification portfolio is next tested for *feasibility* (3) by comparing it with the resources available, as determined in the competitive analysis. If the scope is not feasible, it is reduced and again tested for critical mass.

Alternatives which pass the feasibility test are next classified for their growth-vector properties by constructing a matrix similar to Figure 10.2, which shows different logical paths by which a firm can expand beyond the limits of its traditional business portfolio.

Identification of the growth vectors implied by the alternative portfolio serves three purposes:

1. Within an industry a sub-division into several related product-mission

combinations helps sharpen the choice of product-market scope. Thus, a firm which originally had electronics as a diversification alternative, may split this into several distinct alternatives, such as military and space systems, conventional components, exotic components, materials and consumer products.

2. Within a portfolio, the growth-vector matrix relates different industries to each other with respect to their economic and technological foundations. This makes it possible to rank portfolios on the economic and cost of entry objectives.

3. The common thread delineated by the matrix permits synergy estimates for each portfolio.

The next step is to rank the respective portfolios on *synergy* (4). Synergy estimates must be made between each industry in a diversification portfolio and the key synergies in the firm's historical portfolio of businesses.

These analyses produce an estimate of the potential synergy of the respective diversification portfolios with respect to the traditional businesses. They also provide *common synergistic threads* which would guide the future development of the firm, if a particular diversification portfolio were to be chosen.

The set of portfolios defined and measured against the diversification objectives with the assistance of the growth vector is next *ranked* (5) *on each major objective*. The result is a list similar to the overall rank list (16) of Figure 9.1, but containing alternative portfolios, rather than industries, for its entries.

Choosing the Preferred Portfolio

The stage is set for a major decision point at which the firm commits itself to a particular portfolio scope and growth vector. At first glance this would appear to be quite simple; the portfolio which offers the best performance for the firm's objectives is the one to choose. In practice this turns out to be a difficult process. Each portfolio is measured by at least four ratings: one each on proximate, long-term, flexibility and synergy objectives. These are in the nature of apples, pears and oranges. Each contributes to a different aspect of the firm's performance; each is measured by a different yardstick; and an increase in one usually involves a decrease in the others. There is no obvious way in which they can be combined to produce a single figure of merit for each scope.

This dilemma of reconciling non-commensurate and non-colinear objectives is not an issue in the behavioural theory of the firm. There it is asserted that real-life firms do not deal with multiple objectives, but seek to satisfy one objective at a time. Thus, no combined figure of merit is needed.

While there is evidence (cited by Cyert and March) that some conservative firms do behave this way, there is also evidence that more progressive firms do not. Further, since our interest is in improving and not just in describing decision processes, it is our strong recommendation that firms should by all means take advantage of opportunities to select alternatives which meet a range of objectives, even though the selection process may be complex and imprecise.

This, however, leaves us with the problem outlined above. One helpful feature of our method of strategy formulation is the multi-stage process of narrowing of the field of alternatives, which reduces the final list of portfolio scopes to a relatively small number, sometimes to a single acceptable alternative. Another useful feature is the assignment of priorities to the respective objectives, since these can be used as 'weights' to compute an overall weighted rank for each of the remaining alternatives in a manner similar to that illustrated in Table 10.1. It must be recognized, however, that different numerical weights may lead to different choices. Several weighting schemes should be tried, therefore, and further subjected to consistency tests, such as the Churchman-Ackoff Test.[1]

The result of these evaluations may be a dominant choice which is not sensitive to reasonable weighting schemes. More frequently, several alternative 'best' choices will emerge depending on the weights. Mathematical manipulation stops here and the full range of results and assumptions should be presented to the responsible executive for his final decision. Thus, while management science can offer help in clarifying choices, the final decision and the responsibility for it remain with the executive.

The choice of the preferred portfolio makes it possible to identify the key components which will guide the selection of future projects: the scope of the preferred portfolio (6) identifies the SBA's (insofar as they are known at this point) in which the firm will do business, the growth vector (7), competitive advantage (8), synergy (9), strategic flexibility (10), and the make-or-buy-strategy (11).

Acquisition vs. Internal Growth – the Make-or-buy Decision

The process of strategy selection was carried out without reference to whether the firm will grow by acquisition or develop from within. The

Table 10.1. Internal Development versus Acquisition

Synergy		Preferred method	Applicable growth vectors	Exceptions
Start-up	Operating			
Strong	Strong	Internal development	Market development, product development; technologically related horizontal and vertical diversification	1. Timing is of essence 2. Acquisition of good management 3. Acquisition of needed capacity 4. Low-cost product acquisition 5. Stable market shares; no room for new entry
Strong Weak	Weak Strong	Internal development Combination of acquisition and internal development	Unrelated horizontal, and vertical, diversification	
Weak	Weak	Acquisition	Concentric diversification	1. Timing of no importance 2. Incipient demand 3. No competent firms available 4. High price/earnings
None	None	Acquisition	Conglomerate diversification	

decision on whether to 'make or buy' (11) new product-markets is needed before strategy can be implemented.

Both acquisition and internal development assume many forms. The former varies from licensing, to purchase of developed products, to mergers with another firm; the latter, from addition of new products to major organizational changes to make room for new skills and competences.

Two primary variables influence the choice between the major alternatives. These are the start-up cost and the timing. In internal development the costs are incurred by product development and introduction, and by building new facilities and organizations. The price of acquisition will include those costs; however, over and above them is a premium which frequently has to be paid as a compensation for the risks which had been taken by the seller to develop the property and the competences being sold.

Because of this premium, it is sometimes argued that internal development is cheaper. This is not necessarily the case, because, in risky undertakings, budgeting for internal development has to include a risk allowance to provide for the variances in the estimates and the uncertainties of the results. There are cases, however, in which the premium paid on acquisition may not be an accurate reflection of the risks which have been taken. Thus, a firm which seeks to diversify into a currently glamorous growth industry is forced to pay a premium which may be excessive.

In some cases the choice between acquisition and internal development is forced in favour of the latter. This will occur when the current price/earnings ratio in the new industry is much higher than that of the firm itself. A desire to avoid large dilutions in earnings per share may make acquisition out of the question. The choice may also be forced by lack of attractive acquisition opportunities in the new industry. The choice may be forced the other way when the competitive structure in the new industry leaves no room for a significant new entry.

In internal development the timing of entry consists of two elements: (1) The normal product-development cycle. This may vary from six months to four years depending on technological and marketing complexity of the product. (2) The time span required to acquire new skills and competence. This can vary from one to five or six years. The total time span will depend on the degree of synergy between the new product-market and the firm.

In acquisition of a firm the delay is theoretically only as long as the time taken to consummate the transaction. In practice a time delay is added during which the acquisition is introduced into the parent organization. However, even after this provision it generally takes much longer to develop than to acquire a firm. If a product, rather than a firm, is being acquired, the time span may vary from the time it takes to tool and market, when synergy is strong, to several years, when a complete range of supporting competences has to be developed.

The pros and cons of acquisition versus internal development can be related to the components of synergy, as shown in Table 10.1.

As the second column in the table indicates, internal development is indicated when the start-up synergy is strong, even if operating synergy is weak. Although there may not be operating economies, the firm's competence pattern assures a fast start and low risk. Exceptions in favour of acquisition may occur (1) when the needs of the firm or instability of the market make a quick entry important, (2) when the firm needs or is offered opportunity to acquire competent management. (3) when the firm will have to enlarge some of its capacities anyway, (4) when a product developed outside the firm costs less than it would to develop internally, and (5) as mentioned above, when the market shares in the new industry are stabilized, making it very difficult for a newcomer to take away business from established competitors (as would be the case, for example, in mature industries such as automotive, meat packing, and electrical machinery).

Weak start-up synergy generally makes acquisition preferable. However, if operating synergy is strong – indicating applicable unused capacities – a combination of acquisition and internal development is indicated.

Absence of synergy points to acquisition in most cases. An exception is a situation when the premium on timing is low. This may occur, for example, when the move is being made in support of a very long-term objective and when the firm prepares to serve a still incipient demand.

The middle column in the table relates the method of expansion to the growth vector. The high synergy strategies will usually be pursued through internal development. Synergy can vary in horizontal and vertical diversification and so will the appropriate growth methods. Conglomerate diversification usually calls for acquisition.

Allowing for Risk and Uncertainty

The weighting procedures described above do not resolve a problem which has a major influence on the final choice. This is the problem of risk.*

---

* In the following we shall use the word risk in a non-technical sense to denote the impact of imperfect information on decision making. As discussed earlier (see p. 115), in mathematical literature risk is a condition under which either the occurrence or the outcome of alternatives is not certain but is assigned probabilities.

Risk enters the problem in two ways. First, we have to recognize at the outset that our ability to foresee the future in any detail is limited to only certain foreseeable events and that we have every reason to expect that other events, unforeseeable at present, have a high likelihood of occurring. The weighting process provides for unforeseeable events through the flexibility objective.

However, the foreseeable events also contain several elements of risk. First, assuming that our projections of future business conditions are accurate, the expectations of the firm's success in any given industry are at best probability judgements. The probable may not materialize, and the firm may perform very differently from expectations. It may do much better than expected, or it may fail altogether. Second, the projections of business conditions on which these expectations are based are themselves estimates of probable events. Third, the activities contemplated by the firm will impinge on those of other firms which may react through competition and try to minimize the effectiveness of our actions.

Thus the expectations from respective diversification or internationalization prospects depend on three sources of uncertainty: uncertainties in estimation of results, uncertainties in projecting the environment, and uncertainties in competitive reaction. To a limited extent we have sought to provide for the third through analysis of competitive conditions and of the cost of entry. If the contemplated entry is into an industry in which market shares are widely distributed and no major competitor dominates the industry, the provisions made in competitive analysis are probably adequate. However, if the entry will have a major impact on the industry and if it is to be made against major competitors, an analysis of competitive consequences needs to be made.

As discussed earlier (see Chapter 6), there is a body of mathematics called *game theory* concerned with problems of competitive conflict. As a tool for the solution of business problems, game theory has achieved limited success. The fault is in part with the mathematical part of the theory which is still capable of solving only very elementary games and in part with management theory, since it has failed so far to construct more than a few 'games' of practical value.

While still far from being a practical management tool, game theory offers an extremely powerful and useful concept for analysis of strategic problems in which interaction among competitors has a strong influence on choice of strategy. Therefore, if any of the product-market scope alternatives do pose major competitive implications. they should be examined from the viewpoint of game theory, if only to define and recognize the counterstrategies which the competition may employ. As a result of such study, the respective ratings and hence the ranks of the product-market alternatives should be adjusted.*

Rules for Decision

During the competitive and portfolio analyses the uncertainties of estimation and of prediction have been handled without an explicit recognition of probable errors in the estimates. A 'most likely' environment was constructed and the 'most likely' performance ascribed to the firm. This was necessary to avoid overcomplicating an already complex analysis. However, at the short strokes of strategy selection, consideration of risk must be introduced more explicitly.

There is another considerable body of mathematical literature, generally referred to as *decision theory*, which is concerned with decision-making under imperfect information.[2] It is based on a variety of what W. T. Morris[3] calls 'principles of choice' – decision rationales imputed to the decision-maker. Unfortunately, there is at present very little understanding of the extent to which these rationales correspond to the ways in which a business decision-maker actually does make decisions. A major point of contention among the various theories is the manner in which the executive compares the risk-gain properties of one alternative with those of another.

Nevertheless, decision theory is useful as a 'truth and consequence' device. By tracing the consequences of different risk-gain assumptions the decision-maker can see what the resulting strategy would be under different principles of choice.† To provide such perspective we shall briefly describe several of the most common decision rules found in the literature.[4]

The alternative approaches are shown in Table 10.2. The *aspiration level decision rule*, briefly referred to earlier, merely sets a minimum performance level required of an alternative. Alternatives which are below the level are rejected, those which equal or exceed it are accepted. The rule works when one alternative is being examined at a time. When several alternatives are being considered, the method has no way of discriminating among them.

The *goals-threshold method*, which we have introduced and discussed in

---

* An interactive computer-assisted approach to handling both risk and the game theory aspect of competitive analysis can be found in Chapter 8, note 3.

† The actual application of the model is not something the manager himself usually would do. Most would require the help of a trained management scientist.

detail in this book, is a step beyond the aspiration level. It rejects undesirable opportunities below the threshold, permits us to assess relative desirability of a *single* opportunity by its place within the threshold-goal range, and permits comparison of several alternatives.

Both of the preceding rules measure the returns and say nothing about the probability of occurrence. The *most probable choice method*, shown third, selects the portfolio which will perform best in the most probable environment. This rule is used frequently and typically by firms which use 'single-line' forecasts without regard to other possibilities. A problem arises, however, when some low-probability event neglected in the strategy has the potential of causing a complete disaster for the firm. Thus, by placing all of its bets on boom conditions, the firm may lose liquidity to a point, where, say, a mere 20 per cent drop in sales could lead to bankruptcy. Thus, no provision for risk is made.

The *expected value approach*, (4) in the table, assumes that all decision-makers balance risk versus gain in the same way and that they compare alternatives by the product of the return and the probability of its occurrence.

Finally, the *rating-probability exchange method* differs from the expected value method in that the choice of an equivalent risk-returns combination is left to the decision-maker and is not assumed to be measured by the product of the two.

The expected value method suffers from the deficiency that no course of action is rejected outright because it may contain a particularly unfavourable outcome. However, in selecting its strategy the firm will probably want to reject alternatives which have a substantial probability of losing money, even though their expected value may be attractive. This kind of provision is made in the rating-probability exchange method, in which portfolios which will have negative outcomes can be rejected even if these outcomes have low probabilities.

It is seen from the preceding that the weighting, the game theory and the decision rules are addressed to complementary aspects of the problem. The first deals with a combination of incommensurate yardsticks, the second with actions by competition, and the third with the uncertainties in the action outcomes and in behaviour of the environment.

For the purpose of strategy selection, we recommend an approach which is a combination of weighting, game theory, goals-threshold rule, and expected value, or the rating-probability exchange rule. It would proceed as follows:

1. The threshold minimums are applied to reject alternatives which do

Table 10.2. Principles of Choice

Approach	Procedure	Selection
1. Aspiration level	Set minimum values to be attained on each objective.	Select portfolio which reaches or exceeds aspiration level for all objectives.
2. Goals-threshold	Set minimum values to be attained and also goal values desired.	Reject all portfolios below threshold. Select strategy which gives best weighted rating.
3. Most probable choice	Make a single-line, most probable forecast of the future prospects. Evaluate alternative portfolios under these prospects.	Select portfolio which is best under the most probable conditions.
4. Expected value	Make several probable forecasts of prospects. Evaluate each portfolio for each forecast. Multiply value of portfolio by the probability of the forecast.	Select portfolio with the highest expected value.
5. Rating/probability exchange	Through judgement determine the combined value to firm of each rating/probability combination of each portfolio.	Select strategy with the highest value.

not meet the minimums established for each objective. This has a secondary effect of eliminating undesirable risks.

2. Wherever appropriate, the rating and hence relative rank of alternatives is reviewed and adjusted through the use of a game matrix which contains possible counter-strategies of competition.

3. Probability is assigned to each alternative for each objective. This is a combination probability which accounts for uncertainties of both estimation and forecasting. It is also a simple-minded probability: its value p_s denotes chances of success of the alternative, its complement $(1-p_s)$ the probability of failure. The rank of an alternative for each objective is weighted in accordance to the weight of priority assigned to the objective. The 'value' of each alternative is computed using either expected value of judgement on the probability-returns exchange for each alternative-objective combination. The alternative with the highest 'value' is selected.

The following presents a simple example.

Table 10.3

Portfolios	Objective			
	Proximate (2)	Long-term (1)	Flexibility (3) ◄	Priorities (3 is highest)
P_1	(1,0.7)	(3,0.9)	(1,0.4)	
P_2	(2,0.6)	(1,0.8)	(3,0.2)	
P_3	(3,0.8)	(2,0.5)	(2,0. 9)	Probability Rank (3 is highest)

The computation of the expected value would look as follows:

$$P_1: (2 \times 1 \times 0.7) + (1 \times 3 \times 0.9) + (3 \times 1 \times 0.4) = 5.3$$
$$P_2: (2 \times 2 \times 0.6) + (1 \times 1 \times 0.8) + (3 \times 3 \times 0.2) = 5.0$$
$$P_3: (2 \times 3 \times 0.8) + (1 \times 2 \times 0.5) + (3 \times 2 \times 0.9) = 11.2$$

P_3 is clearly superior to the other two product-market scopes. Other priorities would be tried in a similar manner.

The evaluation scheme proposed above is one of many similar ones which can be constructed. No particular merit can be claimed for it, other than the inclusion in one evaluation of all the major factors which affect the decision. In actual strategy selection, it will be useful to evaluate the alternatives in several different ways and to present to the decision-maker the sensitivities of outcomes to different assumptions.

Competitive Posture

The portfolio strategy specifies *where* the firm intends to do business. It remains to decide *how* the firm will attack each strategic area in order to optimize its objectives in the face of competition. The answer to this question is the firm's *competitive strategy* in each strategic business area.

In the early days of the mass-production era, when demand for goods was growing rapidly in every market, the products offered by firms were largely undifferentiated from one another. Firms competed on price since the sales went to the lowest bidder. To make low prices possible it was necessary to produce in the largest possible volume, and to produce in the largest volume it was necessary to have the largest market share. Therefore, *maximization of market share through pricing* was the commonly used competitive strategy.

By mid-century the competitive scene became much more complicated: many markets became saturated, products became differentiated, customers no longer purchased on price alone and foreign competition from low-wage countries began to take markets away from domestic producers. As a result, maximization of market share became only one of a number of success strategies. And, even when maximization of market share was appropriate, it became one of several mutually supporting components of competitive strategy.

A competitive strategy can be described by three principal components: *growth thrust, market differentiation*, and *product differentiation*, all shown in the left-hand column of Figure 10.3.

Growth thrust defines the activities through which the firm will assure its future growth. As mentioned above in the early part of the twentieth century, there was no need to worry about the source of growth. But during the second half of the century, growth of demand slowed down drastically in many industries, and firms which want to grow faster must resort to deliberate growth-enhancing actions. The several entries to the right of growth thrust in Figure 10.3 describe several possible alternative growth-enhancement strategies.

The task in strategy formulation is twofold: to identify the alternatives which will produce success in the business area being analysed and then to choose the alternative which is best for the firm. We shall say more about this process later on.

The second component of strategy is *market differentiation*, which defines the way in which the firm will differentiate itself from competition in the eyes of the *customers* as well as the relative market-share position it will seek to occupy. Again, the entries are generic alternatives, some of which will be the key to success in the future.

The third component is *product differentiation* which defines the manner in which the firm will differentiate its products and services from those of its *competitors*.

A competitive strategy can be constructed with the aid of Figure 10.3 by selecting one or more mutually consistent components for each of the major sub-strategies. Two examples are given in the figure. The first of these, connected by a double line, is the classical success strategy, prescribed in micro-economic theory. As can be seen, this strategy is 'capture a dominant market share, and offer an undifferentiated product at the minimum price'.

Another strategy, illustrated by the elements connected by the single lines, is the 'Rolls-Royce' strategy: 'segment the market, occupy dominant share in your segment, offer service, performance features, and reliability, which together project an image of exclusivity, comfort and snob appeal'. Interestingly enough, technologically, Rolls-Royce has been a product follower and not an innovator.

The two examples illustrate the important fact that, to be effective, the *sub-strategy components must be consistent with and supportive of one another*. For example, in a mature market the firm cannot hope to gain a dominant market share if its growth thrust is passive. As another example, trying for market differentiation through minimum price, while at the same time seeking product differentiation through innovation, is difficult, if not impossible.

As discussed earlier, in the environment of the last quarter of this century, the traditional competitive strategy in the firm's traditional business areas must be challenged even if it has been a great success in the past.

In fact, the challenge to the very successful strategies must be more determined than challenges to the moderately successful ones. The reason is that successful strategies acquire a momentum and the allegiance of the managers who have made them successful. Unless challenged by corporate management, these strategies will persist even in the face of evidence which shows that past successes are going to become the failures of tomorrow. Thus, as already mentioned, Henry Ford's refusal to recognize the end of the Model-T era had cost him his dominant leadership in the automotive industry. This phenomenon of rejecting unwelcome future prospects has

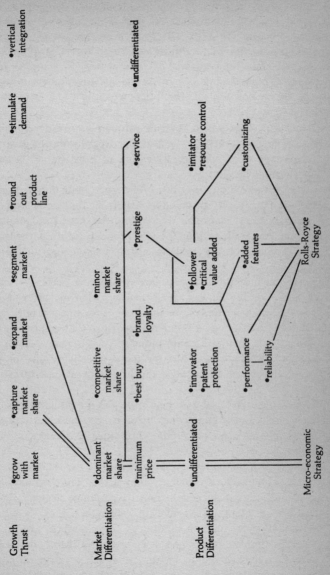

Figure 10.3. Competitive Strategy Factors

been so prevalent as to acquire the name of *strategic myopia*. In the next part of the book we will have more to say about strategic myopia.

If the firm proposes to enter new strategic business areas through acquisitions, the acquired firm will come with an already articulated strategy. An examination of the future validity of this strategy must be a part of the pre-acquisition analysis. If the strategy is likely to require major changes, the acquiring firm must include investments in strategy revision in the calculation of the price which will be paid for the acquisition.

If the new business entry is to be made through internal development of products/services and markets by the firm, the overall competitive strategy, and the costs associated with implementing it, must be of paramount concern in the entry decision.

Repeated experience shows that firms tend to estimate only the product or service development costs and tend to neglect the frequently larger costs of analysing the new markets, developing the new production and distribution capabilities, launching the new product, incurring the learning costs in the new business and gaining customer acceptance of the firm's offering.

A failure to include this massive part of the cost 'iceberg', which is usually invisible 'below the waterline', has led to many grievous over-estimates of the ultimate return on the firm's investment from the new markets. What is even worse, a failure to recognize that major changes in strategy will very likely require a substantial revision of and addition to the firm's capability to implement the strategy typically results in major implementation problems and delays, and in unprofitable performance in the market-place.

As unfavourable experience with new strategies accumulates it becomes evident that the selection of a new competitive strategy must be accompanied by identification of the *capability profile* which must be developed to assure the strategy's success.

Figure 10.4 shows, on the left, the components of capability and, in the body of the table, the various capability alternatives. The capability profile which the firm will need to support the micro–economic strategy of Figure 10.3 is illustrated by the italicized items in Figure 10.4.

Thus, formulation of competitive strategy for a business area must be coupled with a determination of the new capabilities which the firm will have to develop to implement and support the strategy. Furthermore, both strategy *and* capability must be costed to determine the *strategic investment*

General Management	*efficiency* • *growth* • innovation • maturity • creativity • diversification • large risks • technology • project management • multinational • societal
Finance	*controllership* • financing • credit • currency/tax • cash management • capital investment • inflation management
Marketing	*sales* • advertising promotion • pioneering market research • *sales analysis* • product introduction • market expansion • cross-cultural markets
Production	*inventory* • distribution • purchasing • *industrial relations* • mass production • tailored production • *automation* • product changeover • *technology adaptation*
R & D	research • creativity • innovation • adaptation • *incremental evolution* • imitation • styling • industrial engineering • *production technology*

Figure 10.4 Capability Factors

which will have to be made. We shall refer to the combination of the competitive strategy, the supporting capabilities and the strategic investment as the firm's *strategic posture* in a strategic business area.

Decision Flow in Competitive-Posture Decisions

The flow is illustrated in Figure 10.5. Step (1) is identification of the growth and profitability prospects which will be available in the business area to the *most successful competitors* (and not necessarily attained by the firm). Analysis of future prospects will have already been performed in competitive and portfolio analyses (see Figures 8.1 and 9.1.) and the results can be used again at this point.

The second step (2) is to identify the strategies which will be successful in the business area during the next five to seven years. As in the analysis of prospects, *it is essential at this stage to focus attention on strategies which will succeed in the future, and not on the traditional strategy of the firm.* If the environment is expected to be an extrapolation of the past, these strategies can be identified by an analysis of historical successes in the business area. The computer-based PIMS approach is one very useful technique for analysis of historical success patterns. Another approach is *competitor analysis*, widely used in business firms.

In extrapolative environments, the analysis of the future success capabilities is typically made through identification of the strengths (in general management, marketing, finance, R&D, etc.) which were responsible for the historical successes.

If the future environment is expected to be significantly different from the past, historical analyses are of limited value and it becomes necessary to construct scenarios of *future success factors* and use these to identify alternative success strategies.

One technique for competitive posture analysis in turbulent environments is described in detail in Chapter 2.2 of Ansoff, *Implanting Strategic Management*. A personal computer-based approach, known as ANSPLAN, has recently become available (see Chapter 8, note 3). This approach involves responsible line managers, assisted by staff and guided by the computer in a detailed analysis of probable future success strategies and capabilities.

The preceding analysis of the future environment is performed in parallel with an analysis of the firm. As Figure 10.5 shows, this involves identification of the firm's present posture (3) and its objectives (4) for the future.

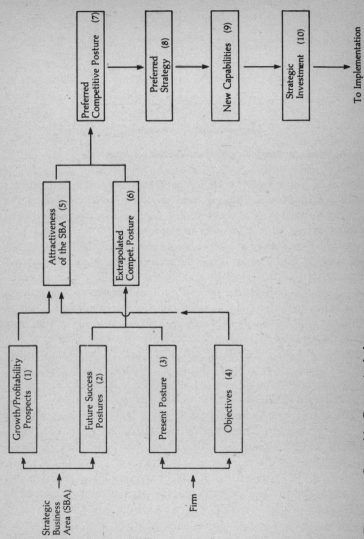

Figure 10.5. Competitive Posture Analysis

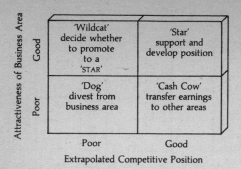

Figure 10.6. Matrix for Positioning the Firm in Business Areas

As the discussion above shows, competitive-posture analysis separates the future opportunities and success strategies in the strategic business area from the historical strategy of the firm. The purpose is to give management an unbiased view of what is in store for the future.

As also discussed above, unless the separation is made and enforced, an unbiased view of the future is usually difficult to achieve during strategic-posture analysis, particularly in historically successful firms. The tendency is to see the future through the eyes of the firm's traditionally successful products, technologies and marketing strategies. The tendency is also to assume that 'our' customers will remain faithful to us even if a new technology invades the market and makes the product obsolete.

The analyses of the environment and of the firm are next combined in two ways. The first (5) is to apply the firm's objectives to the prospects in the environment to determine how *attractive* the business area will be to the firm, in terms of its ability to satisfy the firm's objectives.

The second way (6) is to compare the future success strategies with the firm's previous strategy to determine how successful the firm is likely to be if it persists with its previous strategy and capability. This is called *extrapolated competitive posture* in Figure 10.5.

In recent years, a very useful graphical comparison of attractiveness and competitive position called the *positioning matrix*, has been pioneered by The American Boston Consulting Group (BCG) and subsequently improved by others.

Figure 10.6 illustrates a version of the positioning matrix, in which the attractiveness of a business area is plotted vertically and the firm's extrapolated competitive position horizontally. Each strategic area is shown as a dot or a circle in the matrix.

As the figure shows, strategic business areas which fall in the upper right-hand section are 'stars': they must be supported and developed; the ones in the lower left-hand section are 'dogs': the firm must divest from them.

The lower right-hand section contains business areas in which the firm will remain successful, but which are unattractive. The implication is that they should be treated as 'cash cows': the firm should transfer profits to other strategic business areas and let the activities in that area run down.

Finally, the upper left-hand section is problematic: the business area is attractive but the firm will be a weak competitor: the problem is whether there are time and resources to convert its position into a 'star'. The Boston Consulting Group called such strategic business areas 'wildcats', after 'wildcat' oil wells.

The matrix of Figure 10.6 is simplistic: useful for exposing the basic concept but too crude to permit realistic business decisions. Since its invention by the BCG, the matrix and the methods of its analysis have advanced very substantially to make possible a decision on the competitive position the firm will seek to occupy in the business area. This step is labelled *preferred competitive posture* (7) in Figure 10.5.

Once the competitive posture is chosen, it becomes necessary to determine the strategy through which the firm will attain the preferred position.

The future success strategies in the business areas have been determined by step (2). Therefore, choosing the preferred strategy (8) involves a comparison of the firm's previous strategies with the successful ones in order to determine the strategy which, on the one hand, will be successful and, on the other hand, will involve the least change and investment by the firm.

Following the selection of a strategy, the changes in the firm's marketing, management, capabilities (9), etc., which are necessary to support the preferred strategy, are determined.

The final step in the competitive-posture analysis is to determine the investment which will have to be made in changing the present strategy, developing the capability and acquiring the necessary facilities and equipment. The sum of the three investments is the *strategic investment* which the firm intends to make into the strategic business area.

Summary

The make-or-buy decision completes the chain of steps which we have followed in developing a theory and a methodology for strategic decision-making. In Chapter 2 the method was described as a 'cascade' of decisions, starting with highly aggregated ones and proceeding toward the more

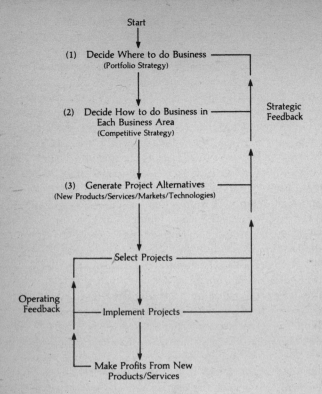

Figure 10.7. Action Cycle in Strategic Development

Level (1), (2) and (3) are Strategic Decision Levels

specific. This is demonstrated in Figure 10.7, which presents the overall decision and implementation flow in strategic activity. The 'cascade' property is illustrated by the progressive convergence of the decision process, which starts with the very broad choice of the firm's future business areas and progresses to selection of specific products or markets with which the firm will serve these areas.

Chapter 2 also discussed the feedback between stages of the decision. This is illustrated by the feedback arrows in Figure 10.7. As the figure shows, whenever unfavourable experiences at any decision level are repeated, thus questioning the wisdom of higher-level decisions, the higher-level decisions are reconsidered.

Figure 10.8. Determinants of Strategy

Chapter 2 had promised that the strategic analysis method would exhibit an 'open constraint' property, which means that objectives lead to the choice of opportunities, but the potential offered by these opportunities, in turn, modifies the original objectives of the firm.

This interaction between objectives and opportunities is illustrated in Figure 10.8 which also shows the key variables which determine the strategy. The need to balance four variables against one another (the environmental threats/opportunities, the firm's objectives, its present capabilities, and its future resources) during formulation of strategy explains much of the complexity of Figure 8.1 and Figure 9.1.

Finally, Chapter 2 promised that the strategy analysis method would be a 'gap reduction' approach. This is illustrated in Figure 8.2. Figure 8.1 determines the competitive gap which the firm can expect to close and Figure 9.1 determines the diversification/internationalization gap.

CHAPTER 11

Uses of Strategy

The fat is in the fire, the die is cast, the jig is up, the goose is cooked, and the cat is out of the bag.

JAMES THURBER

The Problem

The strategy formulation framework is completed. Starting with the philosophical issues which underlie objectives, we have traced the process to the point at which the firm commits itself to specific business strategies.

Two tasks remain. The first is to develop a procedure for evaluation and selection of projects which are triggered by strategy. The second is to show how strategy can be used within the overall periodic planning process of the business firm. Before embarking on these, we shall briefly recapitulate and focus the entire process of strategy formulation.

An Overview

Figure 11.1, shows the main building blocks of a strategic plan. Using this schematic we shall now briefly retrace its development.

As Figure 11.1 shows, one way to start the strategic planning process is to make explicit and to review the near and *long-term objectives* (1) which the firm will pursue in the future. This is the starting point which was used in the early days of formal strategic planning.

Experience has shown that it is difficult to set realistic objectives without an understanding of the future prospects and possibilities which are offered by the firm's business portfolio. An alternative starting point is to perform the *competitive analysis* (2) and then use the results to establish the objectives for the present portfolio, as well as tentative objectives for diversification/internationalization. This approach is indicated by the dashed lines in Figure 11.1.

The diversification/internationalization objectives are firmed up as a result of *portfolio analysis* (3) which, as we have seen, determines the respective resource commitments the firm will make to its traditional business and to diversification/internationalization.

The next step is to make a decision on the importance which will be assigned to synergies in portfolio expansion. The synergy decision commits the firm to an evolution of the organizational structure in a way consistent with the desired *synergy* (4).

As Figure 11.1 shows, formulation of the *portfolio strategy* (5) and of the *competitive postures* (6) in the respective business areas may be conducted sequentially or in parallel, depending on the relative priorities which are assigned to the respective activities. Firms which are secure in the future of their present portfolio and the effectiveness of their past strategies, may assign high priorities to the portfolio strategy improvements through diversification/internationalization. On the other hand, firms which see major strategic challenges in their traditional business areas may decide to 'put their house in order' before venturing into a new business.

Concern with *technology strategy* (7) (which assures that the firm's R & D is coherent with the firm's portfolio and competitive strategies) and with its *societal strategy* (8) (which assures that the firm will be responsive to the socio-cultural-political prospects in the firm's business areas) is relatively recent, but is rapidly growing in importance. (See Chapters 2.4 and 2.5 in Ansoff.)

All four (portfolio, competitive, technology and societal) action strategies place demands on the *administrative strategy* (9). In Part 2 of this book we shall discuss in detail the relationship between the action strategies and the administrative strategy.

Implementation of the respective action strategies, and building of the capabilities required by the administrative strategy, *require a strategic budget* (10), and the budget, in turn, will depend on the availability of financing which is articulated in the *financing strategy* (11).

The financial strategy will specify the rules and means by which the firm will seek to finance growth and expansion. A decision of major importance is the division of the firm's cash inflow between payment of dividends and reinvestment into the firm. This decision is clearly influenced by the other strategies and, in turn, has a major impact on business strategy. Thus, both the finance and the administrative strategy are influenced by, and in turn influence, the business strategy. In the preceding analysis we have used this interdependence several times. Thus, the resource projections and limitations (which are determined in major part by the finance strategy) were used in both competitive and portfolio appraisal to set overall limitations on strategic activity. Later, the same constraint was used in determining the feasibility of product-market scopes. The synergy-structure

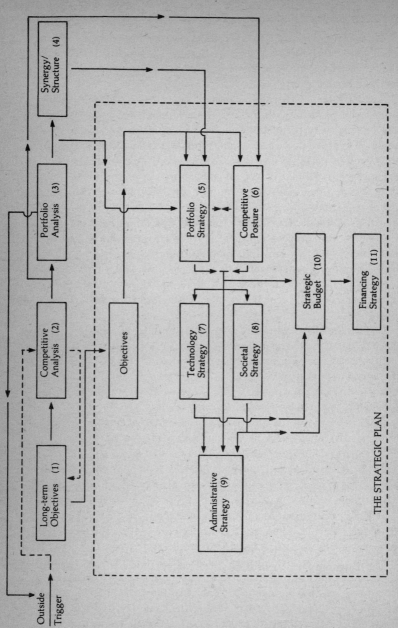

Figure 11.1. The Strategic Plan

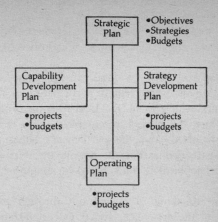

Figure 11.2. The Family of Plans

decision which has a major effect on product-market strategy is a key part of the administrative strategy.

There is much more to the formulation of these two strategies. Each deserves an analysis comparable in length to the analysis of the product-market strategy presented in this book.

Family of Plans

The strategies contained in the strategic plan, shown in Figure 11.1, are the basic guidelines for developing the firm's external posture and its internal capabilities. Before these guidelines become a 'bottom-line' reality in terms of profits and growth, specific projects must be generated, planned and executed. Furthermore, the strategic activity must be coordinated with the operating activities.

Thus, the strategic plan is a starting point for three related plans which translate strategic intent into specific plans for the strategic implementation. The family of four plans is shown in Figure 11.2.

The capability and business development plans contain project and supporting budgets which will change the internal configuration of the firm and its posture in the external environment. The 'bottom line' of these projects is an enhanced potential for future profits.

The operating plan, frequently comprised of short-term and long-term plans. contains programmes and budgets through which the firm intends to continue making profits.

It is important to note that strategic development and the operational profit-making are very different activities: differently organized, managed and controlled.

Strategic development must be done through projects which have a limited time duration and which require participation of all the functional competences: general management, R & D, marketing, production, finance, personnel, etc. Once the project is completed, the temporary project organization is dissolved, and the participants either return to their respective functional organizations or regroup to start another project. Thus, strategic development is fluid, based on temporary organizational structures.

Operational profit-making is carried out through programmes and budgets for each of the permanent functional organizational structures. While strategic projects have different durations, operating programmes are planned on the calendar basis: short-term programmes for a year, long-term programmes for three years or more.

Control of the strategic activity is different from control of the operating plan. The former is based on entrepreneurial risk-taking, the latter on performance according to profit goals.

In the early days of strategic planning, the difference between strategic development and operational profit making was poorly understood, and it was typically assumed that strategic plans will be implemented in the same manner as operating plans. A frequent result was 'paralysis by analysis', a phenomenon we shall discuss in Part 2 of this book.

Project Evaluation

A key element in strategic activities is the process by which projects are evaluated and selected.

It was seen in Chapter 2 that evaluation of product-market-technology opportunities differs from evaluation of capital investment projects. There are two major points of difference.

1. Because of conditions of partial ignorance, product-market projects cannot all be examined at the same time, but have to be evaluated in a continual stream. This evaluation has to take account of:

a The present product-market position.

b The projects currently under way.

c. Other projects which are being held in reserve against availability of resources.

d. Potential future projects which may develop within the budgeting period.

2. Because of the multi-dimensional character of objectives and because of shortcomings in measurement and forecasting, evaluation of a project cannot be based solely on a net cash-flow measurement. Other measurements must be added in order to make sure that the opportunity:

a. Meets the objectives.

b. Fits in with the firm's strategy.

c. Is assessed accurately enough to provide for effects not measured by cash flows.

Using the concepts and results of the preceding chapters, we can now construct a method for project evaluation which satisfies all of these requirements. An outline of the method is shown on Figure 11.3. The decision flow in project evaluation is divided into three main parts: (1) screening, (2) preliminary evaluation, and (3) final evaluation.

The first step in screening is to subject the opportunities to the *threshold-goals* (1) test (see Chapter 4). An opportunity which is below the threshold on all of the major dimensions of the objectives is rejected. If it substantially exceeds at least one of the major goals, it is retained for future study, regardless of whether it passes the subsequent strategy screening. This provision enables the firm to recognize outstanding opportunities which do not fit the current strategy and thus to remain alert to desirable changes in strategy.

If the opportunity lies within threshold-goals range, it is subjected to three successive screenings to determine its fit within the *growth vector* (2), its compliance with the *competitive advantage* (3), and the *synergy* (4) strategy components.

Two screening steps follow – one against the *finance strategy* (5), and the other against the *administrative strategy* (6). In each case a determination is made of whether the opportunity is consistent with the overall guidelines for the firm's growth and change.

Preliminary evaluation, similarly to the external appraisal (see Chapter 7), measures the opportunity against *economic* (7), *cost of entry* (8), and *synergy potential* (9) criteria. It was shown earlier (Chapter 8) that full realization of the synergy potential depends on the administrative strategy of the firm. Therefore, the synergy potential is next adjusted by applying the constraints of that strategy to produce a measure of *expected synergy*

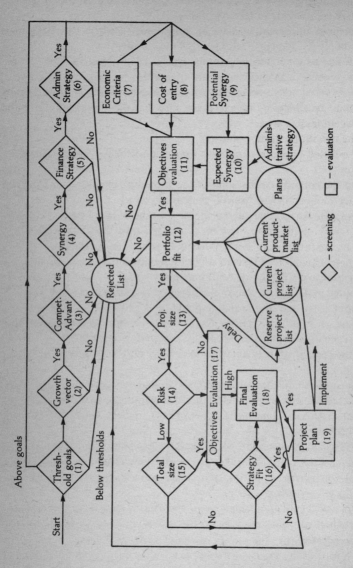

Figure 11.3. Decision Flow in Project Selection

(10). The three criteria ratings are now combined into an *overall project evaluation with respect to the objectives* (11).

It will be recalled that, because of the manner in which threshold-goals are established (Chapter 4), this is a twofold evaluation:

1. Of the merits of the opportunity.
2. Of its relative scarcity.

However, it does not yet include a comparison with the other projects of the firm. Such comparison is now made in a *portfolio fit* (12). This stacks the new project against the following:

1. The present strategic posture of the firm.
2. The list of currently active acquisitions and development projects.
3. The list of projects not currently active, but which had previously been evaluated, found acceptable, and put 'on the shelf' to await availability of manpower, and other resources.
4. The product-market plan of the firm in the area of the present project.

This comparison leads to one of the following conclusions:

1. Reject the project, because it overlaps with and is not superior to another project already on the books.
2. Provisionally accept the project for implementation.
3. Add it to the reserve list of approved projects.
4. Remove a project on the reserve list and replace it with the present project.
5. Remove an active project – discontinue it and provisionally accept the present project.

If a project is provisionally accepted, it is next screened to determine whether further evaluation is necessary before proceeding with a project plan and with implementation. The screening is on four variables:

1. *Project Size* (13). If the estimated cost of the initial investment of the project is within established maximums, it is passed to *risk evaluation* (14). If the estimated initial costs of the project exceed the established maximums, the project is then tested for a second time against the objectives of the firm in an *objectives evaluation* (17).

2. *Risk Evaluation* (14). If the initial size of the proposed project is acceptable, it is then tested for the level of risk involved. If the anticipated level of risk is acceptable, then the project is passed to the *total size test* (15). If the project is estimated to entail a level of risk which is beyond that considered acceptable for normal projects, then the project is passed to *objectives evaluation* (17).

3. *Total Size* (15). If a project has passed the evaluations for initial investment size and risk, it is then evaluated for total size. This test involves consideration of all estimated probable and possible 'follow-on' costs which might accrue over the total life of the project. If all possible costs are within ranges which even in the 'worst case' condition are considered to be acceptable, the project is then passed to *strategy fit* (16). In the event that possible 'downstream' costs are considered to be unacceptable, the project, as above, is passed to *objectives evaluation* (17).

4. *Strategy Fit* (16). This screening is primarily for projects, which, because of their promise of major benefits, were allowed to by-pass strategy screening in box (1). Such projects, having passed all of the preceding criteria, are next evaluated for strategy fit. If, after exhibiting a fit with corporate objectives, the portfolio which the firm wishes to obtain, and previous tests for size, risk and total size, the project is considered to support the firm's strategy, it is then considered as a project which will be undertaken and is moved to the position where a *project plan* (19) is developed. If, on the other hand, the project does not fit clearly into the firm's strategy, it is moved to *objectives evaluation* (17) as was the case for projects which failed any of the previous three evaluations.

If, for any of the above reasons, a proposed project is passed to *objectives evaluation* (17), the promised performance is there compared, once again, to the firm's objectives. If the project promises to make an outstanding contribution to the firm in some way, it is subjected to a *final evaluation* (18). Otherwise, it is rejected and placed on the *rejected list*.

Final Evaluation (18). If the project does not fit the firm's present strategy, a strategy re-evaluation must be made before it is finally accepted or rejected. This is of particular importance in the case where a project, although promising major benefits to the firm, is outside the design of the firm's strategy as developed in Chapters 4 and 6. The danger at this point is that due to the unusually desirable nature of a particular project, major portions of the firm's resources may be committed to a project which is outside of the common thread of the firm's desired portfolio strategy. A decision must be made as to whether, due to the desirability of one project, the firm's portfolio strategy should be changed.

If the unusual or significant benefits of a particular project are such that the portfolio strategy is changed, or if the decision is made to invest a portion of the firm's resources outside of the common thread of the portfolio strategy, the project is moved to *project plan* (19). Otherwise, the project, in spite of its desirability. is passed to the *rejected list*.

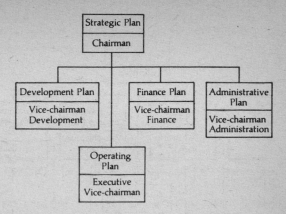

Figure 11.4. Planning System under Functional Organization

In the preceding pages we have been concerned with the application of strategy to the evaluation of projects one at a time, as they are searched out and discovered by the firm. Another and equally important role of strategy is in the overall periodic planning process of the firm. This, too, involves evaluation of projects – in this case of the ongoing projects and projects foreseeable at budgeting times. Strategy is also a key to the overall behaviour of the firm in its search for opportunities, resource acquisition, allocation and conversion processes.

Organization for Planning

In Part 2, we shall be discussing the vector of capabilities which is necessary to support strategic development. In this section we present a brief discussion of one of the capability components: the organizational structure through which strategic work is done.

Organizational structures of modern business firms evolved in response to challenges which were primarily operational in nature. When strategic work became important, the organizational arrangements for conducting it were implanted in the existing operations-oriented structures. Two widely used resulting structures are shown in Figures 11.4, and 11.5. (In North American business jargon, the word 'chairman' in the figure should be replaced with 'president'.)

The *functional structure* shown in Figure 11.4 came into existence early

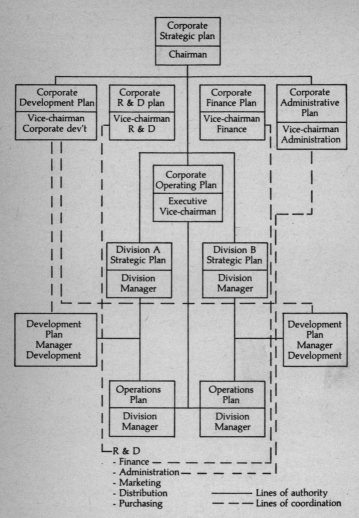

Figure 11.5. Planning under Divisional Organization

this century. It evolved in response to the challenge of mass production and its major strength lay in maximization of production efficiency.

In the functional structure responsibility for strategic development must, of necessity, be centralized at the top, because there is no point on lower levels of management where the range of knowledge and competences needed for strategic activity come together.

As a result, the chairman of the firm has to concern himself both with the daily profitability of the firm and with its strategic development. Operating problems therefore compete with strategic ones for the chairman's attention. As will be discussed in greater detail in Part 2, the operating concerns usually prevail over strategic ones. Thus, the functional structure is not a hospitable environment for strategic activity.

The *divisional structure* shown in Figure 11.5 evolved in the 1920s in response to the challenge of mass marketing. The need for faster (than in the functional organization) and more effective response to competition and demands of the market had led to decentralization of both strategic and operating authority/responsibility.

Thus, two levels of strategic activity exist in a divisional firm: the corporate level responsible for the overall strategic portfolio of the firm, and divisional level responsible for the competitive posture in strategic business areas entrusted to the respective divisions.

For the purpose of strategic development, the divisional form is more effective than the functional, because the strategic work-load is now shared by the chairman and the divisional managers. However, it retains the major shortcoming of the functional form in the fact that each of the general managers must manage the conflict between the strategic and operating demands on himself and his organization.

To deal with this conflict, firms which became heavily involved in strategic activity developed several organizational structures designed to protect the strategic work from the encroachment of daily operations.

One of these forms, called the *project-matrix form*, was invented by large American aerospace companies. The matrix form adds a project-management sub-organization to either the functional or the divisional form. The project-matrix organization manages and executes all of the strategic projects. It has its own budget but it may draw some of its manpower, on assignment, from the operating units. When projects are completed, the new products or services are transferred to the operating units of the firm charged with profit-making.

An extension of the project matrix is the *multi-national matrix*. As the name implies, this form has evolved to handle far-flung operations in many countries.

In the multi-national matrix, there are three types of inter-acting organizational units:

1. Country organizations, charged with success in local markets.

2. Product-group organizations, charged with global strategic development of the major product lines of the firm.

3. A logistics group, charged with optimizing the firm's global production and distribution.

While the project-matrix organization is a very effective way of managing strategic development, the multi-national is less so, because of the problem of having to reconcile the strategic interests of the particular national organizations, which want products tailored to their respective markets, and the interests of product groups which want to design products to a single global standard. (For an approach to resolving this conflict, see Chapter 2.6 in Ansoff, *Implanting Strategic Management*.)

Finally, there is an organizational form which resolves the incompatibility and conflict between the operating and strategic activities by separating the firm into two different groups, each with its own management and resources. One of the groups is charged with profit-making and the other with generating the future profit potential. Unlike the other forms discussed above, this *dual structure* has been used on a limited scale.

A variant of the dual structure is the recently developed *multiple structure* in which the profit potential group is subdivided into several centres of distinctive strategic effort. An interesting feature of this form is that, to assure a truly entrepreneurial, risk-taking spirit, the strategic work centres may be set up with an independent equity, part of which is awarded to the entrepreneurial centre managers.

The purpose of this brief discussion of organizational forms is to alert the reader to the organizational implications of introducing strategic planning into the firm. We shall have more to say about this problem in Chapter 18 of Part 2. (A comprehensive discussion of organizational design can be found in Chapter 4.3 of Ansoff.)

PART 2

Strategy Implementation

Part 2 is based in part on an updated and expanded version of a chapter from a book, entitled *From Strategic Planning to Strategic Management*,[1] which I wrote with Roger P. Declerk and Robert L. Hayes. This part introduces capability planning as the second corner-stone (the first being strategic planning) of the process of strategic management.

CHAPTER 12

The Need for Entrepreneurial Capability

... It is no trick to formulate a strategy, the problem is to make it work.

The Problem

In the mid-1950s many American firms were confronted with disturbing symptoms which could not be readily remedied by available management techniques and which had no precedent in recent experience. For some firms the market demand began to level off and could not be restimulated by even the most energetic marketing and promotion. For others the demand began to decline in the face of substitute products offered by new technologies. Still others saw their traditional markets invaded by vigorous foreign competitors.[1]

The managerial techniques of long-term budgeting, financial control, even the then popular long-term planning, appeared inadequate for dealing with the new symptoms. In the inventive tradition of American business, firms turned their energies to the development of new management approaches to the new and perplexing problems. A number of leading firms and consulting companies, working independently, found themselves converging on a new approach towards the end of the 1950s. The result, developed through trial, error and exchange of experiences, was strategic planning, which was discussed at length in Part 1 of this book.

Some thirty years of experience in companies has shown that the results of strategic planning are difficult to translate into practice. Not only is the translation difficult, but attempts to install rigorous strategic discipline typically run into 'resistance to planning' – an organizational inertia which frustrates the efforts to translate plans into action and even rejects planning, as a 'foreign antibody', from the firm.

Again, in its typically inventive fashion, management started a search for an antidote to organizational resistance which would make strategic planning acceptable and palatable. The first answer was found in the commitment of top management: it was argued that strategic planning would work if it originated with top management and if it received continuing attention and support from the corporate office.

Experience has shown this to be a workable, but a temporary, solution. Indeed, the initial enthusiasm of the chief executive has been instrumental in launching many firms on the road to strategic planning. But organization-wide involvement waned as soon as the chief executive shifted his interest to other priorities.

The impermanence of this antidote was dramatically illustrated by Robert McNamara's efforts to install PPBS (an advanced version of the strategic planning system) in the US Department of Defense. So long as Mr McNamara was able to overcome resistance to planning by force of his personality and enthusiastic support from Presidents Kennedy and Johnson, PPBS was used, albeit reluctantly, throughout the Department. As soon as Mr McNamara left, the pent-up inertia and resistance began to transform planning, returning to the previous political, incremental process, which does not even vaguely resemble strategic planning.[2]

In summary, early experience with strategic planning encountered three serious problems:

1. 'Paralysis by analysis' which occurred when a series of strategic plans produced little by way of results in the market-place.

2. Organizational resistance to introduction of strategic planning into the firm.

3. Ejection of strategic planning from the firm as soon as erstwhile forceful support of planning by top management was withdrawn or relaxed.

One reaction to these experiences, expressed by both managers and academics, was to argue that strategic planning was an unproductive invention, and that it did not produce the intended results.

In response to this reaction, several research studies have been carried out during the past twenty years, addressed to the question: does systematic strategic planning improve financial performance of the firm?

The first of these studies, performed by this author and his colleagues, reached the statistically significant conclusion that, when properly used, strategic planning does produce significant improvements in the firm's performance. (For a brief report on the study, see Chapter 3.2 of Ansoff, *Implanting Strategic Management*. For a detailed description, see Ref. 3. Most of the other studies reached conclusions similar to ours.

While these studies did prove that, when properly used, strategic planning can be effective, they did not explain the three problems diagnosed above: paralysis by analysis, resistance and ejection of strategic planning from the firm.

An explanation and suggestions for making strategic planning effective and stable are the subject of the remainder of this book. Briefly stated, the explanation which has emerged during the past twenty years, is that strategic planning is only one of three processes which must be brought together to assure effective strategic adaptation. The other two processes are: management-capability planning and management of the overall process of strategic change. The totality of these three closely interdependent processes has been named *strategic management*.

In this chapter we reproduce the first paper, published in 1972, which called attention to a need for the broader perspective of strategic management.

Re-emergence of Entrepreneurial Behaviour

As discussed in Chapter 2, the firm relates to its environment in two distinctive ways:

1. Through operating behaviour in which it seeks to make profitable the goods/rewards exchange with the environment. It does this by attempting to produce as efficiently as possible and to secure the highest possible price and market share.

2. Through strategic behaviour which replaces obsolete products/markets with new ones which offer higher potential for future profits. The firm does this by identifying areas of new demand, developing responsive products, developing appropriate manufacturing and marketing capabilities, market-testing and introducing new products to the markets.

In Part 1 we also discussed two varieties of strategic behaviour:

1. Incremental, in which product and markets evolve through stepwise improvement, following the historical logic of the firm's development.

2. Discontinuous behaviour which changes the logic of the historical evolution through technology substitution, divestments, diversification and internationalization.

We have had much less to say about operating behaviour. It is now necessary to recognize that operating behaviour can be incremental, in other words prices, quantities produced and capacity change slowly and in steps. But, similarly to the strategic behaviour, operating behaviour can also be discontinuous, as evidenced by firms which launch price wars through drastic price reductions, or by the current CAM (computer-assisted manufacturing) revolution which has drastically changed the way in which goods are manufactured.

Thus, as Figure 12.1 shows, there are four significant variants of the firm's behaviour. For purposes of exposition simplicity, in this chapter we compare two extremes of behaviour: the operating-incremental and the

Type of behaviour	Type of change	
	Incremental	Discontinuous
Operating	Competitive	
Strategic		Entrepreneurial

Figure 12.1. Varieties of Strategic and Operating Behaviour

strategic-discontinuous. As Figure 12.1 shows, we have named the former *competitive behaviour*, and the latter *entrepreneurial behaviour*. (The reader will note that the two definitions are consistent with the way they are used in micro-economics.)

Since the competitive mode is profit-producing and the entrepreneurial profit-absorbing, it is to be expected that the firm should gravitate towards the former, so long as the potential of its existing markets is perceived adequate for satisfying growth and profit objectives.

Analysis of historical behaviour confirms this expectation. The period of the Industrial Revolution, from 1820 until roughly 1900, witnessed the birth of the firm. Far-sighted entrepreneurs linked new technologies to the emerging demands. The linking body was a new social entity – the business firm. The emphasis of the Industrial Revolution was on the *entrepreneurial activity* – creation of profit potential where none existed before.

By the 1900s firms had staked out their technological and product positions and established linkages with profitable and growing national markets. For the time being, the entrepreneurial work was substantially done, and focus began to shift to *competitive behaviour*, where it remained for the next fifty years.

Entrepreneurial behaviour did not disappear, but it substantially changed its shape and importance. Early in the century leading firms, notably the American Bell System, General Electric, Du Pont and Westinghouse, internalized technological innovation by establishing R&D laboratories. These began to spawn new products and processes which enabled firms to better satisfy customers and extend market horizons.

But even in the most active firms, this remained a secondary activity. In most firms competitive behaviour replaced entrepreneurial. The environmental linkages evolved through logical extrapolation of previous, successful products. The original basic linkages were viewed as the natural boundaries of the firm's relationship with the environment. Steel companies were in the 'steel business', petroleum companies in 'petroleum', etc. The growth prospects and opportunities seemed bright enough to justify this position.

Since the mid-1950s the relative importance of the two types of behaviours began to change. Competitive challenges became more demanding than ever, as markets became global, new aggressive competitors came into the market-place, and government, environmentalists, and consumers put increasing demands and constraints on management.

But success in competitive behaviour no longer guaranteed growth and profitability. In some of the first-generation industries demand reached saturation. In others technology substitution began to displace traditionally successful firms from their positions of leadership. A new generation of industries was spawned by novel technologies and by the rapid emergence of the service sector.[4]

As a result, entrepreneurial behaviour acquired an importance to a firm's continued success and survival that was comparable, if not greater, than the competitive behaviour. The management had to face a dual challenge:

1. To raise the entrepreneurial behaviour from a secondary to a primary role within the firm.

2. To assure a peaceful co-existence within the firm of the entrepreneurial and competitive activities.

From the 1970s on it was increasingly recognized that entrepreneurial behaviour and competitive behaviour were very different and that the administrative structures required by each were also different. We will now summarize these differences through a series of tables.

Table 12.1 illustrates the characteristics of environmental challenges which require the competitive and the entrepreneurial behaviours. Competitive challenges are seen to relate to the firm's previous experience, while the entrepreneurial challenges are novel and discontinuous from the past.

Table 12.2 shows the characteristics of the organizational profile which are effective in responding to the respective challenges. The table shows that the objectives, rewards, information, leadership styles, organizational structure and problem-solving process required to support the two behaviours are not only distinctive, but frequently incompatible.

Table 12.2 suggests that the profiles of the managers who guide the entrepreneurial and competitive behaviour should be different. These differences are illustrated in Table 12.3.

Three important conclusions follow from the tables:

1. When a firm, whose focus has traditionally been on competitive

Table 12.1. Competitive vs. Entrepreneurial Challenges

Attribute	Competitive	Entrepreneurial
Occurrence	Serial and continual	Random and episodic
Direction of change	Continuation of past	Discontinuity
Size of change relative to the past	Small	Large
Relevance of traditional capabilities	High	Low
Problem familiarity	Related to experience	Novel
Cost of information	Low	High
Problem structure	Well-structured	Ill-structured
Predictability of outcome	Risk and uncertainty	Partial and total ignorance
Risks	Low–medium	Medium–very high

behaviour, decides to become entrepreneurial, it needs to develop a new vector of competences which consists of management skills, systems and structures.

Strategic planning is only one component of this vector, and, if introduced without the other components, will not be effective in changing the firm's behaviour.

2. In addition to changing the problem-resolving competences, the firm needs to develop a new entrepreneurial culture which encourages change and innovation and risk-taking.

In the absence of an entrepreneurial culture, the historically entrenched competitive culture will be a source of resistance, not only to strategic planning, but to the basic idea of entrepreneurial behaviour. In the following chapter we shall deal with the problem of diagnosing the culture and the competences which the firm will need in the future.

3. The entrepreneurial competence and culture are different and incompatible with the competitive culture. Therefore the firm needs to make provisions for their harmonious and supportive coexistence. We shall deal with the problem of integrating entrepreneurial behaviour and competitive behaviour in Chapter 14.

The preceding discussion explains why historical efforts to introduce entrepreneurial strategic planning into competitively oriented firms triggered a rejection syndrome, similar to the body's rejection of a transplanted organ.

Individuals lack the motivation, the skills and the risk propensities not only to plan, but to follow planning with appropriate actions. The organizational culture is focused on near-term profit realization and not on

Table 12.2. Comparison of Organizational Profiles

Attribute	Mode	
	Competitive	Entrepreneurial
Objective	Optimize profitability	Optimize profitability potential
Goals	Extrapolation of past goals modulated	Determined through interaction of opportunities and capabilities
Reward-and-penalty system	(1) Rewards for stability, efficiency (2) Rewards for past performance (3) Penalties for deviance	(1) Rewards for creativity and initiative (2) Penalties for lack of initiative
Information	(1) Internal: performance (2) External: historical opportunity space	(1) Internal: capabilities (2) External: opportunity space
Problems	Repetitive, familiar	Non-repetitive, novel
Leadership Style	(1) Popularity (2) Skill to inspire greater effort	(1) Charisma (2) Skill to inspire people to accept change
Organizational Structure	(1) Stable or expanding (2) Activities grouped according to resource conversion process (3) Activities loosely coupled	(1) Fluid, structurally changing (2) Activities grouped according to problems (3) Activities loosely coupled
Planning System	Long-range planning	Strategic planning
Management Problem-solving		
(a) Stimulus to action	(1) Drive to fulfill goals	(1) Search for new opportunities
(b) Search for alternatives	(1) Reliance on past precedent	(1) Creative alternatives

creation of long-term profit potential. The system and the structure are geared for competitive activities and are not capable of rapid entrepreneurial response. The available information is totally inadequate for generating the necessary strategic alternatives. The reward-and-value system actually punishes, rather than rewards, entrepreneurial risk tactics.

In this perspective, the wonder is not that competitively competent organizations will resist strategic planning; the wonder is that top-management coercion can sometimes force strategic planning to take root in the organization. The stubborn resistance and ultimate demise of strategic planning encountered by Robert McNamara is more likely.

Table 12.3. Comparison of the Managers' Profiles

Competitive	Entrepreneurial
World Outlook	
Intra-firm	Environmental
Intra-industry	Multi-industry
Intra-national (regional)	Multi-national
Intra-cultural	Cross-cultural
Personal Values	
Economic rewards and power	Economic rewards and personal fulfilment
Stability	Change
Conformity	Deviance
Skills	
Experientially required	Acquired throughout career
Popular leader	Charismatic and political leader
Participative	Political and charismatic
Goal-setter	Vision-creator
Familiar problem-solver	Novel problem-solver
Intuitive problem-solver	Creative problem-solver
Familiar risk-taker	Novel risk-taker
Convergent diagnostician	Divergent diagnostician
Performance controller	Creativity guide
Extrapolative planner	Entrepreneurial planner

CHAPTER 13

Diagnosing General Management Capability

First we shape our structures, and afterwards they shape us.
WINSTON CHURCHILL

Aggressiveness of Behaviour

So far we have discussed two extremes of business behaviour: the entrepreneurial and the competitive.

But, as discussed in the preceding chapter, in practice, one finds variations of behaviour within each mode: operating behaviour varies from no-holds-barred, all-out, aggressive competition to bureaucratic unresponsiveness to customers of established monopolies; strategic behaviour ranges from reluctant imitation of competitors' new products to a continuing stream of innovations.

The basic proposition of strategic management is that: *To succeed and survive in an industry, the firm must match the aggressiveness of its operating and strategic behaviours to the changeability of demands and opportunities in the market-place.*

In the following discussion we shall refer to the degree of changeability of environmental challenges as the level of *environmental turbulence.*

The level of turbulence is determined by a combination of numerous factors:

- changeability of the market environment
- speed of change
- intensity of competition
- fertility of technology
- discrimination by customers
- pressures from governments and influence groups.[1]

The more turbulent the environment the more aggressive must be the firm's response. But common experience shows that some firms take full advantage of the opportunities offered by turbulence and some lag behind. The factors which contribute to the differences in behaviour among firms are their past history, their size, their accumulated organizational inertia, the relevance of their skills to the environmental

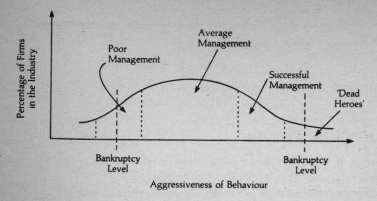

Figure 13.1. Typical Distribution of Behaviours

needs and, particularly, the ambitions, the drive and the capabilities of management.

Figure 13.1 illustrates the distribution of behaviour in an industry, plotted against the observed aggressiveness of behaviour. As the figure shows, some firms lag behind the minimum aggressiveness level (labelled 'bankruptcy level') at which it is still possible to make a profit. These, and the firms just above the bankruptcy level, are poorly managed. Near the other extreme of the scale are aggressive firms (labelled 'successful management') whose aggressiveness is responsive to the environmental turbulence level. These firms have the best potential for success.

The position of the success region implies that the industry environment is very turbulent, as it was some years ago when computer technology reached a point at which the hitherto large mainframe computers could be reduced to a desktop model. Jobs and Wozniak perceived this breakthrough opportunity and invented the Apple computer, thus starting a new industry.

But, as the extreme right-hand part of the graph indicates, managers who are premature, and overestimate the future turbulence of the environment, quickly come to grief. Thus, Henry J. Kaiser, of the American Kaiser Aluminum Co., who pioneered the introduction of the compact car some twenty years before the environment was ready for it, paid for his mistake by becoming one of the 'dead heroes': managers who exhibit a level of aggressiveness which exceeds the environmental turbulence.

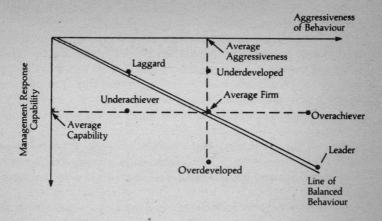

Figure 13.2. Capability and Aggressiveness

It should be pointed out that, while Figure 13.1 shows an industry whose whole success region is at a high level of aggressiveness (implying a highly turbulent environment), the same relationship pertains to industries on a low level of turbulence. Thus, Henry Ford I remained a leader in the automotive industry from 1906 to 1929 by remaining at the lowest level of strategic aggressiveness thus matching the market need for standardized, low-cost, reliable automobiles.

Aggressiveness and Capability

In the light of the discussion in the preceding chapter, it is reasonable to expect a relationship between the aggressiveness of the external behaviour and the internal management capability of the firm. This is illustrated in Figure 13.2.

The vertical and horizontal broken lines intersect at the point labelled 'Average firm'. This is a firm which enjoys average growth and profits in the industry.

The 'line of balanced behaviour' suggests that, whatever behaviour the firm chooses to pursue, there is a level of internal capability adequate to support this behaviour. Thus, for example, the 'laggard' firm, which invests less in promotion, selling and advertising, does not need a marketing department which is as strong or as well-trained as the 'leader' firm, which seeks to be an aggressive marketer.

On the other hand, a firm which is an average competitor/innovator in the industry may be 'overdeveloped': it has potential capability for being much more aggressive. but the potential is not realized and is 'locked in the firm' by the complacent, non-aggressive management. The opposite description applies to 'underdeveloped' firms in which the management and the organization are stretched in an effort to behave above their means.

The firms located on the horizontal broken line illustrate another type of unbalanced behaviour in which the aggressiveness of behaviour is either below or above average, but the capabilities are adequate for balanced, average success.

The varieties of behaviour illustrated in Figure 13.2 suggest both an explanation and an approach to the strategic problem. When a firm finds itself 'out of tune' with the environment, one possible explanation lies in the aggressiveness of its environmental behaviour: it needs to become more aggressive, either to catch up with competition (when the environment is still potentially promising) or align the firm with more promising fields of opportunity (when the present fields of opportunity are in the process of becoming unpromising, like an exhausted oil well). This problem is tackled by strategic planning, discussed in Part 1 of this book.

Another explanation of the maladjustment may lie inside the firm: the strategic aggressiveness is in tune with the future environment, but the capability is out of tune with the strategy.

A third explanation is the most far-reaching: both the strategic position in the environment and the capabilities need to change. When this occurs, and the firm focuses on strategic planning alone, it is neglecting the potentially more important need to change the internal culture and competence in a way which prepares it to live in the new type of environment.

What is now needed is a methodology for a deliberate redesign of the firm's strategy and its capability in anticipation of the demands of the future environment. In Part 1 we have already dealt with redesign strategy. In the following pages we shall deal with the capability.

Environmental Diagnosis

We shall develop the methodology in several steps. First, we turn our attention to the environment. For diagnostic purposes we shall deal separately with the competitive and the entrepreneurial characteristics of the environment.

The columns of Table 13.1 show four distinctive types of competitive environment. The lines identify eleven key attributes which cause environmental turbulence. These attributes will not necessarily vary together, however. Notice also that the values of the attributes vary according to the turbulence levels. The values in Column (1), labelled 'stable', describe a placid, non-turbulent competitive environment. Column (4) (initiative) is a highly turbulent environment.

The procedure for diagnosing environmental turbulence is to circle the observed values which best describe the condition of each of the eleven attributes. For purposes of capability diagnosis, the circled values should represent the anticipated condition of the environment five to seven years into the future. This is because little can be done to change capability within a shorter period of time.

In Table 13.1 future *competitive turbulence* is expected to be between levels three and four. A current example might be the expected turbulence in the personal-computer industry between 1987 and 1990.

Table 13.2 can be used to diagnose future *entrepreneurial turbulence*. The same four turbulence levels are used, but the entries in the table describe the strategic changeability expected in the environment. It should be noted that the first line in the table deals, not with the product life cycle, but with the basic *demand* cycle which is characteristic of all markets. In addition, other determinants of entrepreneurial intensity include technological rates of change, societal pressures, and demand growth rates. Again, in order to diagnose an environment, the applicable intensities of the line items are circled. Taking the personal-computer industry as an example, Table 13.2 illustrates a range of probable entrepreneurial turbulence from 2 to 3.

By combining the results of the diagnosis of the competitive environment and the diagnosis of the entrepreneurial environment, it is possible to locate on Figure 13.3 a *region of probable future turbulence*.

Capability Diagnosis

Tables 13.3 and 13.4 can be used to diagnose the general management capability. Table 13.3 is concerned with the firm's *management culture*. This includes attitudes and drives towards a particular type of organiz-

Table 13.1. Types of Competitive Environments

Attributes	Environmental Turbulence Levels			
	Stable (1)	Reactive (2)	Anticipatory (3)	Initiative (4)
(1) Market structure	Monopoly	Oligopoly	Oligopoly	Multi-Competitive
(2) Customer pressure	None	Weak	Strong	Very Strong
(3) Demand growth rate	Slow and stable	Increasing and stable	Declining/Oscillating	Fast/Oscillating
(4) Stage in industry life cycle	Maturity	Early Growth	Late growth	Emergence
(5) Profitability	High	High	Moderate	Low
(6) Product differentiation	None	Low	Moderate	High
(7) Product life cycles	Long	Long	Short	Short
(8) Frequency of new products	Very low	Low	Moderate	High
(9) Economies of scale	High	High	Moderate	Low
(10) Capital intensity	High	High	Moderate	Low
(11) Critical success factors	Market control	Market Share and Production Costs	Customer Perception and Distribution Service	Anticipation of needs and opportunities

Table 13.2. Types of Entrepreneurial Environments

Attributes	Environmental Intensity Levels			
	Stable (1)	Reactive (2)	Anticipatory (3)	Initiative (4)
(1) Stage in demand life cycle	Late growth or maturity	Early growth	Late growth	Emergence or Decline
(2) Growth rate	Slow	Accelerating	Decelerating	Fast (+/−) Acceleration
(3) Change in technology	Slow	Slow	Fast	Discontinuous
(4) Change in market structure	Slow	Moderate	Slow	Discontinuous
(5) Likelihood of breakthroughs	Low	Low	Moderate	High
(6) Societal pressures	None	Moderate	Strong	Very strong
(7) Diversity of technologies	None	Low	Moderate	High
(8) Demand for growth capital	Low	High	Moderate	Very high
(9) Profitability	High	High	Moderate	Low
(10) Rate of technological obsolescence	Low	Low	High	Discontinuous
(11) Technological intensity	Low	Low	High	High

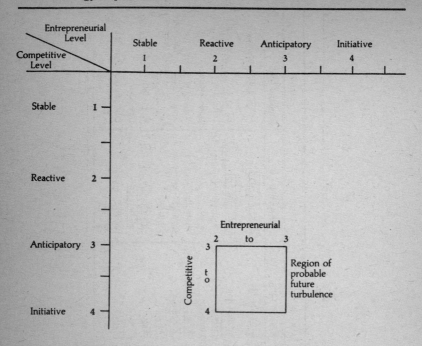

Figure 13.3. Diagnosis of Future Environment

ational behaviour: the values that prevail, the focus of management attention, reaction to change, etc. These are shown to vary from the stable mode, which is found in many bureaucracies, to the active initiative mode, observed in the behaviour of entrepreneurial firms. It should be noted that, for purposes of comparison, we are using in Tables 13.3 and 13.4 the same column headings as we did in assessing the environment, but the labels now apply to the internal characteristics of the firm.

Table 13.4 is concerned with the firm's *management competence*: the ability of the firm's management to execute effectively the respective types of behaviour described by the problem-solving competence, power structure, organizational structure, etc.

As is evident from the tables, the *respective types of competence and culture (stable, reactive, etc.) equip the management of a firm to respond effectively to the corresponding types of environment described in Tables 13.1 and 13.2.*

Table 13.3: Types of Organizational Cultures

Types of Culture Attributes	Internal characteristics			Initiative
	Stable	Reactive	Anticipatory	
(1) Management values	'Don't rock the boat'	'Roll with the punches'	'Plan ahead'	'Dream ahead'
(2) Focus of behaviour	On repetitive operations	On efficiency	On synergistic effectiveness	On global effectiveness
(3) Trigger for organizational response to change	Crisis	Unsatisfactory history of performance	Anticipation of threats and opportunities	Continued search
(4) Reaction to change	Reject	Adapt	Anticipate	Seek
(5) Source of alternatives	Random	Past experience	Past experience and extrapolation into the future	Totality of future opportunities including those unrelated to past experience
(6) Risk preference	Reject	Accept familiar risk	Seek familiar risk	Seek trade-off between risk and gain
(7) Goals of response	Restore status quo	Minimize disturbance of organizational efficiency	Improve on past performance	Best possible performance potential

Table 13-4. Types of Management Competence

Types of Competence Attributes	Internal characteristics			
	Stable	Reactive	Anticipatory	Initiative
(1) Problem-solving	Problem-triggered trial and error	Problem-triggered diagnostic	Anticipatory well-structured optimization	Ill-structured creative
(2) Power focus	Production	Production/ marketing	Marketing/R & D	General management
(3) Management system	Policy and procedure manuals	Control, capital budgeting	Long-range planning and budgeting	Strategic planning, venture management, capability planning
(4) Management information system	Informal precedents	Formal, based on past performance	Potential future in the historical environment	Global future potential
(5) Environmental surveillance	None	None	Extrapolative forecasting	Trend analysis, economic-techno-socio-demographic scenarios
(6) Management technology	Industrial engineering	Ratio analysis capital investment analysis	Operations research computerized transaction analysis	'What if modelling', acquisition analysis, impact analysis, Delphi, multiple scenarios

Furthermore, for a fully effective capability, the respective attributes of competence and culture must all come from the same columns. *If one or more attributes are out of line, the organizational effectiveness is degraded.*

It should be recalled that in this part of the book we are dealing with the *general management capability* to guide the firm in a way that is responsive to the demands of the environment. The required capability is determined by the future turbulence level in the environment.

In addition to the general management capability which guides the firm, the firm also needs *functional capabilities*: skills, knowledge and facilities in R&D, production, marketing, purchasing, etc.

These functional capabilities have already been discussed in Part 1. A comparison of Table 5.3 in Part 1 with Tables 13.1 and 13.2 in Part 2 will show that, while the required general management profile is determined by the environmental turbulence, the functional profiles are determined by the competitive profiles required for success in the market-place (see the section on competence and competitive profiles in Part 1, Chapter 5 p. 94). For a more detailed discussion of general management functional capabilities, as well as more detailed diagnostic instruments, see Chapters 3.3 and 3.4 of Ansoff, *Implanting Strategic Management*.)

Returning to Tables 13.3 and 13.4, which describe the general management capability, the next step in the diagnosis is to construct the profile of the general management of the firm by using the same attribute-circling procedure as was used for the diagnosis of turbulence.

In many firms both the competitive and the entrepreneurial behaviour are guided by the same general management organization. In such cases, only a single diagnostic pass is needed. In decentralized organizations the general management groups guiding the entrepreneurial and competitive activities may be different and in such cases separate diagnoses need to be made in the respective organizations.

Figure 13.4, which adds the results of the capability diagnosis to Figure 13.3, illustrates the latter case, again using the personal-computer industry as an example. In the firm illustrated, the historical entrepreneurial capability has been at level 4 and marketing at level 2. This is typical in technology-driven firms in which R & D activity dominates marketing and manufacturing.

The arrow from the capability pointing into the region of future turbulence indicates the dimensions of the firm's tasks, if it is to be strongly competitive in the future environment:

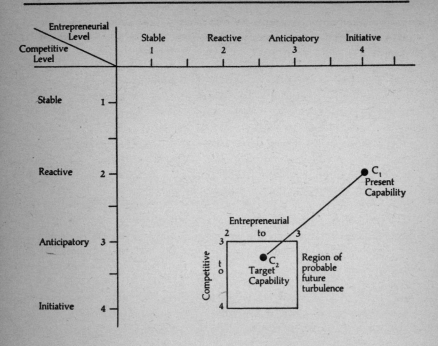

Figure 13.4. Diagnosis of Capability

1. The entrepreneurial capability must be cut back from level 4 to between levels 2 and 3. This means that, instead of frequent historical technology improvements in its products, the firm will succeed better by reducing the frequency of technological advances and, between the advances, improve its products in incremental steps. (For further explanation of this strategy, see Part 1, Chapter 5, note 2).

Accordingly, the entrepreneurial capability must move to levels 2 to 3 which means, for example, that the power centre must move from the creative technologists to marketing-oriented general managers. (This has been vividly illustrated by the recent changes in the Apple Computer Co., where the founding entrepreneur, Steve Jobs, has been replaced by John Scully who came from Pepsi-Cola.)

2. While the aggressiveness of the entrepreneurial capability must be reduced, the aggressiveness of the competitive capability must be enhanced to between levels 3 and 4. This means, for example, that the previously

reactive marketing culture must be transformed into an aggressive one which anticipates customers' needs and develops creative ways to respond to them.

CHAPTER 14

Planning Strategic Posture Transformation

Only the very wisest and the very stupidest never change.

CONFUCIUS, *Analects*

Capability Transformation

The capability diagnosis discussed in the preceding chapter identifies the type of capability change required, but is not specific enough for managerial action.

To specify these changes it is first necessary to translate the general attributes of capability of Tables 13.3 and 13.4 into specific characteristics of the firm which can be modified by managerial action.

Such a translation is shown in Table 14.1. The table shows five categories of management capability components:

1. Organizational values and norms.
2. Managerial skills, knowledge and risk propensities.
3. Structural relationships: authority, responsibility, information, power, task.
4. Process relationships: problem-solving, communication, motivation, control.
5. Technology: formalized systems, information acquisition, decision analysis, computer applications.

Prior to using the table, the first step is to perform the capability diagnosis described in the last chapter and identify the *target capability* which the firm will seek to develop. This is identified as point C_2 in Figure 13.4, and is shown as a vertical line at the right in Table 14.1.

The next step is to use Table 14.1 to identify the *present capability profile*. The zig-zag profile at the left of Table 14.1 is typical of the profiles which could be found in many American firms in the 1950s–60s.

A firm analysing its own capability transformation would, of course, start with a blank set of forms and diagnose the current status of the respective components. The distances between the present status and the target capabilities are the gaps which must be closed through programmes such as training, organizational development, changes in structure or systems, etc.

Table 14.1. Diagnosis of Managerial Capability

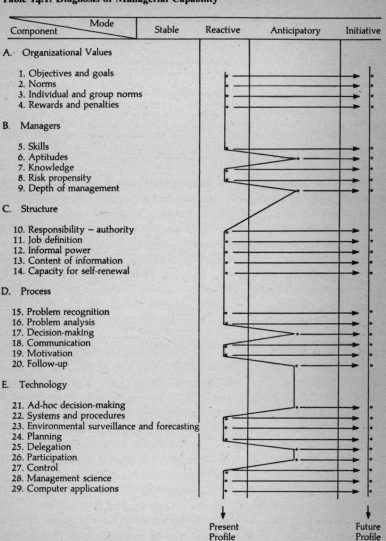

Component / Mode	Stable	Reactive	Anticipatory	Initiative
A. Organizational Values				
1. Objectives and goals				
2. Norms				
3. Individual and group norms				
4. Rewards and penalties				
B. Managers				
5. Skills				
6. Aptitudes				
7. Knowledge				
8. Risk propensity				
9. Depth of management				
C. Structure				
10. Responsibility – authority				
11. Job definition				
12. Informal power				
13. Content of information				
14. Capacity for self-renewal				
D. Process				
15. Problem recognition				
16. Problem analysis				
17. Decision-making				
18. Communication				
19. Motivation				
20. Follow-up				
E. Technology				
21. Ad-hoc decision-making				
22. Systems and procedures				
23. Environmental surveillance and forecasting				
24. Planning				
25. Delegation				
26. Participation				
27. Control				
28. Management science				
29. Computer applications				

Present
Profile

Future
Profile

Table 14.2. Capability Development Plan

YEARS	1	2	3	4	5	6	7	8	9	10
1. Development of plan	—									
2. Organizational development	——————									
3. Reward system		—		—						
4. Training			——————————							
5. Ad-hoc planning			——————————							
6. Information system			————————————							
7. Structure		—		—						
8. Plan planning	—									
9. Operation plans				—————————						
10. Control system				————————————					
11. Strategic plans				—————————						

If the work-load generated by the projects turns out to be substantial, it becomes important to schedule and coordinate the several projects. This is made more necessary by the fact that there is a natural sequence of component development which can make the organizational transformation effective and less resistance-laden than it would be if the natural sequence is not followed. (For a description of natural and unnatural sequences see Chapter 6.2 in Ansoff, *Implanting Strategic Management*.)

In such cases it is highly desirable to prepare and follow a *capability development plan*. Such a plan is illustrated in Table 14.2.

Phasing Strategy and Capability Transformation

Strategy analysis, which was discussed in Part 1, typically generates a series of programmes and projects for product and market development, changes in competitive strategies, development of new technologies and diversification into new businesses. The capability analysis discussed above may similarly generate a heavy project load of organizational changes.

The two sets of projects call on the same organizational resources, which are already heavily committed to competitive profit-making activities. Therefore, if the total strategy/capability change work-load is substantial, it becomes necessary to assign priorities to capability and strategy transformation. Determination of priorities is illustrated in Figure 14.1.

The problem does not arise if, as shown on the left of the figure, the firm needs either a strategy *or* a capability change. When both are needed, the next issue to be examined is the urgency of the change in strategy.

Changes in strategy may be urgent, if the firm's competitive environment

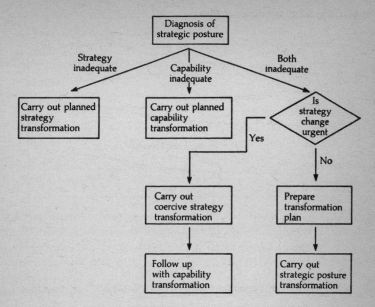

Figure 14.1. Alternatives for Strategic Posture Transformation

is changing very rapidly, or if the firm has been slow to respond to change and now has little time left to regain its competitive position.

In such cases, strategy transformation must be given first priority. But it should be recognized that the change will be carried out by an organization which lacks the necessary capability and that the strategy-change process will be competing for time and resources with the ongoing competitive profit-making activities. As a result high costs will be incurred and schedule slippages will be likely.

In addition, the strategy change will encounter organizational resistance. As a result, the change must be *coercive*, involving the use of power to overcome the resistance.

Finally, a coercively executed change in strategy will be unstable and subject to cultural and political forces which will try to roll back the change.

Therefore, to assure long-term stability of the new strategy, strategy transformation must be followed by a capability transformation, as shown in Figure 14.1. (For a detailed discussion of how resistance should be managed during a coercively executed change, see Part 6 of Ansoff, *Implanting Strategic Management*.)

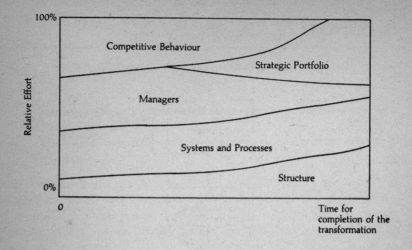

Figure 14.2. Allocation of Resources during Strategy/Capability Transformation

The last alternative, shown in Figure 14.1, is when both capability and strategy need changing, but the urgency is low. This makes it possible to transform the two in parallel, in a mutually supportive manner.

The allocation of effort should be planned to take account of the size of the gaps to be closed and of the interrelationships between the components of capability and the increments of change in strategy.

Figure 14.2 illustrates a possible distribution of effort among five activities *described in the figure*: transformation of competitive behaviour, of the strategic portfolio, development of managers, development of systems and of the organizational structure. The horizontal scale is the time over which the transformation is to take place.

CHAPTER 15

Assuring Coexistence of Competitive and Entrepreneurial Activities

Tomorrow we will get organized and plan. But today, there are profits that need to be made.

The Problem

In Table 14.1 the example used for the target capability (the vertical line at the right) was level four. This corresponds to the future highest probable level of competitive capability which was diagnosed in Figure 13.4. But the terminal capability for the entrepreneurial activity shown in Figure 13.4 should be between levels two and three.

Such conflict of target capabilities is not unusual, because, in a given environment, the competitive and entrepreneurial turbulence frequently are at different levels. This is illustrated in the preceding chapter by the example of the personal computer industry.

Thus, a firm may encounter the problem of conflict between developing a competitive capability, which will produce optimal short-term profits for the firm, and an entrepreneurial capability, which will optimize the firm's future profit potential.

As discussed in Chapter 12 during the first hundred years of the modern firm (in the United States) this conflict did not arise, because the entrepreneurial and competitive challenges occurred sequentially.

From the beginning of the First Industrial Revolution until the beginning of this century, the challenge was primarily entrepreneurial, as great entrepreneurs struggled to marry new technologies to the needs of the markets.

Early in the century, the profit potential was in place, and firms turned their attention to inventing and elaborating their competitive capability.

But, starting in the mid-1950s, American firms progressively discovered that the profit potential developed by the nineteenth-century entrepreneurs began to be exhausted, and, furthermore, that the novel and proliferating technologies of the Second Industrial Revolution began to displace traditional technologies.

As a result, an increasing number of firms felt the need for a revival of the entrepreneurial capability. But, unlike in the past, the need for the

Table 15.1. Success Conditions for Capability Alternatives

Capability Alternatives	Success Conditions	
	Competition	Length of Product/Technology Life Cycles
Competitive capability dominant	Intense price competition	Long
Entrepreneurial capability dominant	Price insensitive demand for advanced technology	Short
Average capability	Competition not intense	Long
Dual capability	Intense price competition	Short

competitive capability also increased, as a result of intensified global competition. Thus, the problem of *capability conflict* became a major concern of management, because, when the two capabilities are left unprotected from each other, one begins to dominate and suppress the other. (For further discussion, see 'Gresham's Law of Planning', p. 404, Ansoff, *Implanting Strategic Management*).

There are three alternatives for resolving the conflict:

1. Let one capability dominate the other.
2. Build an average capability.
3. Assure constructive coexistence between the two capabilities.

Table 15.1 suggests market conditions under which the above strategies will assure profitable performance.

As the table shows, the applicable alternative is determined by the intensity and character of competition on the one hand, and by the longevity of the profit potential (as measured by the duration of the product and technology life cycles) on the other hand.

Dominant competitive capability was a success capability during the first half of the twentieth century in the United States. Dominant entrepreneurial capability was characteristic of the last half of the nineteenth century and again during the second half of the twentieth century in firms born of new technologies such as aerospace, pharmaceuticals, computers, biogenetics, etc.

As Table 15.1 shows, the average capability will work in an environment in which the firm is not under pressure to become an aggressive competitor.

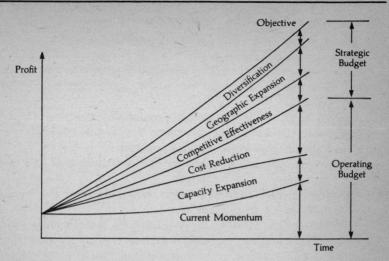

Figure 15.1. Dual Budget

Since the 1960s (in the United States) many firms in the first-generation industries have been progressively forced to start developing the dual capability. Since the beginning of the 1980s the new technology-driven industries are also increasingly under pressure to develop a dual capability.

Introduction of a dual capability into a firm poses two problems:

1. To plan and install the missing type of capability. This problem has been discussed in the preceding Chapters 13 and 14.

2. To assure an effective coexistence between the entrepreneurial and the competitive capabilities. We discuss this problem in the following sections.

Dual Budgets

An effective way to reduce interference between entrepreneurial and competitive activities is to partition the overall budget of the firm into two parts: an *operating budget* and a *strategic budget*. This is illustrated in Figure 15.1, where expected profit contributions from each budget are plotted against time. As can be seen in the figure, each of the budgets is further subdivided according to activities which make distinctive contributions to profits.

The operating budget is further divided into sub-budgets:

1. Support of continued profit-making using the current capacity of the firm (such as marketing and production budgets).

2. The investment in capacity expansion.

3. The investment in increasing profits through cost reduction.

The strategic budget categories are:

1. Investment in improvement of competitive posture in the present strategic business areas (SBAs (such as product and market development budgets)).

2. Addition of related SBAs through geographic expansion.

3. Addition of new SBAs (and divestment from undesirable ones).

The dual budget offers the following advantages:

1. It effectively sets aside resources for entrepreneurial work and thus protects it from operating encroachment.

2. The subdivision into the major budgets helps balance the investments in short-term vs. long-term profitability.

3. The particular graphic presentation is helpful in assessing the wisdom of resource allocation among the sub-activities. If the funds allocated to the respective sub-budget categories are written into the figure, the sizes of the profit wedges can be instantly compared with the budgets assigned to them to produce the return on the respective investments. For example, if profit improvement through capacity expansion turns out to be a relatively narrow wedge, but will absorb a substantial percentage of the operating budget, the wisdom of capacity expansion immediately comes into question.

4. Finally, the graphic presentation shows the comparative timing of the respective profit contributions.

The Crosswalk

Dual budgeting is relatively easy to install, because it does not interfere with the existing organizational structure. Its major shortcoming is that, while it provides the money for strategic activity, it does not assure that, under daily operational pressures, management will devote the time and energy to spending the strategic budget. In other words, dual budgeting is only one of the conditions necessary for assuring balanced attention to the two activities.

A complementary approach has been through structure arrangements. One of the earliest was tried by Robert McNamara when he was United States Secretary of Defense under President Kennedy.

Recognizing that the functional and political nature of the Defense Department made it impossible to plan the future of the nation's military structure in a rational and logical manner, McNamara created interdepartmental teams which were charged with preparing strategic plans for the major strategic business areas (called *mission slices* by the military) of the Defense Department.

Once the planning was completed and approved by McNamara, the plans were 'cross-walked' to the respective services, which is to say that each branch of the military was assigned its appropriate strategy implementation tasks.

The cross-walk approach suffered from three deficiencies. The first was the separation of the responsibilities for planning from implementation, which caused demotivation and lack of enthusiasm on the part of the implementers.

The second was the conflict between the operating and strategic work within the respective services.

The third and major shortcoming of the crosswalk approach is that it separated strategic planning from operations planning, thus aggravating a problem which has chronically plagued the United States Defense Department.

The Project-management (Dual) System

An approach which avoided the above shortcomings was developed and used extensively in American aerospace firms. It is illustrated in Figure 15.2.

Under this approach, all organizational units of the firm participate in the preparation of the strategic plan. One of the main results of the plan is an allocation of priorities and budgets among the strategic and operating activities.

The strategic planning process also produces two sets of goals and objectives: operating for short-term profit-making, and strategic for development of future profit potential. As Figure 15.2 shows, in the dual system the goals, objectives, and strategies are next used to generate two sets of action plans and supporting budgets. The profit goals are converted into *operating plans*, and profit-potential goals into *development plans*.

The operating plan is a set of operating programmes and budgets which are prepared for each operating unit in marketing, production, etc. A distinctive characteristic of these programmes/budgets is that they have the same and repetitive time horizon, usually one year given in detail and, frequently, three to five years specified in less detail.

The development plan contains *projects* which differ from the pro-

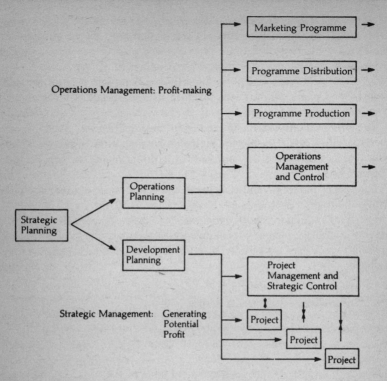

Figure 15.2 Dual System

grammes in five significant ways:

1. They have different time horizons and different durations.

2. As shown in the figure, they are not launched all at once, but are spread throughout the year.

3. *The projects are problem-focused, not unit-focused* and typically require contribution from all of the key functional areas (production, R&D, marketing and finance).

4. Unlike the operating units, the projects are impermanent. They are launched when needed, and disbanded when their strategic goal is achieved.

5. Most importantly, management *control of strategic projects must be very different from control of operating programmes* (see below).

As Figure 15.2 shows, two different centres of line-management responsibility are created in a dual system.

Implementation of the respective plans is carried out by different types of units. The operating plans are implemented by the functional units. and the projects by what has become known as the *project-management group*.

The project-management group draws on a pool of functional and technological experts in strategic development. In some cases, these specialists are borrowed from the functional units; in others, they are permanent members of the project-management group.

The specialists join project teams and conduct the projects. When a project is completed, they return to the pool. Thus, the organizational structure of project management is a fluid one with individuals moving from the resources pool to projects and back. This type of organization has been named the *project-matrix organization*.

Strategic Control and Entrepreneurial Rewards

Experience has shown that the operations-control system used for managing operating programmes and budgets is ineffective and even inimical to managing strategic projects. It is, in fact, one of the major causes of the 'paralysis by analysis' syndrome. Therefore, project management uses a different control system.

The distinctive character of *strategic control* is illustrated in Figure 15.3, which represents a typical cash-flow profile for a strategic move, such as the introduction of a new product line, conversion to a new technology, entry into a new SBA, etc.

The process starts with planning, and is followed by product-technology development, market research, market-testing, building production, marketing and distribution capabilities, and eventually launching the new product or service. The project is terminated after a full-scale market entry has been made.

The part of the solid curve (A), which lies below the horizontal axis in Figure 15.3, traces the negative cash flow which is generated by the strategic activities.

Roughly around the point where cash flow turns positive, the exploitation of the new entry is turned over to the operating units, which make profits and cash from the potential generated by the strategic project. As the solid curve shows, eventually the cash flow returns to zero when the product/ service is taken off the market.

The original decision to launch the project is based on the ratio of the

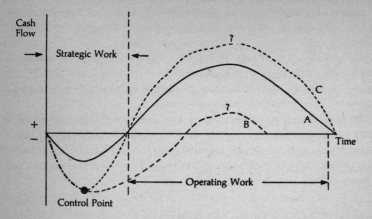

Figure 15.3. Control of Strategic Projects

area under the solid curve above the horizontal axis, to the area below. As the reader can easily verify. this ratio is a measure of the return on the firm's investment over the lifetime of the entry.

When a strategic project is launched, many uncertainties typically surround its probable outcome. Therefore, the solid cash-flow line is highly conjectural and the probability is very high that the actual course of events will not follow the line.

Suppose that the actual evolution follows the lower dotted line in the figure, and that a major review of the project is about to take place at the *control point*, say three years after the project is started.

If the typical operating-control philosophy, based on a comparison of incurred to planned costs, is followed, the project is clearly in deep trouble because of a 100 per cent cost overrun.

But from the strategic point of view, *the historical performance is much less relevant than the future prospects*, which can now be assessed more accurately than was possible when the project was started.

If the new assessment of the future follows the lower dotted line (B) in the figure, the project is indeed a disaster. Not only did the project manager grossly overspend, but he also delayed transition to the operational status to a point where the firm will be late in the market and will, therefore, not be able to recover its investment.

On the other hand, if the best estimate at the control point now follows the upper dotted line (C), the project promises to be a success in spite of the cost overruns and, possibly, precisely due to the fact that the larger early investment made possible an earlier market entry and thus increased the size of the positive profit area. In this case, the project manager should be rewarded for overspending his budget!

The preceding discussion suggests the following principles for strategic control:

1. Because of uncertainties and imprecision of estimates, a strategic project can easily (and frequently does) become a 'free-spending boon-doggle'. This must be prevented, and costs must be tracked against promised accomplishments. But unlike the typical practice in operating control, *the focus must be on ultimate cost-benefits and not on tracking the budget.* In fact, if early progress shows promise of very high benefits related to costs, it may be desirable to encourage overspending of the original budget.

2. At each control point, an estimate should be made of the return on investment over the project lifetime. So long as the probable return remains acceptable to management, the project should be continued. When the return falls below the cut-off level, a comparison should be made with other opportunities and serious consideration given to discontinuing the project.

Unlike the operations control, strategic control is based on uncertain and sometimes vague estimates, and not on concrete results. Strategic control is as much an entrepreneurial decision process as the original decision to launch the project. Therefore, a typical financial-control manager will not have either the risk-taking propensity, or the requisite skills for the job. *The role of the strategic controller must be played by an entrepreneur* who will not only encourage but also participate in the entrepreneurial risk-taking.

But the strategic controller must also be a tough-minded change manager. He must continuously be aware that members of the project are frequently driven by excitement of discovery, fun of the game, allegiance to the project team, and they are quite likely to be indifferent to the ultimate profitability of the strategic move, (particularly since they are unlikely to bear the responsibility for the ultimate profit-making). Therefore, the strategic controller must be prepared to be ruthless in terminating a project, once he has convinced himself that it will not be profitable.

It should be clear from the preceding discussion that the rewards based on past performance used in operating control are not only inapplicable but are suppressive in strategic project management. The characteristics of the appropriate strategic-reward system should include the following:

1. Entrepreneurial risk-taking must be encouraged. This means, in part, that project failure must not be indiscriminately penalized. On the contrary, a *failure to fail periodically should be punished*, as a sign of a lack of entrepreneurial spirit.

2. In part, entrepreneurship should be encouraged and rewarded through the freedom to undertake projects without bureaucratic and lengthy approval procedures.

Firms which have succeeded in encouraging entrepreneurship have set up budget pools on which entrepreneurs can draw freely, provided they do not exceed a set limit for a project. Once the limit has been reached, continuation of the project is either approved by higher management or it is written off.

3. Private entrepreneurs frequently take risks because they expect to get rich. There is no reason why the same incentive cannot be offered in large companies. In some firms inventors participate in the royalties on their inventions. On several recent occasions, entrepreneurs have been made equity participants in the ultimate success or failure of their projects.

4. Strategic activity is stifled and demotivated by the bureaucratic rules which are necessary in profit-making activities. Some firms have solved this problem by setting up strategic 'skunk works', isolated from the bureaucracy and free to engage in creative strategic work. (See the section on dual structure, below.)

5. Finally, for entrepreneurially minded managers who are frustrated by operating work, a significant motivator is provision of 'free' time to engage in strategic activity.

The SBU Substructure

While the dual-system approach removes many of the objections to the cross-walk, it has one major disadvantage in the fact that authority and responsibility for strategic development are separated from the operating authority/responsibility. One typical result of such separation has been failure by the project managers to anticipate and deal with problems which arise when a new product or service is turned over to operations.

As a solution to this problem, the American General Electric Company pioneered the concept of the Strategic Business Unit (SBU) substructure which does assign complete strategic and operating responsibilities to selected sub-units within the overall organizational structure.

The General Electric approach was to leave intact the existing organizational structure which had evolved to support operational profit-making.

Within this structure units were identified (on different levels of the hierarchy) which offered a natural focus point for both strategic and operating profit-and-loss responsibility.

The newly selected S B U managers were made responsible to two different bosses, one for strategic development and the other for profit-making.

Since the pioneering work by General Electric, many firms around the world have adopted and successfully used the S B U concept.

But its application is not without problems, because introduction of the S B Us on top of an existing organization creates two sub-structures, both of which are staffed by the same group of managers. Thus, managers have to learn to 'wear two hats' alternately, and to play different roles when they engage in competitive or entrepreneurial activities.

The two structures must be managed in a supple and flexible manner. In particular, lines of communication between the S B Us and corporate office must be different from the lines of communication used for competitive management. Furthermore, it has become a common practice *within* the corporate office to assign the responsibility for entrepreneurial and competitive management to different individuals (usually entrepreneurial to the Chief Executive Officer, competitive to the Chief Operations Officer).

Dual Structure

The ultimate way to protect the entrepreneurial and operating work from each other is to subdivide the firm into two parts as shown in Figure 15.4. As the figure shows, competitive operations units responsible for profit-making are grouped under an operations manager, and S B Us concerned with developing new businesses are grouped under a strategic development manager.

There are two distinctive ways to make the grouping:

1. To assign all entrepreneurial activities as well as evolutionary R & D to the strategic development group. The operating group is limited to manufacturing, distribution and marketing. This, in fact, is the model which had been used for many years in the Soviet Union with highly unsatisfactory results. The reason is that the strategic development becomes technology-driven with little concern for either the producibility of the prototypes which it delivered to the factories, or for the needs of the market.

2. A more subtle approach is to leave the operating group in control of the strategic evolution of the existing businesses and to confine the strategic development group to development of new businesses.

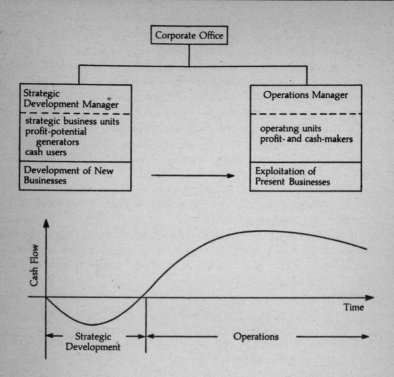

Figure 15.4. Separate Structures

This approach has been used successfully by many American firms. One of the pioneers was the Du Pont Company, which many years ago, set up its Du Pont Development Corporation.

A serious problem with the dual structure is that, in Western firms, transfer of the new businesses from strategic development to operations is difficult for two reasons: the typical cultural NIH ('Not Invented Here') reaction by the operating managers, augmented by their fear that the new businesses will depress profits in the short run, and thus make it difficult to meet short-term profit goals.

In the early days of the dual-structure concept, this problem was resolved by requiring the strategic development group to offer the operating group 'right of first refusal' on all promising new business ventures. But, should the operating group refuse, the strategic development group was free to set up new operating divisions. Experience shows that the fear of turning down attractive opportunities brings strong pressures on the operators to consider the new businesses seriously.

In recent years, as the need for entrepreneurial departures increased, a new approach to dual structure has been developed.

Rather than use a consolidated strategic development group composed of a number of projects, each project is set up as an independent venture, reporting to the corporate management, each with its own equity and necessary resources.

To provide entrepreneurial motivation, the key managers in each venture may be given equity participation.

As strategic development is completed, a venture may be transformed into a new operating unit of the firm, or the new business may be absorbed by an existing operating division.

It can be seen from the preceding discussion that the dual structure is an 'ultimate solution' to the problem of capability conflict in the sense that it permits the respective units to build independent capability profiles which are best suited to their respective needs.

Choosing Among the Alternatives

The different alternatives for assuring effective coexistence of profit-making and entrepreneurship introduce different degrees of complexity into the management of the firm. Therefore, they are not cost free, and should be used only if they are necessary.

The combination of alternatives which should be used depends on two criteria:

1. The importance which management assigns to the coexistence of the entrepreneurial and competitive activities.

2. The degree of discontinuity between the historical businesses and the new businesses which will be created by the entrepreneurial activity.

The left-hand column of Table 15.2 arranges the alternative organizational changes, which have been discussed in the preceding sections, according to the two degrees of disruption they cause in the organization. The remaining two columns show the intensity of the two criteria under which the respective alternatives should be used.

Table 15.2. Applicability of Coexistence Assuring Changes

Alternative Organizational Forms	Applicability Conditions	
	Expected Discontinuity of New Businesses	Importance of Entrepreneurial Activity
Dual Budgets Crosswalk Project Matrix Management SBU Substructure Dual Structure	Low ↓ High	Low ↓ High

CHAPTER 16

Resistance to Change*

There is nothing more difficult to take in hand, more perilous to conduct, or more uncertain of success than to take a lead in the introduction of a new order of things, because the innovation has for enemies all those who have done well under the old conditions and lukewarm defenders in those who may do well under new.

MACHIAVELLI, *The Prince*

Phenomenon of Resistance

Since the emergence of the systematic management of strategy, the attention of both practitioners and students has been focused on two aspects. The first is the logic and techniques of strategy analysis (called strategy formulation); and the second is the design of a systematic process (strategic planning) through which managers interact and contribute to the formulation of strategy.

Prescriptions which were developed for strategic planning were based on three underlying assumptions.

The first was that 'reasonable people will do reasonable things', and that managers will, therefore, welcome new ways of thinking and will cooperate wholeheartedly. When, in practice, the new strategic thinking encountered *resistance to planning*, the resistance was viewed as a temporary aberration due to ignorance, to be removed by strong endorsement of planning by top management.

Since, in fifty years of operations, the firm has justly earned a reputation for the implementation of decisions, the second assumption was that the key problem in strategy was to make the right decisions, and that existing operations-implementation systems and procedures would effectively translate strategic decisions into actions.

The third key assumption was that strategy formulation and strategy implementation are sequential and independent activities. Hence, concern with implementation could start after the strategic decisions were made, and thus not interfere with the already difficult and complex strategic decision process.

* This and the next two chapters are based on Chapter 6.3 in Ansoff, *Implanting Strategic Management*.

The accumulated experience of the past twenty years has progressively cast serious doubts on all three assumptions. When firms diversified from within into novel markets and technologies, the costs of the new ventures typically exceeded estimates, unanticipated delays were encountered, and the organization exhibited resistance to the new departures.

In the field of mergers and acquisitions, case after case led to disappointments. New acquisitions, which were profitable before the merger, mysteriously became unprofitable afterwards; key managers acquired through mergers tended to leave the firm, in spite of attractive financial inducements; synergies anticipated from mergers failed to materialize.

When top management decided to place strategic decision-making on a systematic basis by introducing strategic planning, the organization resisted the new system. Once introduced, many systems exhibited 'paralysis by analysis' or 'death in the drawer' symptoms in which planning languished, or strategies never connected with the market-place. In addition, there was a common tendency to squeeze the system out of the firm and to return to earlier, less radical, approaches to decision-making.

Expressions of support by top management had the effect of temporary coercion. So long as top management applied strong pressure, the organization complied. But when the support was removed, or top-management attention shifted to other priorities, resistance resurfaced.

In summary, practical experience shows that significant changes in a firm's strategic orientation, whether introduced through formal strategic planning or as an informal process, encounter organizational resistance.

Four conclusions follow from such experience:

1. 'Reasonable people do not do reasonable things', if, by reasonable, we mean analytically logical things. Resistance to planning is not a superficial phenomenon; it has a logic of its own, and it cannot be removed by exhortations from top managers.

2. Implementation of strategy does not automatically follow strategy formulation. It exhibits its own resistance which can invalidate the planning effort.

3. Treatment of strategy planning and implementation as two sequential and independent processes is an artificial convenience which neglects the fact that the way planning is done has a determining effect on the eventual implementability of decisions.

4. Resistance to change is not confined to introduction of strategic planning. As the quotation from Machiavelli cited at the beginning of this chapter indicated, resistance occurs whenever an organizational change intro-

duces a discontinuous departure from the previous behaviour, culture and power structure.

Thus, significant strategic reorientations evoke resistance not only to planning but to the entire change process. Resistance is not an aberration but a fundamental problem which deserves attention comparable to the attention previously given to strategy formulation.

Resistance Defined

By resistance, we shall mean a multi-faceted phenomenon, which introduces unanticipated delays, costs and instabilities into the process of a strategic change.

Resistance manifests itself throughout the history of a change. During the change process there are:

– Procrastination and delays in triggering the process of change:
– Unforeseen implementation delays and inefficiencies which slow down the change and make it cost more than originally anticipated;
– Efforts within the organization to sabotage the change or to 'absorb' it in a welter of other priorities.

After the change has been installed:

– There is a typical performance lag. The change is slow in producing the anticipated results.
– And there are efforts within the organization to roll back the effects of the change to the pre-change status.

In Table 16.1 we summarize the remarks which are typically heard in American business firms as they progress through a discontinuous change, showing the attitude behind the remark, and the effect that it will have on the strategic change.

When firms make a major revision of their external strategy, the internal capability becomes maladapted and performance suffers. A firm's strategic response to the environment will be more timely and effective if capability is developed in conjunction with the new strategy which it will support. But while the performance will be more effective after the capability is installed, the process of capability installation more than doubles the organization-disturbing work-load (as compared to installing a new strategy), the impending discontinuities in culture and power structure become more visible and resistance is increased.

Table 16.1. Symptoms of Resistance

Remark	Attitude/Effect
'There is nothing wrong with us that a long production run wouldn't cure.'	Rejection
'Tomorrow we'll get organized and plan . . .'	Procrastination
'Paralysis by analysis.'	Lack of implementation follow-up
'The more we sell of the new product, the more money we lose . . .'	Strategic ineffectiveness
'What the boss doesn't know won't hurt him/her . . .'	Sabotage
'Let's get back to real work!'	Regression
'Death in the drawer.'	Rejection of planning

Seen from the point of view of a strategy analyst, resistance is a manifestation of the 'irrationality' of an organization, a refusal to recognize new dimensions of reality, to reason logically, and to carry out the consequences of logical deductions.

But seen from the viewpoint of a behavioural or a political scientist, resistance is a natural manifestation of different rationalities, according to which groups and individuals interact with one another. In the following sections we identify the sources and the rules of these rationalities.

Resistance and Rate of Change

Two key characteristics of resistance can be inferred from the quotation from Machiavelli cited at the opening of this chapter:

Resistance to change is proportional to the degree of discontinuity in the culture and/or the power structure introduced by the change.

For a given discontinuity, the resistance will be inversely proportional to the time over which the change is spread.[1]

In business language, culture is frequently described as the 'management orientation' or 'management mentality'. Thus, under 'production orientation', which was prevalent during the first thirty years of this century, efficiency of production is the key norm, and success is perceived to come from being able to offer, at the lowest prices, durable undifferentiated products. In the 1930s and 1940s, when production orientation ceased to be the key to success, and a marketing-oriented response became necessary, managements typically persisted in their 'production mentality'. They clung to traditionally successful methods and resisted a transition to a new model of reality based on the marketing concept.

Table 16.2. Effect of Power and Cultural Implications on Behavioural Resistance

Implications of change – – –►	Politically threatening	Politically neutral	Politically welcome
Change in culture	Greatest resistance	Depends on size of cultural change	Depends on size of cultural change
Culturally acceptable	Depends on size of threat	Least resistance	Positive reinforcement of change

The resistance was further augmented by the fact that the transition to the marketing orientation was accompanied by a discontinuity in the power structure: a passing of influence and power from the firm's production departments to the marketing departments. Thus, *when a cultural change is accompanied by a shift of power, resistance is compounded.*

The second part of the above proposition, referring to the speed of the change, is based on the fact that, when change is introduced gradually, only one part of an organization at a time needs to be affected. Resistance is local, and does not receive support from the unaffected parts of the enterprise.

Furthermore, individuals and groups will resist change in proportion to the degree of threat and discomfort caused by the current increment of change only. This is another way of saying that, in resisting change, the affected individuals typically take the short-term view of its consequences, and seldom concern themselves with the cumulative impact of all of the future increments.

As a summary, we present in Table 16.2 the contributing effects of cultural and political resistance. As the table shows, not all strategic changes necessarily provoke resistance: groups and individuals whose culture is reinforced by the change, and/or who stand to gain power, welcome the change and give it support. In Machiavelli's words, they usually '. . . stand to gain under the new order'. But, as he points out, their support is frequently 'lukewarm'. In a later section we shall be exploring the reasons for this attitude, and how those who stand to gain can be won over to more active support.

We can generalize Table 16.2 by means of a single symbolic equation.

$$R_{BEHAVIOURAL} \propto \frac{\pm (\Delta C + \Delta P)}{\Delta T}$$

Where ΔC and ΔP are the signs of the cultural and political disturbance implied by the change, and ΔT is the period over which the change is introduced. (The sign α means 'proportional to'.) The equation expresses in symbols the verbal proposition at the beginning of this section.

An Illustrative Example

A contrast between two similar changes, one of which induced severe resistance while the other did not, is offered by the recent histories of long-range planning and strategic planning. Both were invented within a few years of each other, but their 'track records' are very different.

Long-range planning (LRP), which was introduced in the 1950s, is a method for extrapolating the firm's past into the future. Rather than violate the past, LRP elaborates and confirms the historical model of reality and culture.

Its political consequences are minor, since it is a 'bottom-up' process and does not threaten the established power structure. On the contrary, LRP permits the powerful groups to reinforce their historical claims on resources, and weak groups remain weak.

LRP quickly became popular and, within a few years, surveys began to show that a majority of medium and large firms had adopted LRP (we refer here to the North-American experience).

The history of strategic planning (SP) is different. Despite initial enthusiasm and popularity given to it by articles and seminars, acceptance of SP has been slow, and it was not until the late 1970s that leading firms began to settle into a systematic practice of strategic planning. In the meanwhile, there have been numerous instances in which strategic planning, after having been introduced by enthusiastic managements, either became a process of 'paralysis by analysis', or was gradually sabotaged and disappeared from the organization.

Today (1987), while most major firms in the world regularly practice strategic planning, hardly a month passes without an article by a college professor or a disgruntled professional calling for abandonment of strategic planning.[2]

The reason for this dramatic difference in acceptance is that strategic planning typically attacks both the cultural and the political order of things. Its very purpose is to replace the historical model of reality, and its power implication is a shift of power away from managers who had contributed to the firm's success using the historical model of reality. In the light of the information shown in Table 16.2, this explains the strong resistance to strategic planning.

Resistance by Individuals

The causes of resistance can be traced to reactions by individuals on the one hand, and to common actions by groups of individuals, on the other.

Both experience and literature on psychology show that individuals will resist change when it makes them insecure. This occurs:

– When managers are uncertain about the impact and implication of the change
– When they are called upon to take risks which are uncongenial to them
– When managers feel that the change may make them redundant
– When they feel incompetent to perform in the new role defined by the change
– When they feel that they will lose 'face' with their peers
– When they are incapable and/or unwilling to learn new skills and behaviour

Individuals will also resist change when their position of power is threatened. This occurs:

– When managers expect their share in organizational rewards to be reduced
– When they feel that the change will diminish their position of influence over organizational decisions
– When it will diminish their control over organizational resources
– When it will diminish their personal prestige and reputation

But not all managers are alike. Sime are personally secure, some are prone to anxiety; some are proud, and others less so; some actively seek power and prestige, and others are indifferent to the trappings of power; some are born leaders, and some are content to follow; some are rigid and set in their ways, others are open to change and are eager learners.

Thus, the way in which managers will react to change will depend on the strength of their personality and their personal flexibility.

Therefore, for a given change in culture and power, *the resistance by managers will depend on the strength of their convictions, their preparedness to defend themselves, their power drive, and their predisposition to learn and change.*

Group Resistance

Group reactions to change are traceable, in the last analysis, to the views and convictions of individuals. But, as likely as not, these may be individuals who have long left the organization. Thus, group culture and group power have an existence of their own. Further, they have a stability and permanence which exceed those of most individuals. It is much easier to remove or shunt aside an individual who is a major block to progress, than it is to change the culture of a group, or deprive it of power.

Both sociological literature and practical experience show that:

– Groups of managers who share common tasks and preoccupations develop, over a period of time, commonalities of behaviour and outlook.

– They establish norms and values which reward certain types of behaviour and punish others. For example, in some firms and in bureaucracies, the slogan 'we don't rock the boat' has the power of an edict. In innovative firms the key norm is 'if it's not new it's not good'.

– They develop a consensus on information that is pertinent to their common tasks and information that is irrelevant. For example, there has been a long tradition in business firms that political and social phenomena are not relevant to managerial concerns, because the 'business of business is business'.

– They develop a consensus, which sociologists call a model of reality, on which behaviours produce desirable results and which do not. Thus, during the first part of the century, there was a prevalent view that the way to maximize profits was through producing the cheapest standardized product.

– They develop an allegiance to the common culture and they jointly defend it against encroachment of influence of other cultures.

Political science literature, as well as common observations, shows that groups:

– Coalesce and act as power centres within the rest of the organization
– They seek to accumulate power and influence
– They defend their power positions

In summary, groups will resist a change in direct proportion to which it:

– Threatens the power of the group;
– Violates accepted values and norms;
– Is based on information which is regarded as irrelevant;
– Is based on a model of reality which differs from the model held valid by the group.

CHAPTER 17

Four Approaches to Managing Discontinuous Change

'There are more ways than one of cooking a goose.'
    IONE SHRIBER, *Murder Well Done*

Coercive Change Management

In the early days of strategic planning, support and influence by top management were typically used to overcome resistance to planning. Further, implementation of the new strategy was the first and initial concern, followed by a step by step recognition of the systematic deficiencies. Discovery of the need to change culture and power (if it comes at all) came last.

We shall refer to this method of introducing change, which uses power to overcome resistance, as a *coercive change process*.

Experience shows that coercive change is expensive and socially disruptive, but it offers the advantage of a rapid strategic response. Thus, the coercive approach must be used when urgency is high and rapid response is essential.

But given an understanding of the nature of resistance, it need not be the 'brute-force' approach typically used in the past. Even under pressures of time, resistance can be managed and costs minimized. The typical pitfalls in the 'brute-force' approach are:

1. Failure, prior to the change, to muster the amount of power necessary to assure its completion. The result is frustration of the change, which 'peters out' before the new strategy is in place.

2. Failure to anticipate the sources and strength of behavioural resistance. The results are unanticipated confusion, costs and delays.

3. Failure to attack the root causes of resistance. The result is paralysis by analysis.

4. Premature removal of the power drive behind the change. The result is regression of the change.

5. Failure to follow up implementation instructions issued to resisting units/individuals. The result is sabotage of the change.

6. Failure to recognize the need for new competence and capacity. The results are suppression of change in favour of operating concerns, low quality of strategic decisions, and ineffective implementation.

The pitfalls can be avoided, and the coercive change made more effective, through the following measures:

1. Before launching the change, perform a behavioural diagnosis, along the lines discussed in Chapter 6, to identify the potential sources of cultural and political resistance/support.

2. Muster enough power behind the change to assure its successful completion.

3. During the change, monitor the process for incipient signs of resistance.

4. After the strategy change is made, continue to apply power until the new strategy matches capability, and the change is institutionalized within the firm.

If a firm using the coercive approach lacks a strategic-planning capability, it can save time by using external consultants for strategy formulation. But it should be kept in mind that if the consultants recommend changes which have an impact on the culture and the power structure, they will be unpopular. Top management will need to apply continuous pressure and follow up to assure implementation of the consultants' advice.

Adaptive Change

Firms and other organizations which are not subjected to strategic shocks do, nevertheless, go through discontinuous strategic changes. This occurs through step-by-step accumulation of incremental changes which, over a long period of time, add up to transformation of culture, power structure, and competence. This is a process which sociologists call *organic adaptation* and which is unmanaged from the top and occurs in response to successive environmental stimuli, or to unsatisfactory performance by the firm. More rarely, it is brought about by creative forces within the firm. Organic adaptation usually takes place through trial and error.

If the change is spread over a long period of time, at any given time the resistance will be low, but not absent, because even incremental departures from the 'historical order of things' induce organizational dysfunctions and conflicts. But the required power is correspondingly low. The proponents of the change are change agents, usually below top-management level. Conflicts are resolved through compromises and bargains.

We shall refer to the introduction of a strategic discontinuity through a series of incremental steps spread over time as an *adaptive change process*. The reason for using this name instead of 'organic adaptation' is to underline the fact that incremental as well as coercive change can be managed from the top.

Adaptive change is slow, but has the virtue of minimizing the level of resistance at any given time. Even though it may be argued that this amounts to 'spreading pain over time', the adaptive response belongs in the repertoire of valid responses, because it makes change possible under conditions when very little power is available to the proponents of change.

Like the coercive approach, adaptive change can be made more effective if it is managed. The suggestions made in the preceding section for improving the effectiveness of coercive change apply equally on this case.

Crisis Management

During the last quarter of the twentieth century there is an increasing likelihood that the firm will fail to perceive some rapidly developing and novel discontinuities until they forcefully impact on the firm. When a change appears to imperil the firm's survival and places the firm under severe time pressures, the form is confronted with a crisis. (See Section I. 2.1 in Ansoff, *Implanting Strategic Management*.)

When a crisis strikes, behavioural resistance is replaced by support. But solutions are not obvious, and time pressures are great. The initial task of top management is not to cope with resistance but to prevent panic and to generate a rapid and effective response.

However, as the firm emerges from the crisis, management is confronted by a premature *revival of resistance* which usually accompanies early signs of recovery.

Frequently, a group of key managers convinces itself of the inevitability of impending crisis, while the rest of the firm does not yet see it coming. If this group has sufficient power and influence, it must take recourse to a coercive response.

If the key management group lacks sufficient power for a coercive response, and a crisis is imminent, the managers have the following options:

1. Make a determined effort to convince others of the inevitability of the crisis and launch an anticipatory response.

2. Resign themselves to the inevitability of the crisis and prepare to play the 'saviour' role when the crisis arrives.

3. Trigger off an early *artificial crisis*, usually by inventing an 'external enemy', who threatens survival of the firm. This is an approach which has been used by political leaders throughout history.

The first two alternatives are less risky than the third, which carries not only high personal risk for the leaders, but also severe ethical implications inherent in creating an artificial crisis which will not necessarily transform itself into a real one. But the advantages of an artificial crisis are that it drastically reduces resistance, engenders support for the solution, and enhances the chances of a successful recovery.

Managed-resistance ('Accordion') Method

Of the three approaches discussed above, crisis management should be reserved for emergencies. The coercive and the learning approaches are each an extreme way for dealing with change.

The coercive approach is a 'damn the torpedoes, full speed ahead' way of overpowering resistance. Even when optimally managed, it is costly, disruptive and conflict-ridden, but it is a necessary solution under conditions of high urgency.

The adaptive approach is a 'Rome was not built in a day' way of introducing change; it minimizes resistance, but it is too slow under conditions of environmental urgency.

Hence, there is need for an approach half-way between the two extremes, which works under conditions of moderate urgency and which can be implemented within the time limits dictated by the environment. We shall call this approach *the managed-resistance, or accordion, method* for managing a discontinuous change. We describe it in detail in the following chapter. Its salient characteristics are as follows:

1. It is applicable under conditions of moderate urgency, when there is more time than necessary for the coercive method and not enough for the adaptive.

2. The duration of the change is tailored to the available time. As urgency increases, the method moves toward the coercive extreme. As urgency decreases, it approaches the adaptive change. Hence its name, 'accordion', to describe the stretchable property.

3. This 'accordion' property is made possible by the use of a modular approach: the planning process is sub-divided into modules; at the end of each module appropriate implementation projects are launched.

4. The conventional idea, that planning and implementation must be sequential, is abandoned in favour of parallel planning and implementation.

5. Resistance is minimized at the outset and controlled throughout the duration of the change.

Table 17.1. Comparison of Change Methods

Method	Applicability	Advantage	Shortcoming
Coercive	High urgency	Speed	High resistance
Adaptive	Low urgency	Low resistance	Slow
Crisis	Survival threat	Low resistance	Extreme time-pressure Failure risk
Managed	Medium urgency Recurrent discontinuities	Low resistance Tailored to time Comprehensive capability change	Complexity

The advantage of the managed resistance method is that it tailors the firm's response to the external timing imperatives on the one hand, and to the internal power realities on the other. The disadvantage is that it is more complex than either of the extreme approaches. Furthermore, it requires continual attention from top management.

Because the knowhow necessary for designing and conducting such a complex process will often be lacking within a firm, outside assistance will be needed. However, the contribution of the outside consultants must be different from the coercive method. One of the key features of the accordion method, a feature which is essential for enhancing the acceptance of change, is that the *implementers must also be planners*.

Hence, the roles of the consultants are: to assist in the design of the process, to supply tools of analysis, to train managers, to help monitor the process and to play the devil's advocate.

Choosing an Approach

Table 17.1 compares the advantages and shortcomings of the four approaches to managing. We need to recall that all of these methods are 'heavyweight', requiring considerable attention and energy from management, and that they become useful and necessary only when the change in strategy requires what Machiavelli called the introduction of 'a new order of things'. Incremental changes which do not disturb the order of things are best handled through organic evolution.

As Table 17.1 shows, because of the high failure risk, crisis management is an undesirable substitute for the coercive method, but it has to be used whenever the management either fails to anticipate a crisis, or does not have enough power to force timely response.

The adaptive method is the slowest, but it provokes the least resistance and requires the least commitment of managerial attention and resources. It is useful in environments in which threats/trends/opportunities are highly predictable and the urgency is therefore low.

The managed-resistance ('accordion') method is to be preferred whenever urgency is not so great as to require the coercive change. Its chief advantage is that it strikes the best possible tradeoff between reducing resistance and use of power, within the limits of the available time.

The accordion approach is described in the next chapter.

CHAPTER 18

The Accordion Method for Managing Change

'Passive resistance is the most potent weapon ever wielded by man . . .'
BENJAMIN R. TUCKER, *Instead of a Book*

The Problem

Major strategic changes are frequently introduced without regard for the consequent resistance. The change is planned, 'explained' to those who are responsible for carrying it out, and then launched. When implementation lags and inefficiencies occur, they are treated one at a time, typically on the level of the change process and not at the roots and sources of the resistance.

Control meetings are convened to diagnose deficiencies, remedies are addressed to the process and not to the underlying fears, frustrations and opposition of individuals. Power is used to overcome deficiencies: 'orders' are given to reluctant groups/individuals, punishment is meted out for slipped schedules and cost overruns.

Although inefficient, such unplanned behaviour eventually produces results, provided the proponents of change have the necessary power potential. And the more drastic the change, the more power is needed. If sufficient power is lacking, or if the change managers run out of 'power chips' during the process, the change grinds to a halt, and the organization returns to pre-change 'business as usual'.

If power is adequate to complete the change, the change remains unstable and requires continuing application of power against hostile power centres and the hostile cultures. If the proponents of change relax their vigilance prematurely, a return to the 'good old times' takes place.

This 'muddling-through' approach sufficed in the days when strategic discontinuities were rare, and the pace of change was slow. As the environment becomes more turbulent, managers will need to manage change in a more expeditious and effective manner.

Using the results found in the last chapter, we next describe what we have called the 'accordion' approach to managing resistance.

Building a Launching Platform

Whenever a strategic change requires significant discontinuities in the culture and/or power structure of the firm, time, costs and dysfunctions will be saved if management 'makes haste slowly'.

A desirable first step is to prepare the ground for the change through a series of measures aimed at:

1. Minimizing the start-up resistance.
2. Marshalling a power base sufficient to give the change momentum and continuity.
3. Preparing a detailed plan for the change process which assigns responsibilities, resources, steps and interactions through which the change will be carried out.
4. Designing into the plan behavioural features which optimize the acceptance and support for the new strategies and capabilities.

We shall refer to this pre-launching process as *building the launching platform*. It is similar to the preparatory work done by politicians in preparation for launching a legislative proposal.

The *first step* in building the platform is to perform a preliminary *strategic diagnosis* which determines:

1. Whether the expected discontinuity is singular and will therefore not recur in the near future, or whether it is one of a series which will recur and represents an environmental shift to a new level of turbulence.
2. The time available to the firm (as determined by the speed of change in the environment) for an effective response to the discontinuities.
3. The changes in the management capability which will be needed to provide support for the new strategy. (The procedure outlined in Chapter 3 can be used for diagnosing these changes.)
4. The units of the organization which will be affected by the change.

The *second step* is a *behavioural diagnosis* which determines:

1. The extent of political/cultural disturbance which will occur in the affected units.
2. The key individuals who will support/resist change and the reasons for their position.
3. The support/resistance by culturally/politically coherent groups.
4. The relative importance of individuals/groups to the success of the change.

The results of the behavioural diagnosis are next superimposed on the organizational chart to produce a *cultural/political support/resistance map*.

The *third step* in platform building (using the resistance map as a guide) is to *eliminate unnecessary resistance*:

1. Eliminate misconceptions and exaggerations about the impact of the change by making clear throughout the firm the beneficial consequence of the change or the firm's performance. Groups/individuals which are expected to resist will need special attention, but the entire organization should be informed.

2. Reduce fears and anxieties by making clear to groups/individuals the positive/negative impact of the change on them.

3. Use the resistance map to build a pro-change power base:

   – To the extent possible within the available time, make changes in the power structure *before the change is launched* which will increase the power base behind the change.

   – Include in the power base those who will benefit from the change. In particular, seek to enlist the would-be 'lukewarm supporters'.

   – Neutralize key points of potential resistance through side bargains and payments.

The *fourth step* in platform building is to *design behavioural features into the plan for change*.

1. To the extent possible, exclude from the process individuals/groups who will continue to resist the change.

2. Include in decision-making all individuals who will be involved in implementing the change.

3. To the extent possible, individuals responsible for the success of implementation should also be made responsible for making the corresponding decisions.

4. *Spread the change over the longest possible time which is compatible with the urgency of the external developments.*

5. If time permits, use the *contagion approach*:

   – Start change with groups which are already committed to the change; reward and recognize them.

   – After their initial successes, spread the change to other units.

6. Do not make the assumption that managers have the necessary knowledge and skills to solve problems which are new to them. Build into the plan the necessary education and training programmes. This will not only produce effective solutions, but will relieve fears and anxieties and thus enhance acceptance.

Behavioural Management of the Process

The platform will optimize the launching conditions, but will not guarantee completion of the change. During the period of platform-building, there is seldom enough time to change attitudes, values, norms and perceptions of reality, which will create a consistently welcoming and receptive atmosphere. The preliminary political manoeuvres, while assuring a launching base, will not create a stable pro-change power structure.

Therefore, the *behavioural-change process must be managed*:

1. Monitor and anticipate the sources of resistance during the change.
2. Marshal and use sufficient power to overcome the resistance.
3. Provide participants in the process with necessary new knowledge, concepts and problem-solving skills.
4. Alongside strategy projects, start projects aimed at transforming culture and power structure.
5. Monitor and control the parallel development of the new strategy and new capabilities. If strategy gets too far ahead and generates strong resistance, it may be necessary to stop strategy development temporarily and focus energies on gaining acceptance of the progress made thus far.
6. After the new strategy has been translated into new product/market positions, diagnose the state of the capability. If, as is frequently the case, the capability is not yet fully developed, the capability projects must be continued until the new culture and power structure are supportive of the new strategy. We shall refer to this residual capability development as the *institutionalization of a change*.
7. If the strategic shocks are going to repeat, the firm will have to go through a continual series of change management exercises. Hence, management must institutionalize, not a particular change, but an ongoing change process.

This requires the development of:

- Managers who are seekers or creators of change, skilled in charismatic leadership.
- Power shared by entrepreneurs, general managers, creative R & D and marketing managers.
- A change-seeking culture in which historical models of the business world are continually challenged.
- A high level of positive loyalty throughout the firm, an adventure seeking '*esprit de corps*'.

Resistance and Power

It is only rarely that all of the behavioural resistance can be converted into a positive support of change. This occurs temporarily when an organization is in a survival crisis and everyone rallies around a change which promises salvation. It can also occur when a charismatic leader fires everyone's imagination by a vision of a 'promised land' or the conquest of a 'mortal enemy'.

Under most other circumstances, even after resistance has been reduced to a minimum, there will be points (individuals and groups) of non-reducible resistance to the change.

Therefore, *the change-initiating group must muster and apply enough power to overcome the residual behavioural resistance.* The strength of authority needed will be proportional to the level of resistance to be overcome.

If the power is insufficient to launch the process, the change will never get off the ground. If the 'power chips' get used up in the process, the change will fizzle out during the process.

When resistance to planning was first encountered in the early days of strategic planning, the need for power to overcome the resistance was quickly recognized. A practical conclusion was reached that, to succeed, strategy change must have whole-hearted support and attention from top management.

But, occasionally, this power was used to impose the new strategy on the firm and not to reduce the behavioural resistance. As a result, the managerial pressure and support of the new strategy had to be maintained continuously if the strategy was to remain in place. As already discussed, in many cases, after several years of active support, the attention of top management shifted to other pressing concerns. When this occurred, cultural and political opposition resurfaced, and succeeded in 'rolling back' the new strategy, or suppressing the new strategic-planning system.

On less frequent occasions, when top management remains firmly committed to planning for a long time, a process of cultural and political adaptation gradually takes place: pro-planning managers replace those who opposed it, a new culture supportive of the planning emerges, individuals learn to live and be comfortable with the new view of the world. When this occurs, the new strategy and its supporting capability become gradually institutionalized. But this is a slow process which may take five to ten years.

At the end of such process, no further application of power is necessary to maintain the new entrepreneurial behaviour.

Check-list for Managing Change

(The following is adapted from Chapter 6.5 in Ansoff, *Implanting Strategic Management.*)

I. *Building the Launching Platform*
  1. Perform strategic diagnosis.
  2. Prepare political/cultural-resistance map.
  3. Mobilize political support for change.
  4. Identify and mobilize relevant talent.
  5. Inform and reassure individuals/groups.
  6. Select an approach appropriate to the realities of timing, resistance and power.
  7. Get external help for diagnosis.

II. *Designing the Change Process*
  1. Focus process-design on resolving strategic challenges.
  2. Design the process for implementability.
  3. Use modular design.
  4. Build in strategic decision-making at the end of each module.
  5. Provide for early implementation.

III. *Protecting the Process from Conflict with Operations*
  1. Assign clear responsibilities.
  2. Budget the change.
  3. Provide managerial capacity for strategic activity.
  4. Reward strategic activity.

IV. *Designing Implementability into the Process*
  1. Train individuals in strategic decision-making and implementation at the beginning of each module.
  2. Involve responsible managers and relevant experts in the decision process.
  3. Progressively inform all affected individuals.
  4. Let managers work on problems which are relevant to their jobs.
  5. Control complexity of analysis to be compatible with manager's knowledge and skills.
  6. Provide relevant strategic information.

V. *Managing the Ongoing Process*
  1. Conduct planning and implementation as parallel activities.
  2. Control the planning process to assure balanced progress in making of decisions and on their acceptance.
  3. Launch implementation projects as early as circumstances permit.

VI. *Institutionalizing the New Strategy*
  1. Use a strategy-development master plan to manage the process.

2. After strategy is in place, continue climate-building until after the new culture and the power structure naturally support the strategy.
3. Continue capability-building until all elements of capability are balanced and support the strategy effectively.

VII. *Assuring the Coexistence of Competitive and Entrepreneurial Behaviours.*
Install as necessary:
1. SBUs (dual structure)
2. Dual Budgets
3. Dual Management Systems
4. Separate Structures

CHAPTER 19

Overview of Strategic Behaviours

If you can see things that are out of whack, you can also see how things can be in whack.

DR ZEUSS

The Problem

As discussed on several occasions, systematic strategic management first received attention in business literature in the 1960s. This does not mean that firms first started to behave strategically in the 1960s. Nor does it mean that the systematic strategic management described in this book is the only type of strategic behaviour which will further a firm's success.

Therefore, it is necessary to identify the other observable modes of strategic behaviour and to identify the conditions under which each mode is most likely to produce success in the market-place. This will be our concern in the first part of this chapter.

In the second part we review the key concepts and hypotheses of systematic strategic management.

Modes of Strategic Behaviour

Prior to the 1960s the process of strategic adaptation of organizations had been extensively studied by sociologists. The subjects of these studies were mostly non-profitable organizations, which lack the strong guiding influence exerted by management in business firms.

As a result, most models and descriptions depict strategic behaviour as unplanned, serendipitous and unguided. The terms (borrowed from the theory of biological evolution) which were frequently used to describe such behaviour were *organic adaptation* (in the case of incremental changes) and *mutation* (for discontinuous changes).

Business firms whose behaviour is totally unplanned and unguided do not survive for very long, except in monopolistic or subsidizing environments. Strategic behaviour of firms which do survive is guided and managed, however well or poorly. Therefore, our concern is with the variety of observable *managed strategic behaviours*.

A management style whose strategic behaviour comes closest to the organic is the *reactive mode*. In this mode, under normal conditions, management minimizes strategic changes (recall the edict 'give it [the same model] to them in any colour so long as it is black', issued and practised by Henry Ford I).

When reactive firms incur losses of expected growth or profits, management typically assumes that they are due to operating malfunctions (e.g. inventories out of control, or a price war by competitors) and seeks to redress them through operating measures (e.g. cost cutting, price reduction).

Only when a succession of operating measures fails to improve performance, does management take recourse to strategic measures. These are typically incremental. For example, in 1929 Henry Ford I replaced the Model T, which he had manufactured for the preceding twenty-five years, wth another standard, utilitarian model, the Model A.

Reactive firms typically avoid discontinuous strategic measures, such as a drastic revision of their product or marketing concepts, until the firm is confronted with an imminent crisis.

When a crisis looms, an atmosphere of panic sets in. Historical management is discredited and a search for a 'saviour' who offers a plausible solution ensues. If the solution offered by the 'saviour' works, the firm gradually recovers. If a series of 'saviour' solutions fails, the firm goes into bankruptcy.

When a reactive firm does turn attention to strategic changes, it does not plan the search for alternatives, but follows a successive process of trial and error. The first alternative that starts the firm on the road to recovery stops the search process.

The preceding discussion is not intended to suggest that reactive management necessarily leads to failure. On the contrary, reactive management is the success mode in an environment (characterized in Chapter 2 as being on turbulence levels 1 to 2) which demands standardized, low-cost products or services.

Nor should it be assumed that reactive management is necessarily passive. It is, indeed, passive strategically, but it may be vigorous, aggressive and successful in its competitive operating behaviour (as illustrated by the fabulous success of Henry Ford I between 1906 and 1929).

The behaviour of reactive management in the incremental and discontinuous modes is summarized in the first line of Table 19.1. The second line describes a more vigorous strategic behaviour which we shall call *proactive* or *ad-hoc* management.

The term 'ad hoc' implies that there is no centrally guided, planned

Table 19.1. Modes of Strategic Management

Management Mode	Type of Change	
	Incremental (Product/Service/Market Development)	Discontinuous (Diversification/Divestment/Internationalization/Technology Substitution)
Reactive	Trial and error reaction to unsatisfactory performance.	Panic search for solution in reaction to crisis.
Proactive Ad Hoc	'Bottom-up'. episodic. logically incremental initiatives by R&D and Marketing.	Trial and error search in reaction to a perceived discontinuity. Episodic, systematic anticipation of discontinuities (Issue Management; Crisis Management).
Proactive Systematic	Firm-wide periodic extrapolation of historical trends and performance (Long-range planning; R&D Planning; Strategic Planning).	Firm-wide periodic, systematic revision of the logic of the firm's future development (Strategic Planning; Strategic Management).

strategic development, but the firm is active in pursuing incremental strategic changes. As the entry in the second column suggests. the ideas for such changes are typically generated 'from the bottom up' in R&D, or in marketing departments. The word 'episodic' is intended to mean that the generation of ideas is not preplanned, rather they are invented by forward-looking and imaginative marketers and technologists.

'Logically incremental' calls attention to the fact that the new product and marketing ideas which are accepted for implementation are typically improvements on the earlier products. They represent logical steps in the historical strategic evolution of the firm. Henry Mintzberg, one of the most influential researchers on strategic development. has called such historical logic the *implicit strategy* of the firm; and as we have already mentioned, James Brian Quinn called the ad-hoc management *logical incrementalism.*

As the third column shows, when it comes to handling discontinuous change, the behaviour of ad-hoc management is different from the reactive. Ad-hoc managers are more likely to recognize the need for changes before a crisis strikes and move to deal with the discontinuity in an organized and business-like fashion (for an excellent description, see the Du Pont case [1]). But the search for a solution is reactive through trial and error, without the benefit of a guiding plan.

Ad-hoc management has been observable throughout this century and, since the 1940s, has become the dominant mode of behaviour among progressive firms with strong R & D and market-development departments. It has produced many outstanding successes, and it was advocated as the key to success in the best-seller, *In Search of Excellence*, by Peters and Waterman [2] where logical incrementalism was graphically described as 'sticking to your (strategic) knitting'.

The view in this book is that ad-hoc management is a promising way to manage, so long as the demand and technology in the firm's markets continue to evolve incrementally, strategic discontinuities are few and far between and the rate of change does not exceed the firm's speed of response.

Whenever one or more of the above conditions ceases to be true, a firm which follows ad-hoc management is likely to be 'caught with its strategic pants down'. This may occur either because the speed of the environmental change exceeds the speed of the firm's response, or discontinuties occur frequently, or both phenomena occur at the same time. This assertion has been supported by many case histories and, in particular, by the strategic difficulties which were encountered, just as *In Search of Excellence* was published, in a number of firms which the book recommended as success models to be followed by others.

In the 1970s a modified approach to ad-hoc management of discontinuous change called *issue management* emerged in American business practice. Another approach, called *surprise* or *crisis management* is emerging in the 1980s.

Both approaches apply when the basic logic of environmental evolution remains incremental, but is periodically perturbed by discontinuities. A discussion of these approaches is beyond the scope of this book. (The reader will find a brief discussion of surprise management in Part 5 of Part Ansoff, *Implanting Strategic Management*.)

The final line in Table 19.1 describes the *planned* and *systematic* mode of management. The word *planned* means that strategic decision-making is based on explicit forecasts of the trends, threats and opportunities in the future environment. In ad-hoc management strategic development progresses through a series of (not necessarily connected) strategic moves driven by *implicit* logic. In contrast, planned management makes the logic and the generation of new moves explicit and coordinates its implementation on a firm-wide basis.

The first systematic planning system to receive wide acceptance was Long-range Planning (L R P, sometimes referred to as Corporate Planning, or

Profit Planning). LRP is based on the assumption that the future environment will develop in a logically incremental manner. Therefore, as Table 19.1 shows, long-range planning is uniquely suited for making incremental strategic development explicit, guided and coordinated among the different parts of the firm.

To be sure, the original intent of long-range planning was to enhance the firm's operations management in environments of rapid growth. But a natural offshoot of the planning discipline of LRP was *R&D Planning*. R&D planning in consonance with the underlying assumptions of LRP does not question the basic historical technology of the firm, but it does systematize the process of new product/service generation, evaluation and selection.

The major contribution of *strategic planning* shown in the last column of Fig. 19.1. is that it challenges the historical logic of strategic evolution. If environmental analysis shows that the historical logic does not accurately describe what will occur in the future environment, then strategic planning shifts attention to systematic management of discontinuous change. The first step is to choose the new logic for the firm's future development. In the jargon of this book, this reformulation of logic is called *strategy formulation*.

The new strategy may be such that it can be developed and implemented by using the firm's historical strengths. When this occurs, strategic planning is a fully adequate instrument for guiding the firm's future evolution. If it turns out that the new strategic thrusts are such that the historical strengths are inadequate and may indeed become weaknesses in the future, it becomes necessary to enlarge the perspective of strategic planning to *strategic management*.

The two dimensions of this enlargement have been discussed in Part 2 of this book. The first is the addition of *capability planning* to strategy planning, and the second is the development of a planned approach to introducing discontinuous, and usually unwelcome, changes into the firm.

Strategic planning, which emerged a relatively short time after long-range planning, attracted much attention and generated enthusiasm in the business press. This phenomenon is typical in the United States whenever an attractive-looking, new 'mousetrap' is offered to management. During this period an increasing number of firms turned to strategic planning, including industry leaders. Since the mid-1970s, according to data gathered by this author, some 10 per cent of the world's leading firms have been moving toward strategic management.

However, as we discussed earlier initial application of strategic planning sometimes ran into severe difficulties which on many occasions led to its ejection from firms which had tried to use it.

Two streams of activities resulted. One was a wave of criticism of strategic planning as a 'mousetrap' that doesn't work, accompanied by suggestions that managers had better 'return to basics', in this case 'basics' being the ad-hoc or even organic management of strategic change.

The other activity focused attention on finding out why strategic planning failed to work. This was based on a belief by its proponents (a belief which has subsequently been validated by research findings) that in environments of high turbulence adherence to the historical logic imperils the future of the firm and that it is imperative to redefine its growth logic.

The result of the second activity was a series of developments which were discussed in Chapters 12–18, and which have led to development of systematic strategic management.

The concept of strategic management is still too new to assert with full confidence that it is fully workable in its present configuration. Undoubtedly further developments (such as issue management and crisis management) will enrich it in the coming years.

However, practical experience[3] and research findings[4,5] already suggest that strategic management is a usable concept and that, when used, it produces results.

Which Mode to Use

As discussed above, all four modes of strategic development are observable in practice. Of the four, strategic planning has been and continues to be criticized on several different grounds.[6,7] But it *is* a fact that instances can be cited in which each mode has led to business success. Furthermore, in the preceding section we described the conditions under which the successes typically occurred.

Therefore, the fight between the respective modes, whose proponents would apply their preferred type of management to all firms and under all situations, is divorced from practical reality.

Management and the business firm will be better served if the various fights were converted into a reconciliation process which will identify the

Table 19.2. Optimal Conditions for Management Modes

Management Mode	Environment			Firm's Capability
	Speed of Change	Familiarity of Change	Discontinuity of Change	
Reactive	Slower than firm's response	Recurring	Infrequent	Historical Strengths applicable
Ad Hoc	Comparable to response	Logically incremental		Incremental evolution of strengths
Long-range Planning*	Faster than response ‑ ‑ ‑ ‑→			
Strategic Planning		Novel ‑ ‑→	Frequent ‑ ‑→	
Strategic Management				Novel capabilities

* L R P also optimal for large and complex firms.

conditions under which the respective modes become appropriate for success. Thus management will not only be equipped to select the management mode that is appropriate to their present environmental changes, but will also be able to recognize the need to change the management style when the environment changes.[7]

Table 19.2 presents a brief summary of the success conditions under which the respective management modes are optimal. As the table shows, the choice of the mode is determined by the expected environmental conditions, as well as by the applicability of the firm's capability to the management of strategic change.

As the entries in the Table indicate:

– The reactive mode is optimal when the environment is slow-changing, repetitive and the firm's historical strengths apply.

– Ad-hoc management becomes optimal in a livelier incrementally evolving environment.

– Long-range planning is necessary whenever the speed of change begins to exceed the speed of the firm's ability to respond.

– Reactive, ad-hoc and long-range planning modes cease to be adequate when frequent discontinuities are expected to occur in the environment.

– Finally, when novel strategic challenges require that the firm develop new capabilities, the firm needs strategic management.

Key Hypotheses of Strategic Management

Like all efforts to explain reality, the descriptions and prescriptions offered in this book are based on key underlying assumptions about how reality works. Such assumptions are commonly called *basic hypotheses* (or, in mathematics, *axioms*). In this section we summarize the key hypotheses which underlie this book.[8]

1. Contingency Hypothesis

This hypothesis states that *there is no single optimum prescription for the way a firm should be managed.*

Sometimes the contingency hypothesis is interpreted to mean that, since there is no single universal solution, each firm is therefore unique and must find its own way to its unique truth. This is *not* the form of contingency hypothesis on which this book is built. Our version states that, between a single general solution and a different solution for everyone, lies a middle ground in which different *types* of managerial behaviour can be identified for different types of challenges.

A condensed methodology for matching strategic challenges to management behaviour has been presented in the previous section. Somewhat greater detail was offered in Chapter 13. Still greater detail will be found in Part 3 of Ansoff, *Implanting Strategic Management*.

2. *Environmental Dependence Hypothesis*

This hypothesis states that *the challenges from the firm's environment determine the optimal mode of behaviour.*

This hypothesis is vital during the second half of the twentieth century. It was less compelling during the first half of the century when the business firm had a large influence over its environment.

3. *Requisite Variety Hypothesis*

This hypothesis is borrowed from the science of cybernetics. Translated into business language. the requisite variety hypothesis states that *for optimal success, the aggressiveness of the firm's strategy must match the turbulence in the environment.*

4. *Strategy – Capability – Performance Hypothesis*

This hypothesis states that *the firm's performance will be optimal when its strategic behaviour matches the turbulence of the environment and the firm's capability matches its strategic behaviour.*

5. *Multi-component Capability Hypothesis*

This hypothesis denies the proposition that a single component of management, be it the key managers, the structure, the culture or the system, is a key to the firm's success.

Rather, the hypothesis states that *the firm's capability is the symbiotic result of the several key capability components*, (although under different conditions, one or more components may become more influential than others).

6. *Balanced Capability Hypothesis*

This final hypothesis states that *for each level of environmental turbulence, there are particular combinations (vectors) of components which will optimize the firm's success.*

These hypotheses are focused on the behaviours of a firm which will optimize its success. Common experience shows that only a minority of firms behave optimally. In this book we have not attempted to explain the forces within the firm which result in suboptimal behaviours. A reader interested in such exploration will find an extensive discussion in Part 1 of Ansoff, *Implanting Strategic Management*.

What is the Difference Between Strategic Planning and Strategic Management?

1. Strategic planning is focused on making optimal strategy decisions, while strategic management is focused on producing strategic results: new markets, new products and/or new technologies. To paraphrase Peter Drucker, strategic planning is management by plans, while strategic management is management by results.

2. Strategic planning is an analytical process, while strategic management is an organizational action process.

3. Strategic planning is focused on business, economic and technological variables. Strategic management broadens the focus to include psychological, sociological and political variables. Thus, strategic planning is about choosing things to do, while strategic management is about choosing things to do and also about the people who will do them.

4. Strategic management consists of:

– formulating strategies
– designing the firm's capability
– managing implementation of strategies and capabilities.

REFERENCES

Part 1

Chapter 1

1. H. Igor Ansoff, *Strategic Management*, Macmillan, London, 1979.

2. A. D. Chandler, Jr., *Strategy and Structure*, M.I.T. Press, Cambridge, Mass., 1962.

3. A. P. Sloan, Jr., *My Years with General Motors*, Doubleday, Garden City, N.Y., 1972.

Chapter 2

1. J. Fred Weston and Eugene F. Brigham, *Essentials of Managerial Finance*, 7th edition, Dryden Press, New York, 1985.

2. Weston & Brigham, *ibid.*, and Ezra Solomon, *Theory of Financial Management*, Columbia University Press, New York, 1963.

3. H. A. Simon, *The New Science of Management Decision*, Harper & Row, New York, 1960.

4. H. Fayol, *General and Industrial Management*, Pitman, London, 1959.

5. H. Fayol, *ibid.*

6. Chandler, *op. cit.*

7. Sloan, *op. cit.*

8. H. Igor Ansoff, *Implanting Strategic Management*, Prentice-Hall, Englewood Cliffs, N.J., 1984.

9. H. Markowitz, *Portfolio Selection: Efficient Diversification of Investments*, John Wiley & Sons, New York, 1959.

10. An excellent summary of Clarkson's approach can be found in E. Feigenbaum and J. Feldman (eds.), *Computers and Thought*, McGraw-Hill, New York, 1963. A full treatment is in G. P. E. Clarkson, *Portfolio Selection: A Simulation of Trust Investment*, Prentice-Hall, Englewood Cliffs, N.J., 1962 (The Ford Foundation Doctoral Dissertation Series 1961 Award Winner).

11. Simon, *op. cit.*

12. T. Levitt, 'Marketing Myopia', *Harvard Business Review*, vol. 38, no. 4, pp. 45–56, July–August 1960.

13. W. Reitman, in Feigenbaum and Feldman, *op. cit.*, chap. 2.

Chapter 3

1. M. Kestenbaum, 'The Essential Components of Business Planning', *Planning the Future Strategy of Your Business*, American Management Association, New York, 1956, p. 54.

2. For a critique of micro-economic theory, see R. M. Cyert and J. G. March, *A Behavioural Theory of the Firm*, Prentice-Hall, Englewood Cliffs, N.J., 963, Chapter 3; and M. Shubik, 'Approaches to the Study of Decision-making Relevant to the Firm', *Journal of Business*, vol. 34, no. 3, April 1961.

3. P. F. Drucker, 'Business Objectives and Survival Needs: Notes on a Discipline of Business Enterprise', *The Journal of Business*, vol. 31, no. 2, pp. 81–90, April 1958.

4. F. Abrams, 'Management Responsibilities in a Complex World', in T. H. Carroll, *Business Education for Competence and Responsibility*, University of North Carolina Press, Chapel Hill, N.C., 1954.

5. F. Abrams, *ibid.*; and R. F. Stewart, *The Strategic Plan*, Long-range Planning Service, Stanford Research Institute, Menlo Park, Ca.

6. Sloan, *op. cit.* Chandler, *op. cit.*

7. Cyert and March, *op. cit.*

8. Ansoff, *Strategic Management*.

9. H. A. Simon, 'On the Concept of Organizational Goals', *Administrative Science Quarterly*, vol. 9, no. 1, June 1964.

10. Solomon, *op. cit.*, Chap. 2.

11. A theoretical expression for the procedure is easy enough to write. See, for example, H. Igor Ansoff, 'A Model for Diversification', *Management Science*, vol. 4, no. 4, pp. 392–414, July 1958, reprinted in Thomas L. Berg and Abe Shuschman (eds.) *Product Strategy and Management*, Holt, Rinehart and Winston, Inc., New York, 1963, pp. 288–309.

Chapter 4

1. P. F. Drucker, *The Future of Industrial Man*, The John Day Company, New York, 1942.

2. John C. Chambers, K. Satinder and Donald D. Smith, 'How to Choose the Right Forecasting Technique', *Harvard Business Review*, July–August, 1971.

3. R. L. Collins, 'Scanning the Environment for Strategic Information', doctoral dissertation, Harvard University, 1968.

4. The Conference Board, *Planning Under Uncertainty: Multiple Scenario and Contingency Planning*, 1978.

5. William King and David Cleland, 'Information for More Effective Strategic Planning', *Long-range Planning Journal*, February 1977.

6. Don Lebell and O. J. Krasner, 'Selecting Environmental Forecasting Techniques for Business Planning Requirements', *Academy of Management Review*, 1977.

7. G. M. Kaufman, *Statistical Decision and Related Techniques in Oil and Gas Exploration*, Prentice-Hall, Englewood Cliffs, N.J., 1963.

8. J. F. Weston, *Managerial Finance*, Holt, Rinehart and Winston, Inc., New York, 1962, Chapter 5, pp. 82–98.

9. Simon, *op. cit.*

10. Cyert and March, *op. cit.*, p. 26.

11. J. M. Keynes, 'The End of Laissez-faire' (1926), republished in *Essays in Persuasion*, London. 1931, pp. 314–15.

12. *Ibid.*

13. Ansoff, *Strategic Management.*

Chapter 5

1. 'Combined action or operation, as of muscles, nerves, etc.', *Webster's New Collegiate Dictionary*, G. & C. Merriam Company, Springfield. Mass., 1961.

2. H. Igor Ansoff, 'Strategic Management of Technology', forthcoming in *Journal of Business Strategy*, Winter 1987.

Chapter 6

1. Levitt, *op. cit.*

2. H. Igor Ansoff, Jay Avner, Richard Brandenburg, Fred Portner, and Ray Radosevich, 'Does Planning Pay? The Effect of Planning on Success of Acquisitions in American Firms', *Long-range Planning Journal*, vol. 3, No. 2, December 1970.

3. Clarkson, *op. cit.*

Chapter 7

1. James Brian Quinn, *Strategies for Change: Logical Incrementalism*, Richard D. Irwin, Homewood, Ill., 1980.

2. Chandler, *op. cit.*

3. The five years with the greatest number of mergers (1946, 1947, 1955, 1956 and 1957) had 2,068 mergers. The first wave (1898–1902) had 2,454 mergers and the second wave (1926–1930) had 4,838 mergers. Source: R. L. Nelson, *Merger Movement in American Industry, 1895–1956*, Princeton University Press, Princeton, N.J., 1959, p. 29. Activity as reported by the *Statistical Abstract of the United States, 1964*, p. 101, shows 653 mergers in 1960, 671 in 1961 and 672 in 1963.

4. H. Igor Ansoff and J. Fred Weston, 'Merger Objectives and Organization Structure', *Review of Economics and Business*, August, 1962, pp. 49–58.

Chapter 8

1. Thomas J. Peters and Robert H. Waterman, Jr., *In Search of Excellence*, Harper & Row, New York, 1982.

2. H. Igor Ansoff, 'Conceptual Underpinnings of Systematic Strategic Management', *European Journal of Operational Research, 19*, 1985, pp. 2–19.

3. H. Igor Ansoff, 'Competitive Strategy Analysis on the Personal Computer', *The Journal of Business Strategy*, Vol. 6, No. 3, Winter 1986, pp. 28–36.

Chapter 10

1. C. W. Churchman, R. L. Ackoff, and E. L. Arnoff, *Introduction to Operations Research*, John Wiley & Sons, New York, 1957, Chap. 6, pp. 136–53.

2. Shubik, *op. cit.*

3. W. T. Morris, *Management Science in Action*, Richard D. Irwin, Homewood, Ill., 1963.

4. Churchman, et al., *op. cit.*; R. D. Luce and H. Raiffa, *Games and Decisions*, John Wiley & Sons, New York, 1957; W. T. Morris, *Engineering Economy*, Richard D. Irwin, Homewood, Ill., 1960.

Part 2

1. H. Igor Ansoff, Roger P. Declerck and Robert L. Hayes, (eds.), *From Strategic Planning to Strategic Management*, John Wiley & Sons, New York, 1976.

Chapter 12

1. Ansoff, *Implanting Strategic Management*, Chap. 1.1.

2. A. Schick, 'A Death in the Bureaucracy: the Demise of Federal PPB', *Public Administration Review*, March/April 1973.

3. H. Igor Ansoff, Jay Avner, Richard Brandenburg, Fred Portner, and Ray Radosevich, 'Does Planning Pay? The Effect of Planning on Success of Acquisitions in American Firms', *Long-range Planning Journal*, Vol. 3, No. 2, December 1970.

4. Ansoff, *Implanting Strategic Management*, Chap 1.1.

Chapter 13

1. Ansoff, *Strategic Management*, Chap. 5.

Chapter 16

1. Ansoff, *Implanting Strategic Management*, Chapter 6.1 and Ansoff, *Strategic Management*, pp. 188–195.

2. Robert H. Hayes, 'Strategic Planning – Forward in Reverse?', *Harvard Business Review*, November/December 1985, pp. 111–119.

Chapter 19

1. Chandler, *op. cit.*

2. Peters, *op. cit.*

3. Hans ten Dam and Carlos Siffert, 'Developing Strategic Management in a Diversified Firm', in H. Igor Ansoff, Aart Bosman, and Peter M. Storm, (eds.), *Understanding and Managing Strategic Change*, North-Holland Publishing Company, New York, 1982.

4. Peter Hatziantoniou, 'The Relationship of Environmental Turbulence, Corporate Strategic Profile, and Company Performance', (D.B.A. diss. United States International University, San Diego, California, 1986)

5. Tamer Tamer Salameh, 'Strategic Posture Analysis and Financial Performance of the Banking Industry in the United Arab Emirates', (D.B.A. diss. United States International University, San Diego, California, 1986).

6. Charles E. Lindblom, 'The Science of Muddling Through', *Public Administration Review*, Spring 1959.

7. Quinn, *op. cit.*

8. H. Igor Ansoff, 'The Emerging Paradigm of Strategic Management', forthcoming in *The Strategic Management Journal*.

9. A theoretical discussion of the hypotheses can be found in Ansoff, *Strategic Management*.

SELECTED FURTHER READING

The following list, with one or two exceptions, presents books (and a few timeless articles) which are on this author's list of classic contributions to the field of strategic management.

Part 1

Chapters 1 and 2

1. James G. March and Herbert A. Simon (with the collaboration of Harold Guetzkow), *Organizations*, John Wiley & Sons, New York, 1958.

Chapters 3 and 4

1. Peter F. Drucker, 'Business Objectives and Survival Needs: Notes on a Discipline of Business Enterprise', *The Journal of Business*, vol. 31, no. 2, pp. 81–90, April 1958.

2. Herbert A. Simon, 'On the Concept of Organizational Goal', *Administrative Science Quarterly*, Volume 9, no. 1, June 1964, pp. 1–22.

3. John W. Humble, 'Corporate Planning and Management by Objectives', *Long-range Planning Journal*, June 1969.

Chapters 6 to 10

1. H. Fayol, *General and Industrial Management*, Pitman, London, 1959.

2. Russell L. Ackoff, *A Concept of Corporate Planning*, John Wiley & Sons, New York, 1970.

3. George A. Steiner, *Strategic Managerial Planning*, Planning Executives Institute. Oxford, Ohio, 1977.

4. Derek F. Abell, *Defining the Business: The Starting Point of Strategic Planning*, Prentice-Hall, Englewood Cliffs, New Jersey, 1980.

5. Kenneth R. Andrews, *The Concept of Corporate Strategy*, Dow-Jones/Irwin, Homewood, Ill., 1971. (Revised ed. 1980.)

6. Boston Consulting Group, *Growth and Financial Strategies*, Boston Consulting Group, 1971.

7. Charles E. Hofer and Dan E. Schendel, 'Strategy Formulation', *Analytical Concepts*, West Publishing Company, St Paul, 1978.

8. Michael E. Porter, *Competitive Strategy: Techniques for Analyzing Industries and Competitors*, Free Press, New York, 1980.

9. Eric Rhenaman, *Organizational Theory for Long Range Planning*, John Wiley & Sons, New York, 1973.

10. Richard Norman, *Management for Growth*, John Wiley & Sons, New York, 1977.

Part 2

Chapter 12

1. Peter F. Drucker, *Managing in Turbulent Times*, Harper and Row, New York, 1980.

2. F. E. Emery and E. L. Trist, 'The Causal Texture of Organizational Environments', *Human Relations*, Vol. 18, no. 1, February 1965, pp. 21–32.

3. Daniel Bell, *The Coming of Post-Industrial Society*, Basic Books, New York, 1973.

Chapters 14 and 15

1. Thomas J. Peters and Robert H. Waterman, Jr., *In Search of Excellence*, Harper and Row, New York, 1982.

2. Henry Mintzberg, *The Structure of Organizations*, Prentice-Hall, Englewood Cliffs, New Jersey, 1979.

3. Russell L. Ackoff, *Redesigning the Future: A Systems Approach to Societal Problems*, John Wiley & Sons, New York, 1974.

4. Chester I. Barnard, *The Functions of the Executive*, Harvard University Press, Boston, Mass., 1938.

5. James D. Thompson, *Organizations in Action*, McGraw-Hill Book Co., New York, 1967.

6. Jay R. Galbraith, *Designing Complex Organizations*, Addison-Wesley Publishing Co., Reading, Mass., 1973.

7. H. Igor Ansoff and R. G. Brandenburg, 'A Language for Organizational Design', *Management Science*, Vol. 17, (12), 1971.

8. Ernest Dale, *Planning and Developing the Company Organizational Structure*, American Management Associations, New York, 1952.

9. Alfred P. Sloan, Jr., *My Years With General Motors*, Doubleday & Co., New York, 1972.

10. Seymour Tilles, 'How to Evaluate Corporate Strategy', *Harvard Business Review*, vol. 41, no. 4, July/August 1963, pp. 111–121.

11. Theodore Levitt, 'Marketing Myopia', *Harvard Business Review*, vol. 38, no. 4, July/August 1960, pp. 45–56.

Chapters 16 to 18

1. Alfred D. Chandler, Jr., *Strategy and Structure: Chapters in the History of the American Industrial Enterprise*, MIT Press, Cambridge, Mass., 1962.

2. Henry Mintzberg, *Power in and Around Organizations*, Prentice-Hall, Englewood Cliffs, New Jersey, 1983.

3. E. H. Schein and W. G. Bennis, *Personal and Organizational Change Through Group Methods*, John Wiley & Sons, New York, 1967.

4. Donald Schon, *The Reflective Practitioner: How Professionals Think in Action*, Basic Books, 1984.

5. Chris Argyris and Donald Schon, *Organizational Learning: A Theory of Action Perspective*, Addison-Wesley Publishing Co., Reading, Mass., 1978.

6. Chris Argyris, *Strategy, Change and Defensive Routines*, Pitman Publishers, Marshfield, M A., 1985.

7. Warren Bennis and Bert Nanus, *Leaders: The Strategies of Taking Charge*, Harper and Row, New York, 1985.

8. Enid Mumford and Andrew Pettigrew, *Implementing Strategic Decisions*, Longman, London, 1975.

9. Chris Argyris, *Organization and Innovation*, Richard D. Irwin, Homewood, Ill., 1965.

10. Tom Burns and G. M. Stalker, *The Management of Innovation*, Tavistock Press, London, 1961.

Chapter 19

1. H. Igor Ansoff, *Strategic Management*, Macmillan, London, 1979.

2. Richard M. Cyert and James G. March, *A Behavioral Theory of the Firm*, Prentice-Hall, Englewood Cliffs, New Jersey, 1963.

3. Graham T. Allison, *Essence of Decision: Explaining the Cuban Missile Crisis*, Little Brown & Co., Boston, 1971.

4. H. Igor Ansoff, 'The Emerging Paradigm of Strategic Management', forthcoming in *The Journal of Strategic Management*.

INDEX

Subject Index

READ MORE IN PENGUIN

In every corner of the world, on every subject under the sun, Penguin represents quality and variety – the very best in publishing today.

For complete information about books available from Penguin – including Puffins, Penguin Classics and Arkana – and how to order them, write to us at the appropriate address below. Please note that for copyright reasons the selection of books varies from country to country.

In the United Kingdom: Please write to *Dept. JC, Penguin Books Ltd, FREEPOST, West Drayton, Middlesex UB7 0BR*

If you have any difficulty in obtaining a title, please send your order with the correct money, plus ten per cent for postage and packaging, to *PO Box No. 11, West Drayton, Middlesex UB7 0BR*

In the United States: Please write to *Penguin USA Inc., 375 Hudson Street, New York, NY 10014*

In Canada: Please write to *Penguin Books Canada Ltd, 10 Alcorn Avenue, Suite 300, Toronto, Ontario M4V 3B2*

In Australia: Please write to *Penguin Books Australia Ltd, 487 Maroondah Highway, Ringwood, Victoria 3134*

In New Zealand: Please write to *Penguin Books (NZ) Ltd, 182–190 Wairau Road, Private Bag, Takapuna, Auckland 9*

In India: Please write to *Penguin Books India Pvt Ltd, 706 Eros Apartments, 56 Nehru Place, New Delhi 110 019*

In the Netherlands: Please write to *Penguin Books Netherlands B.V., Keizersgracht 231 NL–1016 DV Amsterdam*

In Germany: Please write to *Penguin Books Deutschland GmbH, Friedrichstrasse 10–12, W–6000 Frankfurt/Main 1*

In Spain: Please write to *Penguin Books S. A., C. San Bernardo 117–6° E–28015 Madrid*

In Italy: Please write to *Penguin Italia s.r.l., Via Felice Casati 20, I–20124 Milano*

In France: Please write to *Penguin France S. A., 17 rue Lejeune, F–31000 Toulouse*

In Japan: Please write to *Penguin Books Japan, Ishikiribashi Building, 2–5–4, Suido, Tokyo 112*

In Greece: Please write to *Penguin Hellas Ltd, Dimocritou 3, GR–106 71 Athens*

In South Africa: Please write to *Longman Penguin Southern Africa (Pty) Ltd, Private Bag X08, Bertsham 2013*

READ MORE IN PENGUIN

BUSINESS

Management and Motivation	Victor H. Vroom and Edward L. Deci
The Art of Japanese Management	Richard Tanner Pascale and Anthony Athos
The Penguin Management Handbook	Thomas Kempner (ed.)
Introducing Management	Peter Lawrence and Ken Elliott (ed.)
The Entrepreneurial Manager	A. L. Minkes
An Insight into Management Accounting	John Sizer
Understanding Company Financial Statements	R. H. Parker
Successful Interviewing	Jack Gratus
Working in Organizations	Andrew Kakabudse, Ron Ludlow and Susan Vinnicombe
Offensive Marketing	J. H. Davidson
Corporate Recovery	Stuart Slatter
Corporate Strategy	Igor Ansoff